C000252851

We had dreams
and
songs to sing

by

Keith Salmon

**Grosvenor House
Publishing Limited**

All rights reserved
Copyright © Keith Salmon, 2009

Keith Salmon is hereby identified as author of this
work in accordance with Section 77 of the Copyright, Designs
and Patents Act 1988

The book cover picture is copyright to Keith Salmon

This book is published by
Grosvenor House Publishing Ltd
28-30 High Street, Guildford, Surrey, GU1 3HY.
www.grosvenorhousepublishing.co.uk

This book is sold subject to the conditions that it shall not, by way of
trade or otherwise, be lent, resold, hired out or otherwise circulated
without the author's or publisher's prior consent in any form of binding or
cover other than that in which it is published and
without a similar condition including this condition being imposed
on the subsequent purchaser.

A CIP record for this book
is available from the British Library

ISBN 978-1-906645-86-1

About the author

Keith Salmon lives in the Isle of Man with his wife Nikki and his son Charlie.

Born in Liverpool in 1965, just after Liverpool's first FA Cup win, the smell of silver polish has never been far away whilst following his football team – Liverpool FC. His passion is as strong as ever and the love he has for his team and his city shines through. Football has defined his path in life and afforded him many wonderful opportunities to travel and meet people from all walks of life.

For more about the author and the characters in the book check out www.wehaddreamsandsongstosing. co.uk

A portion of the proceeds from the book will go towards two truly worthy causes.

The first is dear to all Liverpudlians' hearts and will help support the continued work and focus of the Hillsborough Justice Campaign. For further information please visit www.contrast.org/hillsborough. The fight for justice continues please continue to support the cause.

The second is to support vital research towards finding a cure for Lafora disease. 'Hope for John' is a Jersey registered Charity set up to raise funds for research into the Lafora disease on behalf of John Sharp, a young lad in Jersey.

Lafora disease causes seizures, muscle spasms, difficulty walking, dementia, mutism and is at this moment a terminal disease. The disease is the severest form of human epilepsy and affects one in a million previously healthy teenagers.

To give John hope please check out the website www.chelseashope.org where you can read John's story and help understand the disease.

Thank you

So many thanks need to go to so many people it's hard to know where to start. I will start at the beginning and thank my mum and dad for giving me the best upbringing I could ask for. I thank my dad for my passion for the Reds and my mum for being there when the going got tough after Hillsborough. Their love and support is unquestionable and I thank them from the bottom of my heart. My Scouse brothers 'Our Ian' and 'Our Kev' deserve a mention for looking swell on the front cover, and allowing me to use the picture, if nothing else.

My wonderful wife Nikki, without her unwavering support I wouldn't have made it this far. When it was easier to give up she drove me on and believed in what I was writing and gave me the confidence to believe in myself. For my son Charlie, who though he wasn't there at the beginning, he became the reason to complete the story so he could be proud of me. His lullabies come from the Kop and his love of the Liver Bird already fills me with immense pride.

My companions on my journey with the Reds I thank you all, whether it was one or a thousand games that we shared I dedicate this to you, my favourite times are the times I have spent with you. You will read all about them through the book and a better band of brothers I could not wish for.

My heartfelt thanks and gratitude go to my wonderful proof reader Lynn Lavelle, who went beyond the call of duty, and putting her own needs to one side made sense of my ramblings. Finally, Carole and Sue at work who made me realise that it needed to make sense and be written in English as well as Scouse.

I thank you all!

In memory of the 96 people, who went to a football game and did not come home.

Contents

1

Be the best you can be!

Simply be the best that you can be! Stop worrying about the things you can't affect or alter, do what you can and do your best.

Quite a bold statement but that is exactly what I have tried to do. The following is my story and my story alone. All the events are true and all the feelings are honest, sometimes raw sometimes joyful but always mine. After years of writing I place before you a story of my life. It's taken me three years because I wanted to tell my story from start to finish, and the birth of a little boy slowed me down, but also gave me the drive to complete it. One day he will have his own dreams and songs to sing. I would say his dreams will be red and his songs will be Liverpool songs. From father to son, I give him all that he requires to have the passion that I hold to this day.

Let me take you on my journey, which encompasses the best and the worst of things that happened. Enjoy!

—⁓—

If you are anything like me you are probably in an airport bookshop, or a local WH Smith, taking a sly look at the beginning of this book to pass the time. Your wife or girlfriend is in Next buying all kinds of holiday wear, when she promised she wasn't going to buy anything else as she has everything. You probably have little intention of buying it. Sometimes you may just surprise yourself and get hooked and buy a classic. Don't wait to be surprised, buy it anyway. If you have been given this book as a gift or you have been standing admiring my picture (I am the one on the right) on the front cover, you probably already have a healthy interest in football.

Join me on my journey and I will take you inside the heart and mind of a 'normal' football fan, a man who loves his team and his city. On the way you will find a roller coaster of emotions as football, a simple game, takes me to the heady heights of European football and to the depths of despair as disaster strikes.

My team is Liverpool FC, but my story relates equally to fans of most, if not all football clubs. We are a much-maligned breed, misunderstood and often tarred with the same brush as a minority, the hooligans. I will show the story of a boy who travels from the working class strongholds of northern Liverpool to a nice middle class living as a Bank manager on a rock in the middle of the Irish Sea. The Isle of Man has now been my home for nearly ten years.

There has been a new popularity in recent years for football related books and they have generally come in two forms. Those which detail the link between football, hooliganism and acts of extreme violence, and those by people who lived on their wits or their giros and took part in petty crime. If you're hoping to find similar exploits in this book, you will be disappointed. I didn't fight, I always paid on the train and I didn't steal anything. Not because I am squeaky clean, I just didn't feel the need to or want to. It goes against the way I was brought up. In a time where it seems to be acceptable to write such stories and glamourise such activities, I am proud to state that I went to football to enjoy the beautiful game. I much prefer meeting people than maiming them. It's funny though, as I seem to have an unhealthy interest in reading those books and seeing that type of film. Its like 'car crash TV' you don't want to watch but you just have to. I am interested in their lives but I doubt they are in mine. I would like to think that my experiences have something more in common with hundreds of thousands of football fans, as opposed to the infamous few, who persevere with acts of mindless violence.

You may be asking where did a normal guy get the idea to try and write a book. Well, to help the long hours travelling to and from the European Cup Final in Istanbul in May 2005, I decided to keep a journal and record my experiences. I did it for me, no one else, but it turned into what you now see in chapter 10 as 'the best night of my life', sorry one of the best nights of my life. I stand corrected by my wife. As it turned out, my wife thought my little story was really good and after a little proof reading (I am not admitting to a wholesale rewrite), I passed it around family and friends who seemed to really enjoy what they read. With their encouragement I got to thinking about what else I could document, and 34 years after my first match I had a lot of ground to cover!

You're probably thinking when is he going to get to the sob story where he says 'I could have been playing on the hallowed Anfield turf, if only I had a little more luck?' Well I won't disappoint you and I will let you enjoy the rest of the book. I can't lie; I was never going to be a football player of any decent standard. One man, well one 12-year-old boy, ruined my football career. Colin Walmsley finished me off and he probably never even realised it. Colin played for Liverpool Boys (they were the best players at their age in the city - so he was a star!), and he moved to our school during the second year at senior school. He came with a reputation and, to be fair to the lad, lived up to it. The problem was he played on the wing and that was where I played and all of a sudden, after initially playing for the school in the first year, I was dropped. I had so much to offer, but nobody knew it, not even me!

What did I do? Fight for my place? Did I play Sunday football? No I just gave up and decided the Mighty Red Men were a better bet. My childhood football highlights amount to two moments. The first was as a nine year old cub scout in a grudge game playing for 22nd Walton Pack on the hill cub pack against another grandly named pack who I remember were our big rivals. I scored two goals in a 4-3 win with the second in the last minute. After beating three players, I lifted the ball over the goalkeeper, a la Kenny Dalglish scoring the winner in the 1978 European Cup Final. I did it in 1974, so you could say Kenny copied my style. The second was against another Liverpool Boy's legend in the shape of Sean Martin who was the goalkeeper for Liverpool Boys, possibly even Liverpool FC for while, but they probably dropped him once they found out he got beaten by a 30 yards volley by yours truly in 1979. To be fair it was more like 20 yards but it was an absolute cracker. It was, I admit, only in a PE lesson, and some may not attach much significance to that, but I did and it showed I could still do it once in a while. But at fourteen years of age my football career had burnt itself out.

Oh how I wish I had a bit more guts, I could have been someone on the football pitch. I waited until I was 36 and paraded the touch of Gerrard, the brain of Dalglish and a little of the physique of Jan Molby. All on the hallowed five-a-side pitches of the National Sports Centre in the Isle of Man. The legs had gone but I could goal hang and pass a team to death without moving more than five yards for long periods of time and outthink them with a killer back heel or a Ronaldhino trick (yeah, I know I shouldn't have gone that far - now you don't believe me). I could have played for 20 years in senior football but I chose to watch my heroes play in red, week in week out. Now I think I missed out somewhat, but the lads who played Saturday football missed out on so much more.

—ᴍ—

If I had been a footballer, I would not have been a budding author, unless it was for my autobiography, and then as a star, someone would ghost write it for me. I do however get paid by someone for being myself. As I write this I am sitting on Virgin Atlantic Airbus bound for Johannesburg, South Africa. Better than that, I am actually getting paid to be on the plane, I can't believe it, but then neither can anyone who either knows me or thinks they know me. My job has regularly taken me to America, Gibraltar, Dubai, London, and the Channel Islands. Take it from me, in these days of corporate cut backs, you don't really travel anywhere if you don't add benefit to the company, and the days of the old jolly is gone for most. To be fair, even if it was just for a jolly, I don't think I would bother going as I think it's taking the piss. I would much rather be at home with my wife. Travelling for work is not the same fun as going on your holidays - endless waiting in airport lounges, 5am starts and 10pm finishes, just for a few hours in London. Today is great fun!!! Travelling for more than eleven hours overnight to South Africa, arriving at eight in the morning, oh, and I forgot to say I left the Island at 2.30 on a Sunday afternoon. It was supposed to be my day of rest, but on behalf of my employer, I had already presented the trophies at a local kid's Cup Final in the morning. So no great joy in the travelling then. It's nearly 24 hours since I left home. When I go back, I have to do it all in reverse, arriving back in the Island 24 hours after leaving the office. Doesn't sound like fun, but at least I don't pay for the hotel or my meals, well, within reason, too many people took the piss and I pay the price for it.

For a living I teach people skills that are as simple as talking to people and finding out what they want out of life. It's as easy as that, and yes I get paid to do it, and paid fairly well. But its not about the money, its about doing a good job that people recognise you for. I get that mentality from my Dad. I think being respected is far more valued than being rich. He once said to me "always stay as you are 'a nice guy'". Sometimes it is difficult to identify when you are respected and you have to read between the lines. Not many people will come up to you and say 'Keith, I really respect you and what you do'. When was the last time anyone said that to you? Respect is earnt not bought and that is what I have tried to do, I would like to think I have achieved it too. I have, so I am told, lots of people who have a genuine warmth and fondness for me (well buy the book then). I would like to think that has to do with the fact that I actually like pleasing people for no other reason than I like pleasing people.

Ever since I was little I have been good with the old chat. I never used to shut up as a kid and generally it was going on about Liverpool FC and the latest star, cup glory or just anything to do with the Reds. To put it mildly I was football daft.

South Africa is not the culture shock I expected in some ways, but in other ways it slaps you right between the eyes. Generally it looks like any other place in the developed world. You know the type, your local shopping centres or industrial parks. It looks affluent and believe me, in some areas it really is. But then you see the people and question what lies beneath the façade. I have never seen so many people walking somewhere, anywhere, in the middle of nowhere for no apparent reason and with no apparent destination. On the drive to my hotel (in the best area of Johannesburg) from the airport, I think I saw all sides of South Africa in just 40 minutes. The motorways are well developed, heavily populated and we passed your normal array of out of town shopping malls and industrial units and in between there are vast estates of seemingly decent housing, which, though architecturally interesting, may not be to all tastes. There is even a Las Vegas style casino seemingly inspired by Caesar's Palace. This is where it started to get interesting. The motorway traffic consisted of all manner of vehicles, top of the range BMW's and Mercedes driven by the affluent (and yes, generally white), and then there were the work vans laden with building materials and equipment, loaded with black men atop the materials. All open to the elements and wrapped together for warmth and comfort, the men not the materials that is. Up on the right hand side of the road I could see a rubbish tip. Nothing unusual there, but there were people scavenging upon others leftovers. I stopped looking too intensely as I felt my driver was uncomfortable with what I was looking at, or was it just me that was uncomfortable?

As we left the motorway, I could see a mass of people walking from one side of the motorway to the other. All of the people were black and they were heading towards the towering buildings in the affluent suburb of Sandton. This was South Africa's underclass and they just about exist. They are the cleaners, the bus boys, the maids and the gardeners of the affluent white population. They literally exist side by side with the affluent whites, but in reality they are worlds apart. A stunning statistic I found up was that only 15% of South Africans pay tax, that is because the other 85% don't earn enough to. All along the roadside at major junctions were men sitting forlornly looking at the road in seemingly quiet contemplation. They were actually waiting for work. What work? Any work! It was after 9am and I think at that point, hope must be lost if you are looking for a days work. I had a horrible feeling that if they didn't work they wouldn't eat. My driver confirmed my thoughts - all hope was gone at just nine in the morning. And yes, here I am in a four star hotel on expenses, it's not right is it? Nobody I will be training in the next week is black either. This land still seems to be the domain of the white man, at least for the time being, a fact probably compounded by the fact that virtually every passenger on my plane was white. There doesn't seem to be much of a distribution of wealth, but I suppose Rome was not built in a day. With the disproportionate distribution of wealth, it is clear that security will always be an issue, and you must heed the warnings or face the consequences. The warmth of the welcome from all colours is very strong though.

After eight days in South Africa I had learnt a lot. As I came to the end of my South African odyssey, I left a country that really has a split personality. On one side, it has the first world opulence of the big shopping malls and gated communities where people scurry home and live in secure surroundings. On the other hand is the third world deprivation of the squatter camps. But the people believe in the country, many wouldn't live anywhere else and if ever a place didn't live up to its reputation it was Johannesburg. The problem with Johannesburg is that you are always wary, wary of anyone with a different coloured skin. The hotel I stayed in is linked physically to a shopping mall that is safe and secure and guarded. You are advised not to walk anywhere on your own and be cautious even in your hotel room. I found myself one day staring out of the mall through plate glass windows, contemplating going outside. But not for long. I soon thought 'no I am in a safe area and I am not putting myself in danger like that'. If you think I am being melodramatic, I will just say that a couple of hours later, a woman staying at my hotel was viciously mugged right outside the front door. You have to be vigilant at all times.

The people I was working with all had a story to tell. One lady had at least ten friends she could think of immediately who had been car jacked. Guys in the office had more horrific stories than that, of people they knew of who had been attacked, raped, shot and even murdered. That shows how dangerous a place it can be, but as I said before the people don't want to live anywhere else. It is a horrible feeling, not trusting anyone because they are poor and black, but there is an element that hides within the poor who use the poverty as a reason to attack and kill. One person said that it was not the fact of the attack that concerned her, but it was the sheer level of violence and brutality of it. The first thing the criminals think of is to use as much force as possible against people who are not even retaliating. Criminals in Britain are often only likely to use violence as a last resort, but even that is changing. What I did was to be cautious, but I was also with people with local knowledge who protected me from the real danger. I can honestly say that if you are careful and travel as advised and keep your wits about you it is a great experience. There are some hard nuts that don't care and on my first day I saw one of them. Walking down the road on his own without a care in the world and he was wearing a Liverpool shirt and a Liverpool scarf, in 80 degrees in Johannesburg. How strange (the shirt I understand but the scarf?). Liverpool fans really do get everywhere.

From Joburg, you can get to so many places and see so much that you must. Big game and a country so beautiful - it is a crying shame that fear keeps many people away. Even though on business, the hotel I stayed at was a tourist hotel and there were many tourists taking advantage of what the country had to offer. The cities have great restaurants, European style nightlife, great food and shopping but most of all this country has wildlife that actually lives within its natural habitat.

I always like to take advantage of being somewhere and see the place. I have done it with the football when we have travelled abroad. Barcelona from the Marina and beach to the Ramblas, to the Gaudi Cathedral and then the Camp Nou (when did English commentators stop calling it The Nou Camp). In Cologne (prior to Bayer Leverkeusen in 2002) I saw the Cathedral, well there was not much else left after our forefathers bombed it to bits in the Second World War. Funny, some of the younger ones in the crowd were asking where all the old parts of town were, as it looked like Warrington. Then Istanbul prior to that glorious night, I took in the Blue Mosque and the Bazaar and the Bospherous Tea Gardens looking from Europe to Asia, before striding across the bridge into Asia on foot.

This time I was going back to nature and into the animal kingdom. I had two choices. An all day trip up towards Sun City where I might see the Big Five (Lion, Elephant, Leopard, Buffalo and Rhino), or go to an elephant Sanctuary where I could get up close and personal with the majestic, if somewhat freaky giants. God really took liberties with these creatures. I can see him now, after too much holy wine, saying 'right lets make an animal for fun, massive ears, big nose that reaches the floor, all their teeth fall out and every time they piss they release at least 11 litres, and oh yes their dumps are the size of dinner plates'. Yes, that was a real laugh but as you will see up close and personal they don't hold a grudge.

As you may gather, the elephant sanctuary won the day, on a few points really. It had been a long week in work with a couple of boozy nights out, poor sleep due to the altitude (Joburg is at 6,000 feet), and also because Nikki said I would regret it if I didn't see the elephants. The Sun City trip was a 4.30 am start, so give that a miss, the elephants was a nice leisurely 1pm departure. It was also only an hour's drive from Joburg compared to a four hour journey each way for the big game. To get from the

Hotel to the Sanctuary I hired a driver, a white women, who looked a little like Mrs Doubtfire and gave me mounds of information on the way up to the park. We passed the squatter camps and Government housing projects. It brought the whole place to life, far better than hiring a car. I was off to see Animals in their natural habitat, well with the elephants that's not strictly true as they are in a sanctuary with fences and boundaries and they sleep indoors and are fed by their trainers. There are good reasons why they are here. They have been rescued from being exported to the Americas and China to unlicensed Circus's, or orphaned due to the actions of poachers. Each of the six elephants has their own sad story to tell. But here they are well cared for, protected and eventually the goal is that they are reintroduced into the wild. At the sanctuary people are taught the magic behind the façade of this magnificent beast, sorry beast is an unfair term. You get to interact with them, feed them, feel them (including stroking their tongue) and I even got to ride the biggest, which due to the width of his back is likely to have given me a groin strain that will last a couple of weeks.

Out in the bush on the leathery back of the giant elephant, I was a million miles away from any dangers, perceived or real. I was also a million miles away from what I ever expected, growing up on the streets of Liverpool. I feel privileged to see things that I never thought I would and it would be a massive shame if I wasn't to take the opportunities afforded to me. The streets of Johannesburg are full of people who have little hope of ever seeing my life and the opportunities I have and for that I am humbled. At this point I realised that the world is mine to see and my aspirations and dreams were limitless unless I limited them myself. My story is a story that I thought I would never write, but would love to read. Writing was not for the likes of me, who said so?

South Africa opened my eyes to the inner me. My preconceptions were constantly challenged and it helped me look at my life and myself and showed me that anything is possible if you decide to do it. This book is written and published and is one of my proudest achievements. In this country of so many problems, there is so much hope too. I remember growing up in an environment were hope was limited but still not on the scale faced here. What I found was a positivity, which I could feed off, it was truly a defining moment in my life. I realised how lucky I was and how fortunate I was to be able to see the way others lived. Inadvertently, on the way back to the airport the motorway was blocked due to an accident so my taxi driver with his local knowledge cut through the suburbs. Well I thought he was a taxi driver but all of a sudden I wasn't too sure. In the hotel my original taxi driver hadn't turned up and this guy appeared, whom the concierge seemed to know, and he offered to take me. I thought nothing of it until he turned off the motorway. I nervously looked around the car looking for signs that it was a licensed taxi, which it wasn't. I started to shift uncomfortably in my seat as he headed into a built up area, well built up is not really a good description. It was full of shacks and thronged with people. I was the only white person for miles and there I was in a smart suit, a laptop worth a thousand pounds between my legs and all my best clobber in the boot. The driver looked at me and smiled and softly said 'you OK with me, don't worry, we OK'. I would love to say I had every confidence but I didn't, especially when I saw the sign, which read

Alexandra, which I understood to be the second biggest township after Soweto. What does Soweto mean to you? Think about it, would you have felt the same? The longer we drove, the more packed the roads became, not with cars but with people, and this looked like the Africa of the films with a busy vibrant market place and I was the great explorer. I realised that the driver was right and I wasn't the centre of attention, in fact no one was taking any notice of me. My driver started to explain the nature and life of the township and as we headed out towards the airport I was humbled once again. The dwellings people lived in were no more than shacks, they had three or four levels of breeze block with layers of wood and corrugated iron built up and held together with plastic sheeting and rope. The shacks covered both sides of a path which head a gully running in between, I didn't look closely to the gully as I knew what to expect, it was their drains. Conditions are improving and people are getting electricity and running water and proper housing but it is taking time. On a recent trip, they boasted in Cape Town that 67% of people now have electricity overnight, that sums up the size of the issue and there is still a long way to go. Think about that for yourself - how would you cope with no electric?

In South Africa I found wonderful people of all colours, a lack of prejudice in the white population with very little racism (at least on the surface), and a wonderful will to help (always with a smile) from the black population. I saw for myself a supportive white community in South Africa who appreciate the need to redress the balance. The disparity between the haves and the have-nots is apparently still massive. You don't see poor white people begging by the side of the road, or selling whatever they can at major road intersections. They are all one colour and the colour is black. I think you have to realise that the situation, for so many years under apartheid, cannot be redressed in one fell swoop. Education is the key and that will take some time. With education people will realise they can achieve so much more. In the post-Mandela era there is a void, as the quality that follows can never match his spirit or achievements and that is a concern to all South Africans, black and white.

That brings me full circle in my own thinking. When I was a child, the working class knew their place. You were never really aiming to achieve much more than your parent's did (and there was nothing wrong with that). We didn't realise what we could achieve. We were encouraged, well I was by my parents, to be decent and honest, and they didn't do such a bad job. But reaching for the stars and striving for so much more didn't come into it. I had a job for life with the City Council in Liverpool and that was where I would work forever, get married, live in a terrace street or leafy suburb if lucky and maybe have kids to complete the picture. From the working class environment of the 80s in Liverpool that would have been some achievement, to go above and beyond was not even a dream. Liverpool FC were my dreams and I could not see past my future following the Reds. I was married at eighteen to Football and in particular Liverpool FC and I settled for that, as it was a comfortable marriage.

From the time I could walk I was kicking a ball even though I was a little fat get. I came out weighing ten pounds, which must have nearly killed my mum. I was also a cheeky little bugger, not naughty but mischievous. My mum used to take her frustration out on the couch at some of the things I did, otherwise she said she would have put me in hospital if she took it out on me. I don't remember that! I was a little angel as far as I remember. I wouldn't read and had no interest in learning anything except how to play out with the other kids, which I was good at, and how to kick a ball against the wall, any wall. Football was to play a part in everything. My learning left a lot to be desired and I would now certainly be classed as a slow learner, I wasn't thick or anything (well I am writing a book so that proves I wasn't), I just couldn't be bothered learning, it was boring. I wanted to play out and play with a ball. To get me reading I actually had to read the results out of the Pink Echo (the local papers Saturday football edition) and some of the stories. That's how I improved my reading and spelling. I could read about a Liverpool game no problem and spell Shankly, but schoolwork sucked. I would like to say my mum and dad had a cunning plan to make me read, but I think my dad just got fed up with me making him read the results out to me every Saturday night. The only way I was going to find out what I wanted to find out about the football was to read it for myself.

It's funny but my nephew has learnt to read in exactly the same way. Just add in a bit of technology for good measure with a Sony Playstation and he can tell you how old Steven Gerrard is and how tall Peter Crouch is. Even with an Evertonian for a mum the boy just can't be poisoned. He has ruined the lawn at the back of the house playing football at all hours and in all weathers. He even takes on the toughest of opponents, my dad (well at 72 he has slowed down a touch so he finds him easy pickings). If his granddad scores a goal it is generally offside, but in a game of one on one? It goes to show that he is a little cheat. For some reason, everyone thinks he is a little version of me, well that can't be that bad! The thing is, he is really good for a seven year old and I think I should sign him up now and become his agent prior to the parasites getting involved who will just rip him off. I will look after any future career for only 30%, what a bargain.

In my younger years, football was everything. I ate, I slept and I dreamt football. I wanted to grow up to be Liverpool's centre forward but it was never going to happen. Watching Liverpool's centre forwards was as close as it ever got but I am not complaining. My weeks revolved around what was happening on a Saturday afternoon. If I was going to a match you would hear about it non-stop up until the Saturday, and if I had been, you would hear about it non stop until I could focus on the next one. In my view I have had an amazing journey, even though it was fairly normal, from the mean streets of Liverpool to the life I have and the opportunities afforded to me.

I hope you will see that I have appreciated how lucky I have been and still am to this day. I have a wonderful life with a beautiful wife, wonderful son, and genuine friends. I have also been fortunate enough to have enough enjoyable (and maybe not so enjoyable) experiences to tell you about. The story that follows will help guide you as to what makes me tick, my journey through life guided generally by the round ball and the men in red who kick seven bells out of it every Saturday afternoon.

I hope you enjoy it and maybe even think about having a go at doing it yourself before the grey matter fails you. As someone once told me, if you can read you can write!

—∿—

2

The Anfield Pilgrimage

You always remember your first time! Your first time at
anything. Good, bad or indifferent, and football is just
the same. Your first game, your first away game, your
first Cup Game, your first European game. There is a
rule though, your first reserve game doesn't count. It has
to be the first real first team match. Let's get this right, I
don't remember becoming a Liverpudlian because I was
born a Liverpudlian.

Pilgrimage usually refers to a once in a lifetime religious experiences such as trips to Mecca, Lourdes or
Easter at the Vatican. Football fans are lucky as they
make pilgrimages on a regular basis, for nine months a
year at least fortnightly, this is very fortunate. Have you
seen football fans go cold turkey during the summer
months between seasons? It's not a pretty sight. Watching any sport on TV will generally replace the love of
their life (that is football), indoor bowling from Milton
Keynes on a wet June afternoon is always a winner as is
the Golf from Macau at 4am. No wonder everyone is so
relieved as pre season gets underway.

Even though they don't really count, I do remember
my reserve game outings as they were fairly regular. My

dad used to take me to every reserve home game, as he got in for free with his season ticket. Probably the only thing that stopped me talking about football, was watching it. There were so few opportunities to watch it, no Sky Sports providing 24 hour coverage and live games in those days were generally only Cup Final's. I had to rely on Football Focus (BBC 1) with Sam Leitch and On the Ball (ITV) with Brian Moore. Pundits in those days were only for major shows such as the World Cup Final.

The reserve games were an adventure. A short bus ride from home, and we always got a seat on the bus, a long walk up the hill (or carried by my dad, if I was lucky, really lucky as I was a fat little beggar then at six years old) and we entered into a wonderful world. My wonderful world consisted of an empty stadium, except the main stand, which always held a decent crowd (well it was free to most wasn't it!) and a team on the pitch dressed in all red. Heaven!!! I knew the names of the players as I digested every line of the one page match programmes that cost about one penny. I was watching players like Steve Ogrizovich, a mountain of a man who never really made it at Anfield but had a wonderful career at Coventry City, and Hughie Macauley who was a reserve crowd favourite but I don't remember him making it past the bench for the first team. He ended up working in the Youth set up at Liverpool. The reserves were managed by Roy Evans, later to become first team manager, he was still young and learning following an early retirement from playing. If you were lucky you could see one of the first team favourites returning from injury to get match fit, not just from Liverpool the opposition often brought their stars of the day, whether it was to get fit or as a punishment for going out on the piss the night before a game. The opposition stars would generally be singled out for the wags in the crowd to take the piss out of them. By the way the word wags had a different meaning then. It referred to humorous people, not blonde girls in stilettos spending a fortune in designer shops and leeching off their husbands and boyfriends who just happen to be footballers. If it wasn't bad enough playing for the stiffs they now had a load of Scousers ripping the back out of them. Hand on heart I couldn't tell you which stars I saw except for Ian Callaghan once and that was because he was a hero of my dad's. Generally once the top players like Toshack, Keegan and Hughes were fit they went straight back in to the first team. The teams I watched wore red but contained kids desperate to make it and people who were past their sell by dates.

Reserve days out were great. We went in the turnstiles, which clicked as dad pushed me through the same gate so he didn't have to pay for me. As I ran up (I never walked) the steps, the bareness of the concrete faded as the first landing became a vibrant sea of people. We always seemed to come out by the tea bar, which seemed to have a very limited supply of food in those days and if it came to more than six items I would be surprised. We got tea or Bovril (no coffee, god forbid in the seventies), diluted Orange juice in plastic cartons and a free straw (my favourite), pies, Eccles Cakes (the ones with dead flies in them) and plain crisps. That was it. The tea tasted like piss but the Bovril was great. It was a dad's drink on a cold night as the wind whistled through the stand. The Bovril always took ages to cool down enough so I could take a drink, it was still like molten lava and burnt my tongue for weeks. Health and Safety didn't drive the world then, so the lesson had to be learned the hard way. I tried the Eccles Cake once and besides the dead fly thing it was so dry I never bothered again. Orange juice and plain crisps were my staple match diet unless it was freezing then I would get a grown up Bovril. We could always get served as well, even at half time the queues were surprisingly small. As long as the old bird behind the bar could see me, the pleasing sound of 'what would you like sweetheart' would float over the counter. Even at the age of six, I would go on my own. My dad had it planned, sit near the entrance right by a tea bar, and if I got a bit fidgety, it would be a big honour for him to let me go the tea bar. He could watch the match in peace for five minutes and he never worried about me as I couldn't get out of the ground. It wasn't that he didn't care, far from it. It was that people didn't have to worry in those days. Perverts were not on the agenda and you didn't worry every minute your child was out of view. It was just what you did and it was fine as there was no risk.

By the time the second half had run its course the stands would empty out and a blanket of cold would wrap around us. No matter how warm the day seems, football grounds are cold places when empty, a bit like churches. Once the worship is over there is an emptiness that brings with it an element of coldness. The walk back down the hill towards the Mersey would be a nightmare for my dad as he had to go through every shot and every header of the men in red. I re-lived every second of what was probably uninspiring and disappointing, but to a six year old it was a Cup Final. It was great as Liverpool won a lot (generally they won the reserve league), which means a lot to a little boy. When we got on the bus home, everybody would know where we had been and how the Reds had got on. Once we got home my mum got a re-run and I gloated to my brothers Ian and Kevin, as I was the chosen one who had been on the pilgrimage with my dad.

The next step on the ladder of superiority to my brothers was when I went to my first game where I saw the first team play. Keegan, Toshack, Hughes, Callaghan, Smith, Clemence, shall I go on? I was a reserve regular at six and it was only a matter of time until I went to watch the first team. Maybe a pre-season game, a friendly or even a testimonial is the usual introduction to the first team. Not for me though, I got the full treatment. I got taken to a league game in front of a full house, with the Kop baying for the lambs, well West Bromwich Albion, to be put to the slaughter. I was mesmerised, not by the football but the crowd. The Kop in full effect was as awe inspiring to me then as it is to any onlooker now. I had to keep remembering to watch the action on the pitch while the red tide pounded against the away team's battered defences. It was a good job that one of the goals in the 2-0 win was a penalty so I couldn't miss it, otherwise I might not have realised what made a crowd of people erupt with such unbridled delight.

The game is not what I remember the most; it's the journey that sticks in my mind. The day started like any other Saturday going to watch the reserves play. We put our coats on, me and my dad, walked out of the door almost forgetting to say bye to my mum. Up the street to the bus stop to wait for one of the buses to take us to Everton Valley, where we were then to head up the hill to Anfield. As the bus arrived it was busier than normal with standing room only. I remember standing by the bit where people put their luggage (I've never seen any luggage, just shopping bags). I was holding on to the silver pole like a crap lap dancer, holding as tight as I could, with my dad towering above me and shielding me from the crowd. I was chattering non stop and if I asked him once why the bus was that busy, I must have asked him a hundred times. His reply never faltered 'must all be going to the shops son'. 'God the Kwik Save was going to be busy' I thought.

As the bus pulled up at the bottom of Everton Valley, the doors opened and the first men jumped off before it stopped, doing that little run that makes them lean backwards so they don't fall flat on their face. As I said Health and safety didn't exist in the 70s, if you fell off a moving bus it was your fault, no one else's. As I said before most people would use public transport to get to a game and buses were dropping off their cargo of fans by the minute. This resulted in the mass movement of humanity up Everton Valley and towards the mighty Kop. I was lost amongst the adult bodies and could, from time to time, only catch glimpses of the Kop roof, and normally nothing or no one was in my way. God the shops were going to be busy today!

With my dad keeping a tight grip of my hand we took a left turn down one of the terrace streets near to the Kop, this leads to an alleyway that arrives at the side of the Kop and the Main Stand car park. This way we could miss out on the pushing and shoving and get into the car park without getting separated or crushed. As we turned left at the end of the alleyway there was a mass of bodies, moving against each other - left to right, backwards and forwards. There was no direct route to anywhere, if we had a 20 yard walk it ended up as a 40 yard walk due to the torturous route. I have seen this car park hundreds if not thousands of times over the years and it has never been as busy as that day, or was it just that I was only six years old?

Inside the ground the familiar layout was not so familiar now, with thousands of people pushing and jostling to get to their seats. Even the tea bars were heaving with people in queues, though as you may know there is no such thing as a tea bar queue on match day. It's just a mass of people trying to get to the counter and I made my dad get my plain crisps and orange juice. No dead fly cakes or Bovril as it was spring time and that called for spring rations. Dad stood me by the wall where he could keep an eye on me and try to get served at the same time. If he said don't move I wouldn't. Could you do that now? No! I think you would be terrified. I wasn't scared of my dad or anything, I just knew that if he told me to do something I would do it and not question it. I was also, if truth be known a little scared of getting lost, how would I find him in all those people?

Orange juice in hand, crisps in pocket it was getting to our seats which was the problem. It was at this point that my dad told me we were here to watch the first team play. All my real heroes - Keegan, Clemence and Hughes - not Hughie Macauley and his colleagues. I couldn't wait to get in there. With my dad providing a protective cordon around me, we headed up the stairs and towards the light. The feeling as I head from the belly of the ground into the stand and can see the pitch and the crowd for the first time still excites me to this day. As you head up the ten or so steps, you change worlds. The sky comes into view first, then the top of the stand facing, and then the glorious green pitch (and if you're lucky it has men in red already on it). Then finally your peripheral vision starts to reel in the sights of the terraces (as was) and the seats and bodies. As a young boy the noise was immense and I was smitten, love at first sight. I was sold. There was nothing else for me, and outside of my wife and baby boy, (not forgetting my own family) nothing has ever really come close. I realise it now, right now whilst I am writing this for them.

As the teams came out, that was that, I can't remember anything after the kick in, outside of the Kop swaying and singing and the penalty. Everything else must have been pretty good though as it has stayed with me for over 30 years.

The walk up has changed over the years, more cars than buses, different people, but it is always still familiar and welcoming and like the call to prayer in Istanbul all those years later the ground is whispering or sometimes even shouting 'come on it's time to worship'.

And every week another little boy will be lucky enough to go to his first proper home game with his dad. Just like I did, and like I hope Charlie will one day with his dad. With me!

—◈—

CHAPTER 3

Cultural experiences – away days

Home games were one thing and they only happened once a fortnight roughly speaking, and then for only nine months a year. If you wanted to further exercise every man or child's right to watch his beloved team play, you had to venture outside of your home ground and outside your city.

My first trip away was as surprising as my first visit to see the first team, as it came right out the blue. I didn't even have time to have a sleepless night, as it was a closely guarded secret. My cousin Tony, who you will meet again later on, used to come to all the home matches with me. My dad and his brother in law, my Uncle Len (Tony's dad) were best mates and they used to sit us in the corner of a little pub near Goodison Park. We would be sitting in the corner drinking our bottles of lemonade and eating our KP crisps, usually Beef flavoured for me. With all those e-numbers, I would be bouncing off the walls by the time I got home. I looked like I had really been to the pub. I used to love the smell of stale ale and felt like one of the big boys as I sipped my dads Brown Bitter (a Northerners pint if ever there was one) every time his back was turned or he went to the toilet. We were thick as thieves, me and our Tony, and we would spend as much time together as possible. Usually our one chance to meet was at home games as he lived in Ormskirk, a 20 minute car drive north of Liverpool, and my dad didn't drive. Going to our first away match, it just had to be together.

So it was to be, as one Saturday morning Uncle Len turned up and announced we were going to watch our Tony play football. Nothing unusual, I had been before. Tony played for a crack side in the Ormskirk league (we must have been eleven or twelve at the time). His team had a couple of lads in it who ended up as professional footballers (well sort of - they actually played for Everton). As we got to their pitch, they had only just kicked off and that was half an hour behind schedule. Then the match went to extra time as it was a cup match, and Uncle Len started to mutter under his breath and talking in hushed tones to my dad whilst comparing watches. I thought they were worried about how long they had left to win the match, but they weren't. They were worried about missing kick off. I don't know why they were worried as they usually missed all home kick offs by staying in the pub for one more pint. When the game finished and Tony came over, they dropped the bombshell that we were off to the match. But what exotic location was it to be? I can't glam it up at all - it was Leicester. Leicester City was not the biggest pull on the calendar for some, but for us, Filbert Street, then home of Leicester City, was as good as the Nou Camp or San Siro.

By the time we set off, Tony had been made to have a bath to clean the remnants of the pitch from his legs and knees. My Auntie Ann was not one for letting him out the house with dirty knees, covered by clothes or not.

Another 20 minutes did us no favours with the traffic, the M6 was slow going which was rarer than it is nowadays when you can't get anywhere fast. A succession of accidents and tailbacks delayed our progress and, as the kick off time of 3 o'clock approached (I know, what a novelty; a 3 o'clock on a Saturday), we were nowhere near Filbert Street. The route from the M6 was torturous and we had to make do with the radio commentary to keep us up to date with the action on the pitch. By the time we got to the ground and found a parking space, the streets were deserted and our only company was the pre-match litter. We went right around the ground and you wouldn't know a match was on, not a single turnstile was open and trying to get in was an impossibility, or so it seemed.

Our excitement of midday had all but disappeared, we were fed up kids now and probably a right royal pain in the arse. Then the good lord sent us a gift, a steward appeared from nowhere. Well he wasn't really a steward, as they didn't exist in the 70s. It was some fella who could get in and out of the ground and that was all we needed. Some money changed hands and hey presto! We were in the bowels of the main stand. It looked very similar to the main stand at Anfield, it was dirty and grimy and in need of repair. We heard applause from above filtering down to us at the bottom of the dank concrete steps. It was the end of half time and we had missed the whole of the first half and the ten minutes half time break. Remember ten minute half time intervals? Another thing that Sky got rid of, and don't you just love pundits talking rubbish for fifteen minutes?

We headed to find somewhere to sit. You would expect no seats but these were the days when not all the games sold out and the main stand at Filbert Street was half empty. Leicester were not doing too well and in this game they were already three down to the Reds. Once we sat down, as always, we needed a pee, and me and our Tony headed to the toilets. Big lads us, going away to watch the Reds and going to the toilets on our own. The wind was taken right out of our sails. Seeing a guy with a Liverpool scarf on Tony announced that 'we've only just got here mate you know'. Total indifference and with a shrug the guy was gone. Tony was gutted, we were still only kids but there was no need to treat us like it.

Back up the stairs it wasn't great to watch. At 3-0 up Liverpool were cruising and their foot was so far off the pedal it was in the boot. They still managed to score another though, think it was old carrot head and super-sub Davie Fairclough, rounding off in style to finish the game 4-0. As we clapped the Reds off we were still delighted to be on foreign soil and getting a little wave off the men in red, it always cheered us. I still don't leave until I get the wave.

The journey home was worse than the journey there. Trying to get out of the streets around the old football grounds in England was always murder. It may be a little better with some of the new ground locations, but traffic control is not something the English do well. I was in San Francisco a number of years ago and we took in the San Francisco 49ers playing American Football. The roads outside were made up of four lanes, two in two out, well what's new there? Going to the game, three lanes led into the stadium straight from the freeway and one led out (for emergency purposes I was told). After the game the situation was reversed with three lanes leading to the freeway, which had traffic control allowing easy access. Simple but effective and it allowed 50% more traffic to leave the area of the ground.

Leicester seemed to just be grid locked for an hour after the game. Every ground I go to, I always seem to be in traffic for an hour after a game. As we headed out into the Leicestershire countryside, starvation was kicking in. First stop would be a chippy (also known as a Fish and Chip shop for anyone down south) wherever we saw one. These were the days when there were still plenty everywhere you went. We found one in Ashby de la Zouch. Where's that, France? No, it is actually in Leicestershire. How it got its name is beyond me as it is, or at least was quintessentially English. The fish and chips went down a treat and it fulfilled one of my dad's lifetime ambitions, which was to go to Ashby de la Zouch just to see what was there after years of seeing it on signposts. With the creation of a new motorway, I have never been there again and I am hardly likely to either.

Back at school on the Monday and I was a celebrity. It was a rarity to hear of anyone who had travelled the length and breadth of Britain and come back to tell the tale. This was the shape of things to come - I was going to go everywhere! Well it wasn't, it was very quickly made quite clear that this was a one off, and I cant recall another trip until I was a sixteen year old and went under my own steam.

At sixteen years old I braved the Football Special (the train that is) to Wolverhampton. On a sunny August day, which heralded the start of the season, I took the train down to a welcoming Wolverhampton, where we were playing Wolverhampton Wanderers (the Wolves). However it wasn't the welcome I imagined at all. The Special was met by the whole of the West Midland police force, which seemed a little over the top until we saw the second welcoming committee of thousands of Wolves fans. The escort to the ground and back was fairly threatening but also uneventful with more posturing and gesturing than action. This was something I was to get used to as this was the 80s, and that is the way we generally watched our football. Escorted to and away from grounds, fenced in like animals but kept safe. I knew no different and was there for the actual game so it didn't matter that much. I was OK as long as I got to see the 90 minutes without getting battered. We often spent more time waiting for the game to start than it took to play the thing, and we very rarely wore any club colours, a small enamel badge with a Liver Bird was all that might ever give us away. But this was the path I chose, so I would put up with any hardships to see the Reds. Looking back now, what a way for a civilised society to behave. Tribalism took over the English way of watching football.

As the Football Specials gave way to different ways to get to and from places, things changed. Away games were always something to look forward to, as we had to do more than get the bus to County Road and traipse through the park. There was so much to do; it needed planning, and willing travel companions. The planning was usually down to me. On the rare occasions others sorted the plans, things usually went pear shaped. On one occasion we ended up at the back of the Chelsea member's enclosure and faced a baying mob of Chelsea's members, supposedly their better behaved fans who threatened us for 90 minutes than waited a further hour to threaten us outside the ground.

Generally, I was the ticket king, travel advisor and car driver to hundreds of games outside of the European Capital of Culture. It was great to find out what life was like outside of our own city and gave us a taste of how popular we were in the outlying regions of Her Majesties kingdom. We were not always the most popular guests in town, but outsiders were never really that welcome anywhere. I can trace the away day experience from downright hatred and hostility everywhere we went, through picking and choosing carefully where we went and our form of transportation, and finally a general warm welcoming fan base which, outside the grounds, had become much more accepting of the presence of away fans. Thankfully we now have an environment where we can wear our clubs' colours with pride and not a wariness that results in hiding anything that gives away our homeland.

I love meeting people and getting to know them, so today it is great when I meet opposing fans with a similar mentality. Share a pint, discuss the match, have the craic, sounds great doesn't it. Sadly it was not like that for much of my time following football. I was used to being herded from train stations, car parks and coach parks, to and from grounds with as little human contact as possible. To be fair it was often a relief to get in and be safe, but we always had to think about getting home. These really were, in many ways, the bad old days. Good people couldn't be heard and the hooligan minority often seemed to represent the majority. Now, for a number of reasons, and believe what you wish, things have changed for the better. Some of the theories put forward are as follows

- The Heysel disaster woke people up to the consequences of the mob mentality and the horrendous results of the actions of so few, what happens when people act as a mob and follow people they generally would not.

- Policing is much better than it ever was before. The use of intelligence and infiltration of gangs has been so successful that people who may often be influenced no longer see it as an attractive option to get caught fighting. There is now a stigma to being a football hooligan, where it was previously glamourised.

- The drug culture may be somewhat coincidental, but less reliance upon alcohol and the use of more drugs such as cocaine and cannabis, has in some areas contributed to a more chilled out fan who finds no reason to fight as he is high as a kite and wants love not war.

- Less alcohol is certainly a reason for a reduction in violence, but as a society drink has always blighted our city centres on a Friday or Saturday evening. The funny thing was many of the better-known hooligans shunned drink so their senses were sharper in the fight. What control of alcohol does is change the mob mentality and the "sheep" who follow at the instigation of others.

In my opinion the Hillsborough disaster has contributed dramatically to the improvements of fans' behaviours.

After the Taylor report into the disaster, people finally had to listen to what we, as followers, had said for years. Heavy handed policing, caging fans into decrepit unsafe stadiums, and not ploughing money back in to facilities was an accepted practice by the football authorities in the early 80s. Where had all the money gone? We were treated like dirt and we expected it, put up with it, and in some ways we deserved it. As a group of people, we need to regulate our behaviour ourselves. But if you treat people like animals they are going to behave like animals. Because you were a football fan you were automatically a second class citizen and because of peoples' behaviours through the 70s and the 80s, the authorities looked to be well within their rights to treat us badly. After Hillsborough people gained a voice and people woke up to a terrible tragedy that could have been avoided. People immediately blamed the disaster on hooliganism, but it was the result of incompetence, poor planning and treating people in a way you should never treat people. Regrettably the people who blamed hooliganism never really apologised for the mistruths and myths they created.

Unfortunately 96 people had to lose their lives for people to wake up and smell the coffee and realise that they should not blame the majority for the actions and behaviour of the minority. When you sit in your shiny new stadiums, and the stewards and police treat you fairly and with respect, say a little thanks to our departed fellow supporters. They never had the opportunity we now have, so say a little prayer and be thankful. The thing about Hillsborough was that it could have been anyone that day, not just Liverpool but any club who could have been in the same position. "There but for the grace of God go I". More by luck than design it could have happened in the same place a couple of years earlier to Leeds United, once again in a semi-final at the same ground. Do you know what? No one ever dispelled the myth that that was hooliganism either, because we had no voice. I think people woke up, but also people grew up and realised what was important.

The following pages portray just a couple of my most memorable times following my passion, the good, the bad and sometimes the downright ugly. Pick out your club if you like, you may remember some of the events or it might make you think of your great days out. For anyone who was there with me, don't argue about the events as I was usually the one who was sober and had to drive home, and by the way I had to keep myself awake all the way home while you lot were snoring and blocking out my eighties sounds (yes even in the nineties!)

—⚏—

Milwall 12th of April 1989

Definitely one to remember, this was the bad old days. Note the date – its there for a reason. Three days before our ill-fated trip to Hillsborough for the FA Cup semi final. Liverpool had a great team under Dalglish and we went everywhere expecting a win and the football was often a wonder to behold. Aldridge, Barnes and Beardsley were in full flow and, even though a little off the pace of the league leaders Arsenal, were in with a shout of the league and cup double.

Cold Blow Lane was not the most hospitable of places to go and earlier that year we had a visit in the FA cup that was a fairly naughty affair. All of our coaches had been bricked on the way in and the way out. Trouble had flared for most of the afternoon, but at least Liverpool had won the match well. One of the highlights of the day was when the Liverpudlian's in the crowd spotted Peter Hewitt, the actor who was, at that time, playing the wide boy Joey Boswell in the Liverpool based comedy Bread. Obviously being well known as playing a Liverpudlian, I don't think he was too keen with 3000 Scouse voices singing "One Joey Boswell" and alerting all the hyped up Londoners to his presence. He didn't stay all afternoon - he soon disappeared as fighting sporadically erupted all around him. At the time it was funny because there were 3000 of us, and guarded by police we would be getting escorted out, so no worries there. The problem that day was that all the old faces, who liked a bit of trouble, had travelled and they were quite happy to mix with whoever and whenever. What happened that day was to affect our next visit and it certainly did. You might think I was mad to go, but I had never had a fight following the Reds, I was always careful and my record was intact – I hadn't missed a home or away game since August 1985.

Midweek is never a good time to travel in England and especially during the 1980s, so we decided that, even following our last visit, the coach was the best, and probably still the safest, option. In 1989 a local coach firm, Amberline, specialised in long distance trips to Sunny Spain and had a fleet of expensive double decker coaches. Wanting to get the most from their money they had to use them at every opportunity and the holiday off season was the football season, so we travelled on executive coaches. After years of second rate travel, this was great.

Travel was booked through Barnes Travel on County Road, and over the course of the year they organised travel for thousands upon thousands of Reds fans. This away trip though, the numbers were closer to a hundred - three days before a cup semi-final, a midweek trip to the capital was not on everybody's agenda. This was for the undeterred and hardcore away supporters. The one thing I forgot to say about Amberline's coach fleet was that it was not the most reliable and this was to be one of their unreliable days. A 2 pm departure to the capital was always cutting it fine when you then had to make your way into deepest darkest London. Millwall. I don't think it could be more central, and that made getting to it difficult when you had to battle the London rush hour traffic. 2 pm came and went and the coach didn't move an inch. There was much shaking of heads by the Coach stewards and it didn't look like the coach was going anywhere. Due to a fault they were waiting for a mechanic from their depot, which was in Speke in the south of Liverpool a good half an hour away. It looked like we were going nowhere that night.

With the promise of a full refund we took our lives in our hands and decided to make our own way. There were six of us including Tommy the Butcher, Brian with an ulcer, big Chris, Zil, Our Kev and me, and we had two cars. It cost more in petrol than the coach, and we were cutting it fine, but we could make it. Brian took some convincing to drive that far, and so did his passengers as he was blind as a bat and scared the living daylights out of anyone in the car. We tried not to think about our reception committee at Milwall.

All went well until the Thelwall Viaduct in Cheshire, where we hit a wall of traffic, this certainly was not our day. The traffic was crawling and my hopes of three points and maintaining my attendance record were going out of the window. Then I realised we could get off the motorway and head for Crewe. It was less than ten miles to the train station from the motorway junction. I knew this because we had done it earlier in the year for a cup game. A quick chat to the others in the traffic jam to tell them the plan, you know you roll the window down and talk (for my younger readers mobile phones had not been invented for the likes of us yet). All my travelling companions thought it was a stroke of genius – as there must be at least one train an hour from Crewe to London.

Travelling at 80 miles an hour, and only ten miles to go, should have meant we would be in Crewe in no time at all. Wrong!!! It turned out the delays on the motorways were due to high winds, and the arteries leading on and off the motorways were blocked. How did we find out? It was when we had to drive around or over the top of the branches of fallen trees. This was getting beyond a joke and it was now nearing four o'clock. Only three and a half hours to kick off. After a few dodgy turns and shady manoeuvres we broke through god's natural barricade and hit Crewe. Into the car park like Starsky and Hutch followed by the Dukes of Hazard. Parked up, locked up and hightailed it into Crewe station. Ticket office window 'six returns to Euston please mate' on a single credit card (at that time you had to have money to have credit cards and not many of us really did). British Rail (yes that's how long ago this was, because they have been gone for years) duly obliged, 'When's the next train mate and what platform?' It was leaving in one minute and you guessed it, the furthest platform away from the ticket office. We made it to the platform just in time to see the guard laughing his head off as the train pulled away. Was this it? Had our last chance to make the match had slipped away?

A quick check of the schedules and we could see a five o'clock train to London Euston was a chance and the journey time was an hour and 55 minutes. Get in there! Let's go to the pub! Over the road from the station was a little convenient pub, which must have been called The Railway, they always are. As we were supposed to be on the coach the food of the day was a carry out (packed lunch to others) so we supped a few beers, ate our butties and played some pool and made sure we were back at the platform in plenty of time. Easy this travelling lark isn't it?

It couldn't go wrong now, all we needed was a taxi at the other end and we might only miss a bit of the first half. However, I think the guard must have had his ear to the ground because he decided to take the piss a little bit more. We were just relaxing in our seats when he proceeded to tell us about technical difficulties, which may add an hour on to our journey if it couldn't be sorted out. That put the top hat on it for us so we resigned ourselves to going to Euston and coming straight home again. Finally God, or at least British Rail, gave us some sort of break. The technical difficulty was sorted and we would be in Euston on time.

We moved as far up the carriages towards the front of the train as possible, and hit the ground running at Euston, before the train had even stopped, and we headed to the underground taxi rank. Two taxis, 'There's extra in it for you if you do Milwall by half seven'. That was the cue for a Wacky Races rendition through the busy streets of London, heading to the south of the river and the Old Kent Road. On the way our cabby picked up another passenger, Benny from Oslo (this is no word of a lie). Benny was in London on business and decided to take in a football match and, as with most Scandinavians, he had a love for the Mighty Reds. We were flying through the streets interrogating Benny about Norway and his family, which was how we found out that he had three daughters between 16 and 25. You never know, we could have had our own little exchange programme going. Benny was wetting himself, going to the match and with Scousers as well, he had no idea how dangerous the next part of the journey could be.

With the taxis racing each other it looked like we were actually going to make it, we were nearly there now as we hit the Old Kent Road. Then, right in front of us, a car ran over a dog, the wheels ran right over its back. I can still hear the yelp now. Without wanting to upset dog lovers everywhere, we drove on. I will blame the taxi driver if it makes you think better of me, but none of the lads argued as he left the scene and neared Cold Blow Lane. Thank God, we had made it. 'Cheers mate' we gladly shouted as he dropped us outside the ground. It was only as we saw the mass of unwelcoming faces staring in our direction did we realise he dropped us right outside the home end. Thankfully, as it was literally two minutes before kick off, all we had to deal with were the stragglers, who though moving menacingly towards us, they couldn't stop us heading towards a police cordon and down a side alley to the away end. Five minutes earlier we might have been in big trouble because we stood out like a sore thumb. As we went through the turnstile we heard the whistle blow as the match kicked off and we missed all of the first 30 seconds of the match. As we headed towards the middle of the terrace, still with Oslo Benny in tow, we bumped into some of the lads we met on the coach earlier in the afternoon. On asking how they got there, the reply astounded us all, by coach!! The coach had left with only 20 people on it and by some miracle arrived ten minutes before kick off. Why did we bother!

I would like to say I remember the match, but from what had gone on before, that was never likely. I do remember teaching Benny all manner of Liverpool songs, including such hilarious ditties about London Bridge falling down and songs about a certain Man United player with a rather nasty rash. Funny but Benny loved it. Liverpool did win 2-1 but this may have been the end of an era without us knowing it, things were to go cruelly wrong in the years to come.

As we left the ground we were still celebrating a crucial victory in the Big Smoke, but celebrations were short lived when we hit the tough streets of South London. This was the unforgiving playground of Milwall. They hadn't given us the warmest reception inside the ground, and they were still obviously smart-ing following the alleged liberties that Scousers had taken on their manor in the cup game earlier in the year. 'No one likes us, we don't care' That's what their song is. Its not bloody surprising if that's how you treat your visitors. As we headed into the cool night air following the warmth of an evening football crowd, we expected quite a reception from the locals. At the time, we were safely ensconced in a police escort, so we would be all right. We got no reception at all, the streets around the ground were totally deserted, doors all locked and no bystanders. This was unusual for an escort as usually all the locals at least came out to gawp at the weird Northerners, maybe even shout a few derogatory comments about Scousers being on the dole and robbers. Always hilarious when shouted by someone who looks like one of Harry Enfield's Slobs. As we headed through the deserted streets towards the tube station at New Cross Gate, we were half expecting to be charged at from one of the side streets, but nothing came. Even for someone who abhors the violence that often blighted our experiences, it was seemingly an anti-climax, nothing to tell at work the following day. Then, just 100 yards from the Tube station, everything went mental, Milwall fans came from everywhere and were charging at us desperately trying to breach the escort. People were trying to get at them too from our side, then from behind them someone was attacking them, it was West Ham allegedly. It was mad and this was when I saw the most amazing sight. There was a fella on the floor lashing out at a police dog. What's unusual about that? The dog had the fella's head in his jaws and behind him there were people being slammed into the side of a stationary bus. Then they started firing fireworks into the escort. Thankfully, for me at least, the police managed to get us away from the mayhem and into the station with the violence still raging. Right onto a tube and non-stop to Euston.

Oslo Benny was still with us and, whilst a little shocked, he had still had a great night, I imagine him the following morning at some high-powered meeting when someone asked him if he had a quiet night the evening before. Hopefully he was professional and let people believe he had a quiet night at Pizza Hut. At

4 2

Euston Benny had a short journey back to his hotel but we had to retrace our footsteps back via Crewe to Liverpool.

—✹—

Not all trips held the same excitement as going to Milwall and the general travel experience could often be more banal than exciting. The sheer effort to get to places to see 90 minutes of action on a bit of grass often wasn't worth it. Every trip holds its own memory and I could go on for hours but thankfully due to printing costs I will spare you that. What I hoped to demonstrate was the taste of the travels of the away supporter. Taste was really important, as it was your butties that sustained you on your journey. Various sandwich fillings were to be found, from the Salmon boys' Salmon Sandwiches, drenched in vinegar, to the Corn Beef, Lettuce and salad cream of Jugsy, or the Hoola Hoop sandwiches that popped up once in a while, to finally the four cans of lager for Zil which happened without fail. Zil was never with food but never starved he used to hoover up leftovers and accept peoples' sympathy offerings.

To the away supporter the football is often secondary to the trip, the fun you have outweighs the game and the memories I now have are of the time I spent in good company and only little flickers of football action sometimes spring to mind. For action buy a DVD.

In total I travelled to around 60 football grounds. Considering Liverpool never dropped through the divisions, new grounds only came along on cup runs. That's not bad going. A number of them don't even exist now as the clubs have moved to pastures new.

I am sorry to say it, but there is no space for stories such as when I led the Newcastle Gallowgate end in the singing of 'Sack the board'. With Liverpool cruising against a woeful Newcastle side the message on the big steel bins outside sprung to mind and I started singing to be joined in by a couple of thousand Liverpool fans. Much to our amazement and delight the rest of the ground, some 30,000 Geordies joined in and the chant was deafening.

There's also no space for the tale of our trip to Norwich where, even though we left Liverpool at 6.30am, we missed Liverpool's goal in a 1 – 0 win. It wasn't like we were delayed on the road, we got to Norwich at 11.00am and went straight the pub, a favourite travelling pub of ours called the Compleat Angler. It was only a ten minute walk to the ground but we kept getting reasons to stay. Big Chris who was famous for blowing up condoms on his head (an 80s party trick if ever there was one) was one last breath away from the need for Hospital care as the condom thankfully went pop. His big blue head in the condom was hilarious, that sounds rude on its own though. As we all caught our breath following our laughing fits we headed for the balcony, which hung over the river across from Norwich train station. Some of our travelling band of brothers, rather the worse for wear after hours in our pub, had commandeered a pleasure boat. As Norwich is the entrance to the Norfolk Broads it was always going to happen. We had the sight of a Scouse Captain and his first mate and second and third mates for the matter, trying to steer the boat through a cannabis haze, with a guy in a sailor's cap running up the towpath threatening them with the police. They were not being rude but as they were having fun they politely declined his request and the Norfolk Constabulary were called, the Scouse plan to get to the ground by boat was scuppered. The scallies bailed out a couple of hundred yards up the footpath away from the police and disappeared into the match traffic as the boat gently slid into the bank. Arriving at the ground, going in the wrong end we were to be gently persuaded to leave by the local police, Liverpool scored as we were escorted around the back of the ground. The next 85 minutes bored the life out of us. To make matters worse by the time we got home, Match of the Day had shown the game and we missed the goal again.

I am glad to say there is no space for any stories about Southampton. The old Dell, their home ground, was always a horrendous place to go, firstly the journey was one of the longest on our calendar but when we got there we could end up watching the game from the 'Chicken Run'. A shallow terrace fenced in and we were cooped up, tough to get a pie and a piss and even tougher for Liverpool to pick up any points.

And finally, no place for an iconic moment of the 80s. It was 1984 to be precise Liverpool played Walsall (from the West Midlands) in the Milk Cup and to their credit, the team from two leagues below got a draw at Anfield in the first leg of the semi final. This was a Liverpool team, which included Hansen, Dalglish, Souness and Rush. The return was one of those magical cup nights. A ramshackle old fashioned ground with a nip in the air and all the atmosphere of the cup with a full house (19,000 at the time) roaring both sides on. Liverpool were to win 2 – 0 but as they scored the second, a wall collapsed in the Liverpool end. The shallow terrace meant that whilst celebrating, many people didn't know that anything had happened. With the game delayed the iconic moment arrived. Graeme Souness picked up a child in his arms and carried him to safety. That image was flashed across the newspapers and TV stations. I could have been in an iconic picture of my own if the press had been present an hour after the game under the raised sections of the M6. The ground and the train station was dissected by the M6 motorway and to get back to the special train we were corralled under the motorway in the pitch dark and as always the organisation was so woeful people were getting crushed. So what did the police do? They rode in on horseback to calm the crowd. I was hemmed in by a massive grey horse desperately trying to keep my feet away from the hoofs of the beast. As I was looking down the horse decided it was feeding time and started chomping on my hair, horse slobber is not recommended, it doesn't hold like hair gel and smells of horse piss, I don't know where he had been licking. Imagine that picture over your cornflakes, not as good as Souness carrying a kid is it?

If only I had space to tell you those stories it would give you a true picture of travelling away to watch your team.

—ɯ—

4

A night of shame

The Heysel disaster in May 1985 is a part of the history of Liverpool FC that nobody really wants to admit to. 'It wasn't our fault' is a cry you sometimes hear from the more belligerent of our followers. But it was our fault, well some of us at least. We have to be honest about the part that we, as supporters, played in the death of 39 people. There are a number of reasons for the disastrous events of that night but they still do not represent a defence for the actions of some people. There are people with blood on their hands.

It might surprise you to hear (or maybe not) that I am not admitting to any guilt whatsoever in the death of the 39, mainly Italian, people. Thousands of others will say the same. My defence is that I wasn't even in the ground as the disaster evolved. I was still on the way to the stadium, but I was witness to the chaotic aftermath. In my view that puts me in the fortunate position of not having had to witness any of the graphic events first hand.

Until I started writing this chapter I didn't remember much of the events of Brussels in 1985, but they are becoming clearer as I write. They have been placed to the very back of my mind as unwanted history. Things that I never wanted to think or talk about, until now, at which point I feel almost compelled to.

Liverpool had cruised effortlessly to the European Cup Final as holders, having won the trophy the year before in Rome against the local side Roma. The win, though, was tainted by the brutality shown against the Liverpool fans by their Roman counterparts. The joy of their first win in Rome in 1977 wasn't matched by the travelling Liverpool fans following the 1984 victory. Following Liverpool's victory over the local favourites, organised and systematic attacks against the supporters started as soon as they left the ground. Truth be known the attacks had actually started early that morning and lasted throughout the day as the unsuspecting visiting supporters arrived in the city. That night in Rome, hundreds of fans were hospitalised and hundreds of others headed to the British Embassy when their coaches left the ground with out them. Fans were stabbed and slashed and, into the night, roaming scooter gangs were still attacking groups of supporters heading back to their hotels. The hotels wouldn't even let their guests back in for fear of reprisal. Years later and Liverpool fans still receive the same response in Rome, as do Manchester United, and each time the police have done little, if anything, to stop the Romans acting in such a way. Where was I? Well it certainly wasn't Rome, that's for sure, and from the reports back, mightily relieved I was too. I was in between a rock and a hard place, my dad had stopped going away and none of my mates at that time travelled to watch the Reds. So for me the plan was to stay at home and watch with all the other armchair supporters.

The stories of the attacks and abuse, including one thirteen-year-old boy who needed 200 stitches to facial wounds, had certainly done the rounds in Liverpool. Italian opponents in the final brought an element of scaremongering and fear of reprisal. I was nineteen at the time and had started following the Reds away from home quite regularly and this didn't worry me that much really. 'Go on an organised trip' was always the way I looked at it. Get a police escort in and away from the nutters and I would be alright. The 1980s were undoubtedly the years that were the height of football violence in the UK. Our transport would be routinely attacked, but we'd get an escort to and from the ground by a substantial police presence. We might get abused but not much, well that was my experience at least. I had seen some violence but never been involved in any and 22 years later I can still say the same.

To appease my mum and dad though I went on an organised trip run by a guy my dad knew. Alan Brown used to wander into Anfield as if he owned it. I never quite knew how he was connected, but he was and still is as I still see him nowadays, his head held high marching in through the Directors' door at Anfield. 'Browny' was a top fella, my dad said, and when I met him he seemed to be. He was like a docker with a degree of sartorial elegance. Top to toe pristine and he knew everybody.

My dad used to see 'Browny' after the match over a drink in the company of Roy Evans, who was gravitating up the coaching ranks at Anfield. Good company both of them and my dad would regale stories that started with "Evvo (Roy Evans that is) said that Ian Rush has a sore toe. Kenny Dalglish .... blah blah blah. Well

'Browny' was running a trip for the families of the players, and my dad got him to keep a space on it for me. I was already working (no mean feat in Liverpool in the mid 80s) and whilst it was a little more expensive than a normal trip, it wasn't going to break the bank.

I rolled up to Liverpool airport on the morning of the match and the plan was to fly to Brussels early, travel to our hotel in a town called Ghent and then travel back to the stadium from there. European travel plans especially on Cup Final days never went according to plan though and delays were inevitable. Liverpool airport terminal at the time was some two miles from its current position. It was art deco at its best and has now been converted into a swish Crowne Plaza hotel. Art Deco or not, there was still nowhere to sit, eat or drink. It was a nightmare with thousands of others in the same position. Contingency plans were never made in the 80s, no one gave a monkies then. By the time we were airborne, it was already early afternoon and at least four hours delayed. But I was really excited. I had my best bobble hat and scarf on, properly dressed for a Cup Final. Looking back now I was a walking fashion disaster. According to Nikki I still was when I met her and if she ever needs a laugh she just gets out my old holiday photos. Things that I thought so stylish don't stand the test of time, just ask George Michael and his Wham outfits. As we landed in Brussels it was roasting hot, but the woolly bobble hat stayed on. I wanted to get going to the ground but, as I was in a group, I had to go with the plan. By the time we left the Airport it was mid afternoon and kick off wasn't too far away. We headed up country to the town of Ghent, just under an hours drive. Check-in was a headache, as always, and people were going to freshen up, why?

Didn't they know there was a match to get to? Of course they did but they were not after the same experience as I was. I was after the fans experience and they were there for their sons or brothers or mates who were representing us in red that day. I remember speaking to Bruce Grobbelaar's parents and the parents of Paul Walsh, and they were all great. They were all excited but for different reasons than me. They were proud of the individual and I was proud of my team.

I was an add-on to the families, and as such I ended up sharing with some random mate of some player or other. He was sound but looked unnervingly like Bernie Flint (the Singing postman from Southport who won Opportunity Knocks for an eternity). He had his little lad with him who must have been about nine years old. To be honest, I got more sense out of him than his old fella, who just wanted to blag on about who his mates were. For what seemed an age, we hung around reception whilst the players' families messed around getting ready. I was itching to get going and was cursing under my breath. It was my first European Cup Final and I was missing the whole build up. As it turned out they probably did me a favour, as I am glad I didn't witness first hand what happened next.

As our coach hit the Motorway, the events that were unfolding in the Heysel Stadium would change the football world for years to come.

—ᴧᴧ—

The Heysel Stadium was on the outskirts of Brussels and right next to one of its main landmarks, the Atomium, which was built for the World's Fair of 1958 and symbolises Crystal molecules (or some science type stuff). As we approached the ground, the steel spheres were glistening in the sunlight and it was quite some sight. By 7pm local time disaster struck. The view from the Atomium was to be horrific, overlooking the horrors that had happened within its shadows.

The Stadium itself was a huge bowl with open terraces at both ends and covered seating on each side. The pitch was surrounded by an old running track putting quite some distance between the fans at each end and the goal nets. The stadium was built in 1920 and was to be demolished after the European Cup Final to create a new modern stadium. That says it all. What a choice by UEFA to opt for a dilapidated stadium to host the biggest game in club football. There are stadiums that are being knocked down and stadiums that <u>NEED</u> to be knocked down. Heysel was the latter of the two. The terraces were of the most awful standard, I find it hard to describe to give you a clear picture but here goes.

If you can imagine a piece of concrete on the floor, about two inches in width and a depth of six inches, held in position by steel bolts half an inch in diameter. Behind the concrete was packed sand or rubble, which resulted in an uneven surface that created an imbalance in crowd movements, making it difficult to stand correctly. Even before we got to the terrace, the ground was falling apart. There were little shacks for turnstiles with concrete panels linking them together. By the time I got to the stadium perimeter, the concrete panels were broken and the turnstiles were out of use. The ground just couldn't cope. I still have my full ticket to this day, as no one checked it. People were wandering in and out of the ground at will. I got to the ground about half an hour before scheduled kick off time and there was not a single policeman in sight. That was because all the police resources had been deployed inside as disaster had struck (well they stood on the running track watching events, too frightened to move).

Reports from the day time in Brussels paint a picture of heavy drinking in the sunshine with a generally good natured atmosphere in most of the city centre, although there were reported skirmishes between opposing fans in parts of the city. Police moved all fans to the stadium as early as possible to contain any potential threat, and this threat was supposedly massive. Depending upon who you listen to there were English Hooligans, the British Army (who allegedly often caused trouble abroad), and the Italian Ultras all there in force. If you believe it, English Hooligans didn't actually mean Liverpool fans, there are reports of Milwall, Luton, Newcastle and the West Ham ICF (the famous hooligan Inter City Firm) all present and all hell bent on trouble. I don't know whether to believe it or not as I saw no evidence of it, it may just have been a smoke screen and the 'it's not our fault' mentality.

Blame is a game and there are plenty of players in that game for the Heysel disaster. UEFA, Belgian Police, Juventus Fans but most of all Liverpool Fans.

UEFA, in their wisdom, gave Juventus a whole end of terracing, but Liverpool only about half of the terrace with the other half being sold to neutral fans. Once again Liverpool Football Clubs protests fell on deaf ears. The neutral tickets sold in Belgium ended up mainly in the hands of Italian ex-pats and ultimately on the black market to Juventus fans. The Liverpool section was overcrowded and spaces were evident in the neutral areas. Between the two areas were two lines of chicken wire dividing the two sections with little or no police presence in between. It was an accident waiting to happen. The events are a little unclear as to what started the fateful events, but it was widely reported by many in England, that Italians were spitting and throwing objects into the Liverpool enclosure and the final straw was when they targeted a young child. People on the Liverpool side surged at the segregation fence and it buckled and the Italians retreated away from the fence. Others say that people just got annoyed at the lack of space they had. With a gaping hole in the fence, there was a surge of people heading towards the Italians. Barrages of missiles were exchanged and more English became involved advancing towards the Italians and then retreating to their own enclosure. Nothing new in this maybe, as this had been seen on terraces across Britain and the Continent in many years preceding. The difference was that the Italian fans had nowhere to go and they were penned back against a wall. The sheer weight of numbers and the force created meant that the wall crumbled and collapsed. Men, women and children were crushed and suffocated by the weight of the bodies pinning them down. There, in the sunshine, 39 people died as a result of the actions of a minority. Those who died were not hooligans, they were decent normal people who went to a football match but never came home.

I only know now what happened from the TV reports I was to see later. Our coach was still stuck in the heavy traffic surrounding the ground and it was approaching 8pm local time. As we arrived, I was itching to get inside and as soon as the coach parked up, I was away, not even a goodbye to my fellow travellers. I didn't want to miss out on the biggest match I had ever been to. What I was to find on the other side of the broken concrete fences that surrounded the stadium, totally confused me, and did so for hours, and maybe even days, to come.

As I entered the stadium, my ticket still grasped tightly in hand, there was no one to greet me. I was met with a wall of backs of the people who faced the pitch. The sun was beating down but there was no atmosphere, which was odd as usually the travelling fans would be in great voice by now, especially after a day on the beer. But there was nothing, no action on the pitch. Over the heads of the crowd I could make out the bowl shape of the stadium, and everywhere seemed to be packed solid. The Juventus end opposite us, and the stands on either side seemed to be full to busting. I started to edge myself through the crowds, dipping below the crash barriers as I headed for a decent spec to watch from. Usually half way down would do me, not too near the front so I could see as much of the game as possible. I was more intent on watching my footing on the dilapidated terracing and keeping my balance than to look around any further than the first five yards. I picked up little pieces of conversations from people as I passed 'It wont kick off on time now' ... 'They started it, then they just shit themselves and ran away' ... 'Why don't they let us stand over there now'. When I finally settled and stood firmly in my position, I looked around me and to my right there was a huge swathe of terracing with no one on it, covered in a blanket of dust and litter. In the bottom corner at the far side I could make out a commotion. The Police were on the edge of it and also positioned on the track in front of it. I didn't know at the time, but people were dying there and the commotion was a frantic effort to release people from a crush. In between the commotion and me was 70 yards or more of empty terrace covered in litter, plastic bags, scarves, hats and banners. Look closer and the colours were mainly black and white (the colours of Juventus) and they were scattered around the crush barriers, many of which had buckled.

Finding out what had actually happened was difficult, as people really didn't know what had gone on initially. People knew there had been a massive fight but due to the position on the terrace, only those closest or farthest away had any clear view of what had actually happened. Those in the middle of the crowd generally didn't see much past the heads of people to their right hand side; those in the stands would have seen it all.

What people were focusing on though was the mayhem that was being created at the other end of the stadium. As all the police presence was down at the Liverpool end, the Italian end was left unguarded, and it wasn't long before things started to go wild. Having seen the events unfold at the other end of the pitch and seen their Italian counterparts chased out of the stadium, the Juventus Ultras were looking to exact revenge. Anyone wearing a Liverpool shirt or t-shirt was fair game for a severe beating, and the Juventus Ultras were chasing people out of their end and attacking them pitch side. The victims were beaten severely with fists, feet and flag poles, until they were dazed and bleeding. Many made it to the safety of our end. The Belgian Riot Police showed no interest in the events unfolding with the Juventus fans at the other end of the pitch; they were wholly focused on us and I found that quite ridiculous. Obviously they had real reason to concentrate on us following what had happened but I didn't know that then. The apathy changed when an Italian fan strode purposely out of the

Juventus end and produced a handgun (later identified as a starting pistol), face covered, he aimed purposefully at the banks of Liverpool supporters and seemed to fire off a number of rounds, until slinking back in to the Juventus end and disappearing in to the crowd. At this point the opportunity for disorder on the largest scale ever seen was a huge possibility. As police finally headed to the Juventus end to seal off the pitch invasions, the authorities appealed for calm confirming that the game would be played if and when people calmed down.

The Liverpool end was silent and faced by banks of police on horseback and on foot. The team captains appealed for calm and Phil Neal, Liverpool's captain, was greeted by cheers by the vast majority who wanted order restored. Calm descended in the stadium, enough to actually let the game take place. The buzz around the ground was about what would happen if the game did not take place, there would be absolute mayhem!

The game did take place and the fans supported the team even though there was a massive empty space to our right hand side. No one knew in our end that anyone had died, well how could we? The worst scenes were out of view, people didn't think about where the thousands had gone who had been standing there. We had no BBC commentator or mobile phones to inform us of the unbelievable result of the actions of the minority. We roared on our team as if nothing had happened, we felt cheated when down the far end the Polish striker Boniek was upended outside of the box and the referee gave a penalty. The master craftsman Platini slotted the ball past Grobellaar and won the European Cup for the Italians. The game petered out and Liverpool under performed. After the game, we later understood it was because the players knew that people had died. There is a conflict in a number of stories, certain Liverpool players say they knew people had died, and others say they were unaware. The Italians say to a man they were unaware. Maybe it was easier to play if you didn't believe people had. Liverpool's manager Joe Fagan, about to manage his last Liverpool game after announcing his retirement the day before, was in tears before the kick off. Liverpool keeper, Bruce Grobellaar, said he didn't want to play but was persuaded to carry on with the game in order to ensure things didn't get worse.

As the Italians celebrated we left the ground still unaware of the scale of the disaster. I was worried now, on my own in Belgium and knowing the level of violence that had taken place. I fully expected a rough journey back to my coach. There was a sinister atmosphere and people were on the look out for trouble, but with a sigh of relief I got back to the coach safely. Then I found out people had died. The players' families were virtually all on the coach already, and we were on the move out of Brussels very quickly in the hands of a very nervous Belgian driver. Well if he had been listening to the death of 39 people half a mile from his coach at the hands of Englishmen, he would be nervous wouldn't he? Firstly they were rumours, but they were quickly confirmed, people had died! How many we didn't know exactly, who they were and who they supported all not known. We hadn't even seen it. The families had faced extreme levels of abuse in the stands and that's why many of them were already on the coach. They felt unsafe watching their boys playing the biggest game of their lives.

As the coach sped on to the motorway and into the night it was well past midnight as we headed north to

Ghent. Upon arrival at the hotel, our reputation had gone before us, it was the shape of things to come. We were met by riot police, the bar was closed and the hotel staff very wary of their guests. There was no way of getting a drink or anything to eat, straight to bed but there wouldn't be much sleep. Here were the riot police protecting a hotel from the players' families, which ranged from young children to pensioners. If I was confused as to the evening's events, what chance did they have?

The guy I was sharing with, whilst trying to explain events to his young son (try that for a conversation) made sure he rang home and the little fella spoke to his frantic mum. He asked me if I had rung home yet to let my family know I was alright. I hadn't even thought about a call. It was after midnight in Liverpool – would they still be awake? Of course they would be, they were terrified that I was caught up in things. All they had seen was fighting and people dying on their TV screens. My roommate said 'make the call to let them know you're safe and everyone can sleep'. It was the best advice I'd ever received. I carefully dialled the number, even though I had rung it thousands of times, I had to make sure the international dialling code didn't put me off. I pressed the final digit and waited for what seemed an eternity for it to connect. It only rang once or twice and the voice at the other end of the phone breathless and concerned said 'Hello' to which I said 'Hiya, its only me just ...' I didn't need to say the rest, they knew I was safe. The wave of relief throughout the whole family at home was tangible from Belgium, I could almost reach out and touch it. My mum was so relieved. I could hear her shaking, once they knew I was well away from Brussels and any potential trouble they could sleep well.

My mum, dad and brothers had gone to my Uncle and Auntie's house 40 minutes north of Liverpool to watch the game with my uncle Len (he and my dad did Rome in 1977 and hundreds of other away trips). It was to be a big party to watch the Reds win the cup. Our whole family had done the same the previous year when Liverpool won in Rome. But this time I wasn't there with them - I was in Brussels. They were terrified, they didn't even stay to watch the game on TV, they headed home in case I called (or anyone called). It had been a long night for me waiting and watching, but I knew I was safe and not in trouble, they had no idea. Their night was endless until they got that call.

—⁓—

All I needed to do now was get home and that's all I wanted to do. Without wall to wall coverage, which wasn't available in those days (Sky News didn't exist then), I was still a little unaware of what had actually happened. I knew people had died. I knew there was empty terracing, but nothing prepared me for my homecoming. As we touched down at Speke Airport, I thanked Browny for letting me go with them and my roommate for looking after me and for his good company. Regardless of the events I was thankful. After shaking hands, I headed out of the Arrivals hall and was met by a host of television camera crews and reporters, 'Bloody hell the BBC were there', the cameras, adorned with bright lights lit up supporters giving their events of the night before. This scene was being replayed in all points of entry back to the kingdom of Merseyside. I still didn't know the full extent as I headed past the scrum of press and walked to nearest train station.

I wasn't far from home now, just one train journey but it was one of the longest one-hour journeys I've done. I was still resplendent in my Liverpool colours when I got the shock of my life. An old woman of at least 70 came up to me poked me in the chest and said 'You should be bloody ashamed of yourself'. I said 'Why, what have I done?' The response: 'You killed all those people'. Hold on a minute, I didn't do anything. I wasn't even in the ground when it happened but I had been tried and was guilty in her eyes. Other people just looked away and I could hear the muttering under their breath. I was treated like a leper in my own city, guilt by association, and I still didn't know why. I didn't take off my colours though.

Within an hour of being home, to the relief of my family, I understood why. The local paper was full of it - the shame of the city and rightly so. I saw the pictures that had been recorded and the politicians were already right on to it. We were considered disgraceful working class thugs. All branded, all guilty, no denying it. No wonder the old lady said what she said. The city should be ashamed, but we shouldn't all be considered guilty, I was nineteen years old and I'd done nothing wrong!

Retribution was swift. Liverpool FC pulled themselves out of Europe immediately, well it was sensible. Within weeks, the British Government (under Maggie Thatcher) were pressurising the FA to pull all clubs out of Europe. UEFA seized the day and banned English Clubs from European competitions indefinitely. A further proviso was applied that Liverpool would have to serve a further three years after any ban was lifted. As it turned out the ban lasted five years for all English clubs and Liverpool served an additional year.

The investigations into the causes rumbled on. The excuses of other teams' fans being present were not wholly substantiated. 60% of those charged were from Liverpool, but others came from places like Stoke, Aberdeen and Ipswich, however this doesn't mean too much when our fan base was already wider than the city boundaries. There were 27 arrests following great media publicity, culminating in a five-month trial in 1989 in Belgium. Fourteen people received three years custodial sentences for involuntary manslaughter. One of the lads I went to school with ended up going to prison initially in Belgium before being brought back to Liverpool. Was he a bad lad or had he just got caught up in it? I would like to think the second. The only time I have seen him since was at a Cup Final in Cardiff with his young son, both in Liverpool colours, and no one would never have known his past.

The next five years were pivotal in Liverpool's history. In 1986, they did the double with Kenny Dalglish as the boss. Following the double he built a wondrous team that included Barnes, Beardsley and Aldridge and the fans showed what the majority were like. Just as things were getting better the disaster at Hillsborough struck and shaped the future of football as a whole. If the shape of football hooliganism changed at Heysel the shape of the way we watch the game and the treatment of spectators was changed forever at Hillsborough.

Heysel stadium was demolished in 1995 but no memorial was ever established to the victims by Juventus, which is surprising. Liverpool fans did not wholly forget, but we had our own tragedy now. 20 years later Liverpool, met Juventus on the way to European glory in Istanbul. The first competitive match between the two teams since the tragedy was at Anfield in March 2005 for the first leg of the Champions League quarter final. Liverpool fans extended the hands of friendship and looked for forgiveness, which was accepted by some, and others (mainly the Ultras) who never would accept it. That night, as the teams came out, a mosaic in the Kop simply read 'Amicizia' (Italian for friendship). I was sitting less than 50 yards away from the Juventus fans and the reaction was mixed. The back of the stand applauded the gesture whilst four rows at the front, obviously packed with the Ultras, turned their backs and held their index fingers in the air in a sign of defiant abuse. The interesting thing was that the reaction from the older fans, who could remember the tragedy, was of acceptance and appreciation, whilst the younger element didn't. There was little if any trouble though and the step had been taken to build a new relationship en-masse. Many people had been building smaller bridges for years but this night showed the feelings from all of our supporters, genuine and decent respect and sympathy. The second leg was built up with threats from the Ultras but the only violence involved them and the police, which is not uncommon in Italy. As for Italians, well we played AC Milan in the final and there was no trouble whatsoever. The fans mixed, drank, ate and sang together.

Those 20 years has changed everything, stadiums, attitudes and an increased level of mass supporter travel has allowed people to understand each other more. For me, Heysel was a disaster that could have been averted, but it was inevitable due to the treatment of supporters and the lack of common sense shown by the authorities. But then, things don't change much with UEFA. Their picking of venues for major Cup Final's still has more to do with money than safety and whether the venue is fit for purpose.

On a personal level, Heysel curtailed my European travel opportunities with Liverpool. Over the next five years I didn't miss a game home or away with the Mighty Reds, not a single one, but by the time we got back in Europe, life had changed for me and the opportunities were rare and rarely taken. For me, the most important thing was that the ban drew a line in the sand. We started again and we can travel to Europe and be fairly safe, from fans if not always from the police. It is amazing that some of the stunts pulled by fans on foreign soil from other European clubs lead to fines of a few thousand euros. What are they waiting for another Heysel? You only have to watch Croatian fans running wild in the streets of Milan, or the Roma fans actions against the English to realise there is still a threat, but they still look at it as an English disease. Well, it may have been our disease, but we took the medicine to improve our condition whilst others are getting sicker year on year. Ask the policeman's widow in Sicily whose husband was killed on duty at a local derby match. You only have to watch programmes like the 'Real football factories' where they glamorise the efforts of the thugs round Europe. I can hear UEFA fiddling now …. What's that smell? It's Rome Burning!

'Ee aye adio we won the cup'

Until 1985, Cup Final's were always days of immense joy, usually because we won. Heysel certainly took the edge off Cup Final's for some time, at least until we could write history that would be enjoyable. The TV coverage of a Cup Final was different from normal football matches. There was much more depth to the programming and BBC and ITV made it more exciting. That was years before the introduction of Sky TV and it's razzmatazz, at least in the early days. I remember seeing cheerleaders on the pitch at Goodison Park one Derby Day, fighting for space with massive blow up Sumo wrestlers - some people mistook them for Jan Molby and Mickey Quinn (never short of pie dinners them two boys). The level of abuse they got seemed to persuade the Sky bosses that football fans wanted football, not "It's a knockout" style entertainment.

On Cup Final day the TV took us into the team hotels and helped us to meet celebrity fans such as Jimmy Tarbuck for Liverpool and Freddie Starr for Everton. We were right bang in the middle of it thanks to that little box in the corner of the living room. There was even Cup Final "It's a knockout", where fans of the two teams played each other, with Stuart Hall and Eddie 'up and under' Waring guffawing and struggling for breath through their own howls of laughter. The prelude to the Cup Final would be "Cup Final Question of Sport" and finally, the trip to Wembley with the players on the team coach. If we were lucky they only lost the satellite signal a hundred times between the team hotel and the Twin Towers of the original Wembley Stadium. By the time the match came we were too exhausted to take any interest, but wow, what telly watching! Now we have three hundred digital channels showing us how to cook our way to building our own house just in time to dance on ice or appear in the West End show of our choice. It's up to us! Or you can just turn the TV off and put your DVD or videos on and recall yesteryear. Remember Jimmy Melia, from Liverpool's own Scotland Road, arriving at Wembley as Brighton manager in a helicopter to play Man Utd (and they should have won as well). Everyone has their own memories of great Cup Final's, from Ricky Villa mazy dribble for Spurs against Manchester City to Lawrie Sanchez's header for Wimbledon against Liverpool, which gob-smacked a nation. The glory days of the FA Cup are always synonymous with a walk up Wembley Way, or at least a dodgy "duck and dive" up Wembley High Street.

Who says the FA Cup is not what it used to be? Usually people who don't get to the final, that's who. Don't try telling me as I head to Cardiff for the last Cup Final to be held at the Millennium Stadium (that's if they ever finish the new Wembley) that it's not what it used to be. I have no arguments about Cardiff overall. It's been a good hunting ground for Liverpool, so much so it was renamed 'Anfield South' by the fans.

I have just left the Island en-route to Cardiff for the FA Cup Final and once again it is a sign of the changes to my life and how football now fits in to it instead of the other way round. 2.30 pm on a sunny Friday afternoon and 80 miles of, thankfully, calm Irish Sea lies between me and the normal Cup Final journey. Behind the wake of the high-speed craft the Island fades into the distance. In two and a half hours we will be pulling alongside the Liver Buildings and docking in my hometown. I still love the feeling of 'coming home' even though home is now really the Island.

This could be my last Cup Final. You never know when your team will get to another one or even if you will be able to go. When I was young, I took it for granted that the Reds would be successful, and Cup Final's were just normal events. The older I get, I realise that Cup Final's are for the lucky few. Our opponents tomorrow, West Ham United, have waited twenty-six years to return to the final stage of a cup competition. I know we are spoiled, Robbie's little fella Craig will have already been to the Millennium stadium three times and he's only seven. I am more excited now than I thought I would be.

After Istanbul last year, this is a walk in the park. A two and a half hour boat ride, a four-hour car journey each way, and two overnight stays. There is no such thing as a day out at the Cup Final anymore, it's more like a weekend, and definitely nothing like the weekends we used to have in the eighties.

Cup Final's have always been major events. It's not just another game. It's a special games, a special day due to the support that follows the Reds and the passion generated by those supporters. As Phil from Norris

Green said in Istanbul last year 'we were born to do this'. Liverpool and their supporters are at their best at times like this. The sheer enthusiasm, passion and desire are a sight to behold, belting out classic versions of "You'll never walk alone" with scarves held high and numerous imaginative banners and flags. You could say we like to put on a show!

As I look out of the window, we are just passing my birthplace. Not far from the mouth of the River Mersey, at the Liverpool Bar (no it's not a pub it's the entrance to the River Mersey), is Bootle, fronted by the Seaforth docks. Now home of the Liverpool Freeport, the docks here were firmly established when I was a kid and for me it was my first home. For others, Seaforth was the end of the bus line, the bus terminus. It was a road where the buses parked up next to the enormous grain silos - you couldn't get away with calling it a terminus now. Why anyone who didn't live there would want to end up in Seaforth is a question I can't really answer. I left far too early for that. As I grew up I realised it was a tough, sometimes inhospitable and uncompromising place to be. We used to return quite often to see my Nan and Granddad (on my mum's side). We had moved and taken a step upwards to the north of Liverpool to what seemed like an upwardly mobile place to be. The best thing I could see in Bootle was the people, who were the salt of the earth. The place itself was just a place to go through on the way to the posh suburb of Crosby and that was a different world.

Who knows what I would have turned out like if I had stayed in the area? That's just one of life's little mysteries. Little decisions can radically alter events. I am sure things would have been different, who knows whether in a good

or bad way. I could have been as big a star as Jamie
Carragher, who comes from the neighbouring area of
Bootle. The passion for the Reds would, I am sure, still
have been there, but a Bank Manager? I don't think so! I
think I would have been a little more streetwise. Thanks
to my upbringing I can't see me ever having taken the
wrong path and ending up in trouble. Peer pressure in
areas such as Bootle takes its toll though, as do the higher
levels of unemployment and poverty. I often think to
myself how lucky I am! Recently, I was watching Alan
Bleasdale's classic drama 'Boys from the Blackstuff'.
What struck me was how dated it looks now, but how
true to life it was at the time – the mid-80s - as it resonated
throughout the city. From an area blighted by unemployment (at least 1 in 4 people were unemployed in the
city during my youth) I am happy to say I have only ever
been unemployed for four weeks in my whole working
life. Take it from me, growing up in the eighties, the
Thatcher years in Liverpool that is a great achievement.
Nikki said to me after watching an episode, 'it's a bit
bleak isn't it'. Well, she was maybe too young to realise,
and well protected by her parents to understand, that
life really was like that. I started working in the eighties,
firstly on a government scheme. Youth Training Scheme,
Youth Opportunities Programme, often referred to as
YTS or YOP respectively, call it what you will, it was just
cheap labour and reduced the dole queues. Then, by luck,
I landed a temporary job with Liverpool City Council,
which after a year or so turned into a permanent job.
It was a job for life or so I assumed. If it wasn't for a
number of changes of direction as the years progressed it
probably would have been, and I would be well on my
way to my pension with the Council.

Anyway, back to my Cup Final memories, I can't remember it exactly but I must have pestered my dad constantly to let me go to one. He held out manfully until 1982 when Liverpool were pitched against Spurs in the Milk Cup Final. When I look back now, it must have been a bit of a leap of faith for my dad. He had to stop going with the lads for the weekend and take his son on the football special. Hours of joy on an overcrowded dilapidated train. Usually the train was the poorest rolling stock British Rail (now deceased) had available. To be fair, the trains were notorious for being vandalised on football journeys on a regular basis, so it was understandable that they didn't provide the best quality carriages. The other thing to keep in mind was that hooliganism was rife and the surroundings of Wembley stadium were not always the most hospitable of places when teams from the North played their London counterparts. We were on their turf and a warm welcome was not forthcoming.

Thinking back, the thing I remember the most was the sheer joy of Liverpool winning the Cup, the delirium as the goals went in and I was sucked down the terrace as the crowd went wild. I was then hauled back up the terrace (usually by the scruff of my neck) trying to regain my balance and take my place again. Generally it was not the same place, but often within twenty yards unless the crowd really went wild and then I could end up miles away from the original position. On the day of my first Cup Final Ronnie Whelan scored two and the second was a cracker, which he curled round Ray Clemence, a Liverpool hero following his previous years of service with the Reds. The young kid from Ireland became an instant hero to us all. We stayed to see the team parade the cup right in front of us and it was brilliant. I had seen them win the League at Anfield before, but a Cup Final win was something different! It still is!

Before the match, I had seen problems around the turnstiles areas with little fights breaking out, and I'd heard people talking about trouble on the way from the station. Football specials were often targets for anyone who fancied it, sometimes the whole of London turned out to fight the Northerners. These were definitely the dark days and thinking of it now, my dad must have been really wary of taking me into this lion's den. On the way back to the station, there were gangs roaming around Wembley High Street, Actually getting to the station unscathed was a major achievement. There were enough Liverpool fans willing to mix it to be honest and that seemed to keep the mobs at bay. Generally Cup Final's were about normal fans watching their team, but the hooligans could strike fear into the majority. In those days the violence was much more indiscriminate than it is now, where troublemakers find troublemakers. Picking on innocent fans is, according to most of the new breed of hooligan authors, not acceptable behaviour. I think that's a fair statement after a lifetime of following Liverpool to hundreds of away games I have never been involved in any trouble, probably because I have never looked for it. Sometimes it was a little too close for comfort, most notably at West Ham, Milwall and Chelsea.

—⟶—

Let's start the chapter again. Why? Well, the 2006 Cup Final has just rewritten the history books. After a breathless 120 minutes, we had all witnessed, arguably, the best Cup Final ever. After Istanbul things couldn't get any better, or we thought would ever be equalled, but I think the game against West Ham matched Istanbul, or dare I say, it was even better. Comparing games is never easy and comparing these two is quite difficult. I say that, but statistically there are numerous comparisons. A three all draw, Harry Kewell failing to finish the game again, the opponents missing a gilt edged chance in the final minutes of the game, penalties with Liverpool missing their second and our keeper saving three of their penalties. It may sound ridiculous with all that consistency, but it was a different game completely.

This time Liverpool were favourites to win and win comfortably, if you believed the media. The one thing that was expected was that it should have been a good game, as West Ham will normally let us play football. Well they didn't let us play. They stopped us playing in the right manner, they counter-attacked brilliantly and made our magnificent defence look very ordinary. Within 28 minutes and beyond their wildest dreams, they were two goals up and Liverpool were in disarray. Then calling Captain fantastic, Stevie Gerrard conjured up two magnificent passes to bring the Reds back into the game. Firstly, finding Crouch who calmly slotted the ball home only to find a flag from the linesman had ruled him marginally offside (later to be proved a wrong decision). Not dwelling too much on the decision, he provided a pinpoint pass to Cisse to volley home perfectly. Can't let this go without a mention, Cisse must be the only man to ever have two haircuts in one game, each side of his head had a different pattern on it. He also wore boots of a variety of colours - in the first half, one red one and one white one, whilst in the second half he wore Day-Glo green. That lad really needs to spend some time lying on a couch talking to someone in a professional capacity. Still he brought us back in to the game.

Back in the game, the Reds had taken complete control. Whereas in Istanbul, they were thoroughly outplayed for 45 minutes, here they were two goals down due to a fortuitous own goal and a sloppy piece of goal-keeping. With one in the net for us, I was confident of going on to win it, a two-goal start no problem! Besides an early scare in the second half, it looked like it was only a matter of time before the equaliser came, and sure enough it came within ten minutes of the restart. Crouch nodded down into the area for Stevie G arriving with impeccable timing to hammer the ball in to the top right hand corner of the net with an immaculate finish. Now there could be only one winner with Liverpool looking really dominant. Wrong! With Liverpool well on top, out of nowhere the West Ham left back floats a cross right in to the top corner of our net past the despairing grasp of Jose Reina, 3-2 down. Now, from being on top, we were totally shot, the team had nothing left and with 25 minutes left it looked like West Ham's name was on the cup and they would have deserved it.

Those 25 minutes flew by, as they do when you are anxiously watching the clock and trying to get back into a game, as opposed to when you are hanging on and it takes forever (however long that is). Liverpool huffed and puffed but they didn't seem able to make their effort count with an equaliser. Into the last minute, and follow-ing a punt into the West Ham box the ball came to Cisse, and as he lost it he went down with cramp. The West Ham player nearest the ball kicked it out, seemingly so

Cisse could get treatment. He knew that Liverpool would have to give him the ball back - not so daft eh? Liverpool, and Gerrard in particular, were exhausted and players were struggling with their fitness all over the pitch. The West Ham fans were going absolutely mental, never mind blowing bubbles. They were bouncing up and down and many were on their mobiles planning the biggest knees up the East End had ever seen. As Cisse hobbled to his feet the stadium announcer called out that there were four minutes left. With a desperate roar from the Liverpool supporters for one last effort, the Liverpool throw in returned the ball to the West Ham right back. He punted it up field, but it was a poor clearance and the ball was returned to the edge of the area where, under a Liverpool challenge, West Ham could only help it out of the box. There he was, our Gladiator Steven Gerrard, lurking about 35 yards out. If there was anyone it should fall to it was Stevie G but he was knackered. 20,000 shouts of 'hit it' were barely out of the throats as he caught it with his right foot. Absolutely perfect, it arrowed into the corner of the net past the helpless Hislop in goal. One end of the stadium erupted, as the other end collectively stared in disbelief. People were flying past me tumbling down the stands, hugging and kissing. Gerrard headed towards the red hordes. This was going to be our day again, I could feel it. At 2 – 0 I'd thought it could be, but honestly, at 3-2 down it was a step too far. The season that had started early in July for Liverpool, in order to qualify for the Champions League, looked like it had lasted one game too many. Me of little faith again, why do I ever doubt them?

Extra time was a case of Liverpool conserving their energy, soaking up the pressure and hitting the Hammers on the break. It was heading to penalties, and we had already seen from his career in Spain how good Pepe Reina was at saving them. We were confident West Ham wouldn't be able to get their heads up. But heads up they did for one final chance, a looping header that had Reina leaping arm outstretched, straining every muscle to give him that extra inch that got him to the ball and tip it on to the cross bar and fall away to safety. Just like Istanbul we were saved at the death by an unbelievable save. The penalties were a piece of cake, a one-sided shoot out with Reina excelling again to mark his place in history and let people forget his two earlier errors (I know, I remembered them). As I said before, the slightest thing can alter things drastically. What if Cisse had not gone down, or the clearance didn't fall to a red shirt? There you go, that's the beauty of football. Sometimes it's luck, but often it's brilliance, and that day we had a fair mixture of both. The relief at the final whistle was a little lost in the tumultuous celebrations, but as the teams left the pitch, it hit me, my head was booming, I was physically shaking and my legs were weak. I felt drained. That's how much it means to me!

I was sitting with Our Kev, but we just had to meet up with the other lads who were down in Cardiff. Grown men embracing happens rarely in macho England, but when you win the cup that all changes. Zil, Mongoose, Peter B and as a bonus today our Ian was with us, which was most welcome. He has been unable to share in so many of the glory days, so it was brilliant to have him with us at one of the best ever, especially as he did the driving! Hugs all round Gentlemen! The weird thing is that you see people you haven't seen for years. Degsy (Derek to his mum) from Bebbington over the water (the

Mersey that is) was one of those guys. He was Peter B's mate really and had spent a little while travelling with us in the mid eighties. Most notably, the day we won the title at Chelsea in the double winning season of 85/86, where he spent all afternoon shitting himself. Not because of the Chelsea Headhunters. No, just every time Chelsea got anywhere near threatening our goal. I saw Degsy last year in Istanbul for the first time in nearly twenty years and here we are again, a year later at another Cup Final where after a 3 – 3 draw, we win a cup on penalties. How strange. We saw him afterwards and a big hug and smile was the greeting before he faded away into the past again. That happens so often at football, so many people you see are from the past but for a fleeting moment you are as one again. Just like it used to be, but you no longer know them, and some you never really knew in the first place. We are brought together by one thing and one thing alone -Liverpool FC.

To all the men I have hugged before, I think of you often, but not in a gay way. I can't call you friends as we don't really know each other but 'mate' is a great term. Thanks for everything we shared together. Hopefully you all know who you are.

The Cup was ours and we headed back to Merseyside, worn out emotionally but I knew what I was going to do on the Sunday before I hit the ferry back to the Isle of Man. I was seeing the cup come back home. I know, how old am I? I remembered Istanbul the year before when I was on a train rattling through northern Greece as the trophy was paraded around the city at the most joyous homecoming ever. I had travelled the breadth of Europe and even into Asia and seen the best European Cup win ever and had one of the most amazing nights ever (Nikki, note I have learnt my lesson and don't call it the *best* night ever anymore). But on the train with the sun going down over the Mediterranean and Greek plains, it all felt a little empty, the whole train was quiet as people were hearing news of the homecoming. It's a big thing seeing your heroes return home with the goods.

Sunday came and we took the kids, my nephews - Our Kev's boys Josh (in his pram), and Daniel, complete with kit and flag, and Ian's football mad little fella Matty. As we stood on Queens Drive (Liverpool's inner ring road), they were all there. We were joined by grown men, lots of families, kids and dogs dressed in Liverpool kits (sometimes difficult to tell them apart). There was a real family atmosphere which reminded me of all the times as a kid when we would go with my mum and dad to see the Reds return home with silverware. It had turned full circle for Our Kev and Ian with their own kids. For me it would still be a little while longer. Nikki was at home minding our little boy Charlie, well she had no choice as he was still inside her! It would be another six months before he could sit and watch the West Ham win on DVD with me, what else can you do when he won't sleep at night?

I remember as a child, the excitement of heading to a good vantage point. Here I could see the open top bus for as long as possible. It needed to be somewhere that the crowd would make the bus go slow and not fly past. We would normally head down to Everton Valley, where there was a grass bank, which gave a natural stand from where to watch proceedings. There would be people hanging from lampposts, sitting on top of the local bank or post office, and hanging like monkeys off the bus shelters. A buzz would go around the crowd when the bus was approaching. Anyone with a radio was a mate so we could plot the journey and try and work out how long it would take them to get to us. It never worked out though, as they would always take an age and the excitement would start wearing off as the bus got delayed. The bus always started from the south end of the city and used Queens Drive as its route until it got near to Anfield, where it would head up to the ground and behind the Kop then down to Everton Valley, on to Scotland Road to end up in 'town' (the city centre-always called 'town'). Sometimes, later on in the route the bus would be so late that they would fly past us at 30 miles an hour and we could hardly spot our heroes, never mind the silverware. There would be a number of false alarms but as the bus came into sight the roar would go up. People would then rush down to the road and with a bit of luck, the bus would be forced to crawl through the throng before it could pick up speed at the bottom of the valley. I would be there trying to spot my favourite players, Keegan, Dalglish, Hansen or Joey Jones (everyone's favourite). Often I couldn't spot more than half a dozen before they were gone, but that would do and the silver was obviously the first thing to see.

—⁂—

As I got older, our gang would either not be home on time from our Cup Final travels, or we would give the fans en-route something to cheer before the big event. Whilst they were waiting for the team's arrival with the silverware they could at least have a laugh at us. Cup Final's in my early twenties were a great excuse to go on the ale for the weekend. As it was still a bit naughty in London, we tended to stay out of London and drive in

on the day to Wembley. Our venue of choice was Stratford-upon-Avon in Warwickshire. That's a long way
from London, I hear you say. Well, it was about a two-
hour drive, but Stratford was a great place for a weekend
away. I had started going there on booze ups with my
mates from work, ably organised by Hoges (John
Hogan) who had gone there with his football team on
tour. Yes, the tour included one obligatory game of football against a local pub side, two extremely heavy nights
on the beer and an all day bender on the Saturday. Of
course the football mattered...not!!! Whoever had the
idea should be congratulated as it was stroke of genius.
It was a great place to go. We used to stay in a pub called
the Green Dragon. You have probably heard of lots of
pubs called the Red Lion but a Green Dragon? The
Green Dragon was run by two real characters called Ray
and Jean, and they had the assistance of a barman called
Tracy. Tracy was a man and a big man, built like a brick
out house, nobody took any liberties with him. Nobody,
and I mean nobody, mentioned his girly name. He was a
great fella but he took no messing. He was the pub's
muscle even before the real days of the bouncer. Ray was
a great guy. He would let anything go in his establishment, of the drunken antics sort that is, dead set against
drugs and he ran a clean boozer on that score. The only
rule was that if we broke something, we had to pay the
costs of the breakages. He was canny like that as he put
us in the rooms with dodgy furniture, which invariably
broke, and within a couple of years he had refurbished
all his bedrooms. Drunken horseplay often resulted in
broken beds and chairs. Ray had a massive handlebar
moustache and he was from Cornwall or somewhere
south of Bristol. His wife Jean was a dirty old bird (in the

nicest possible way). If any of the lads tried to embarrass her, it would be them on the receiving end. Often the lads who had been before would goad one of the Stratford Virgins into winding her up. Before long she would have embarrassed the lad so badly that he'd be red and the butt of our jokes for the whole weekend. They were both wonderful people who, though larger than life, cared about each and every one of us whilst in their care. The more often we went the more we realised it.

For the princely sum of £10 per night we would get a clean room, toilet and shower facilities, the biggest English breakfast ever seen on one plate, and a bar at our beck and call before, and after, closing time. The Green Dragon would be home for the weekend and the local clientele would be our mates, no problems on that score. Stratford-upon-Avon as a town was a beautiful tourist trap, used to Americans and the gentile tourist, not rent a mob. Groups of lads were a rarity and that often made us popular with the local girls, though not always the boyfriends, but the local girls like a little Scouse wit. Built on the River Avon, the town boasted enough pubs and clubs to keep us entertained for at least two nights. There was very little trouble and the local police were fairly chilled out as long as we behaved ourselves, which I must say we always did. The only time there was trouble was if gangs came from Birmingham or nearby Coventry, and the locals would end up fighting with them. We never had any bother, we always had a great time. There was one time when we actually got the blame for a stabbing in the town. The word was out that Liverpool fans were in town and that it was probably them that did it. No evidence, just names put in the frame. The police found themselves in front of Ray in the Green

Dragon, and before they could even say 'there has been a stabbing......' Ray gave them what for and vouched for us all, and the police ended up having to apologise for having the temerity to even raise a suspicion. Ray actually went out into Town and found out what had happened and could name the culprits. It had nothing to do with us, and we were none the wiser until the following day at breakfast, when Jean told us. Ray was still fuming that his guests had been blamed. He was a good judge of people. We could get up to our drunken antics but we were never violent.

Drunken antics, of which there were many, kept the Stratford trips alive for many years. It kept them fresh. One of our best trips was the Cup Final weekend of 1992 when Liverpool were strong favourites to beat a poor Sunderland side. On the Friday we left Liverpool at 4pm and headed down South to the traffic jams of the M6 around Birmingham. By the time we were heading towards the Green Dragon, it was after 7pm. Being late, I was getting it from all sides, as I was the mini bus driver. 'Stop the bus I want a piss' from one traveller or 'don't stop the bus we need to get there to go out' from another traveller, with the majority in favour of the latter. Brian was in the first category and as we left Liverpool on the M62 he was already shouting for a piss stop. Two stops later at Knutsford and Hilton Park everybody had heard enough and were shouting for me to drive on. As we headed through Henley in Arden, the next town up the road from Stratford, he was at it again and he was starting to complain about the pain he was in. Tommy the butcher was sitting next to me and started whispering 'hit the potholes'. I fully obliged, well it wasn't my mini bus. I don't know if you have ever had <u>that</u> feeling, as the bus jars the bladder shouts let me out! Do it a couple of times and your bladder is screaming let me out! Brian wasn't happy at all, but the rest of the lads were wetting (pardon the pun) themselves at Brian's plight. I know it's not nice but I found every pothole in Warwickshire, much to the delight of my travelling colleagues except poor Brian. As we pulled into the outskirts of Stratford, he was swearing wildly and his trousers were on the edge of getting a wash from inside. When the lights turned red, he shouted 'how far now?'. I could see up ahead to the Green Dragon, so told him, 'another two miles on the left hand side'. At which point he called me all the names under the sun, and made a dash for freedom up an alley to relieve himself. We waited for him. No we didn't really, I drove on up the road and around the corner, where we all bailed out. As we looked around the corner we could see him realise that we had left him and he didn't know where he was. His face was a picture, then he spied the rest of us laughing in the gutter outside the Green Dragon. I wouldn't like to say what he called us but it should never be said in front of kids.

The night got better, and Brian was right in the middle of it. Brian had been diagnosed with a stomach ulcer (he was only in his early twenties) so it was bit of a blow when the doctor advised him not to drink too much, but Stratford was a big blow out for him. Generally his drink of necessity was a pint of tap water whilst everyone else had lager. Now he had emptied his bladder he was out to enjoy himself, well it was Cup Final weekend wasn't it? As we went from bar to bar, he was well up for a great night out and by closing time he had the munchies. Stratford was a bit thin on the ground for eateries, but there was a shop that served pizzas, those dodgy frozen chips and half cooked kebabs. Brian likes what he likes and what he likes is a Margherita pizza (cheese and tomato for the uneducated). So that's what he ordered, but as he was drunker than he had been for sometime, all he heard was 'pizza' and took it off the counter and headed off back to the Green Dragon. As we walked down the road he found, much to his displeasure that his Pizza had stuff on it. Stuff such as peppers and pepperoni, at which point he declared 'I am not eating this shit'. Everybody else on a belly full of beer was more than satisfied with their own choice so there were no swaps available. Brian couldn't be talked into going back, so that was it he had a cob on (really upset if you speak English not Scouse). 'If no one wants it, I am lashing it' and that's what he did, he lashed it alright, from the middle of the street and right through a random open bedroom window. That was it, we were wetting ourselves, well at least until the light went on and a male voice boomed 'what the Fuck is going on'. Chips in hand we legged it down the street as fast as our wobbly legs could carry us. I can just picture this fella peeling bits of Pepperoni from his face fuming at the miscreants outside.

The match was nothing to write home about really, quite an easy 2-0 win and it looked like the Reds would restore their former glories after a few barren years following the departure of Kenny Dalglish. Graeme Souness had set the tone for the Cup Final by selling an exclusive story about needing Heart surgery to The Sun (of all people). Even though we won the cup, the talk was more about the fact that he should go, resign or be sacked, either way, he should go. The one-time hero of the Kop had betrayed us all. He tried to say he didn't understand the depth of feeling against the Sun, but he had previously been quoted as saying that both he and the players understood the feelings against <u>that</u> paper. Once he had written that article for that paper, his time was up. He had struggled to get anything really decent on the pitch even though he blooded the youthful talents of Redknapp, Fowler and McMannaman. Liverpool were in transition but he had taken an axe to a good Dalglish squad and bought the likes of Neil Ruddock and Julian Dicks to Liverpool. While Ruddock lasted a while (and was a hero to some), Dicks was just awful and not a Liverpool player.

As we headed back up Wembley High Street, it was just another Cup Final win, the first for a few years and we were still fairly blasé about winning things. Little did we know that the cup would be our main saviour in the next fifteen years with no Premiership glory coming our way. That's probably why the cup still means so much. As we passed the tube station, we threw a left back towards the Chequers pub and through the Asian markets, which seemed to be oblivious of the Cup Final happening up the road. The off licenses knew there was a Cup Final though, and they enjoyed their busiest day of the year. Our crew accounted for much of that profit as we loaded up for the journey northwards to the Midlands. With added alcohol supplies the mini bus was rocking all the way back to Stratford.

After Brian's Friday night pizza throwing, you would think that would be enough for one weekend from one man but no, one last hurrah was called for in Stratford that Saturday evening. He found a bike lying outside a pub at closing time and started to ride around the car park area of the pub that fronted onto other pubs and shops. With a willing audience egging him on, he was recreating a scene from Butch Cassidy and the Sundance Kid. In the film Ali McGraw sits on the handle bar of Paul Newman's bike and 'raindrops keep falling on my head' plays in the background. He had no one on the handle bars - well would you let him ride a bike half cut in the road? Also he couldn't remember the words so just rode around like the local loony laughing. He was brought to an abrupt halt as his tyres screeched to a halt at the size ten feet of the local police. The interrogation went something like this, 'is this your bike son?' to which he replied 'er no occifer'. 'What are you doing?' to which he replied 'er Butch Cassidy and the Sundance kid mate'. The policeman was obviously not amused but somewhat bemused, decided that he should put the bike back and nothing more would be said. Could you imagine a charge sheet and all that paperwork? It just wasn't worth it.

The journey home from Stratford on the Sunday was fairly uneventful, two hours drive in a van full of sweating, farting men is never appealing. 'Get those windows open and now'.

—⁓—

Brian saved his most glorious moment for the journey home when Liverpool had been beaten by Wimbledon 1-0 in the biggest upset seen since Leeds were beaten by Sunderland in 1972. We had gone down to London to just pick up the Cup, have a great time, and go home. Wimbledon, known as 'the crazy gang' (more stupid than crazy if you ask me), rewrote the script and the journeyman footballer and now international football manager on his CV (how?) Lawrie Sanchez scored a header and Liverpool never recovered. The always reliable John Aldridge missed his first penalty ever, and of all the times to do it too.

As we headed up Wembley High Street and back to the mini bus, spirits were understandably low. By the time we got back to the van the spirits had lifted somewhat when the shout went up 'lets get pissed'. It was probably Zil as that was his shout for nearly twenty years. Now he has to ask his wife 'can I get pissed love?'. So the off licence got battered and so did the travellers, except for yours truly who was mug enough to drive. As we headed out on the A40 towards the M40 and our Stratford Upon Avon temporary home, the atmosphere was still a bit subdued, the post mortem of the game was in full swing and it was quite depressing.

Then Brian piped up from the back 'I am going to moony' (show his arse if you didn't know) and proceeded to look for victims of his baboon like show. Up ahead there was a roundabout and just before was a car stopped in a lay-by with three fellas standing by the car. 'Ey watch this, just look at their faces'. Brian proceeded to ram his bare cheeks against a side window of the van while shouting out of the window 'oi knobheads, kiss my arse'. He was so engrossed with what he had been doing that he didn't realise who his victims were until someone said 'eh that's Keith's dad'. Trousers up, face of shame and Brian would be quiet all the way home. For twenty years since, he hasn't been able to look my dad in the eye. What made matters worse was that we stopped to speak to them. They had broken down on the way home and they were waiting to get going.

As it turned out, they had a nightmare weekend without Brian's help or his arse. They had left Liverpool and planned to stay in London on the Friday night. The car they had borrowed had other ideas though. The car was that of a doctor in Liverpool that my uncle had been doing building work for. Instead of money being paid and having to declare it for tax, I think he took payment in kind. For some reason you expect a doctor to have a decent car but this guy had well and truly stitched him up. It was some obscure make of car that was hardly heard of in England, probably very big in East Germany at the time, like a Trabant or something. By the time they reached Birmingham, they had already had to stop twice and there was little chance of making London so they had the bright idea to head for Stratford and maybe meeting up with us. On the way to Stratford it broke down again, and they limped into Stratford and found the Green Dragon. There was no room in the pub as we had all the rooms. They had also missed us as well as we had gone straight into town on the lash. Ray though put them onto a B&B over the road from the pub, where they could check in and come back to the pub and get bevvied. Sounded like a plan so they did just that.

Nothing strange in that until the next morning, and my dad still tells this story now. They came down for breakfast after a fairly heavy session at the Green Dragon and the guy met them who booked them in the night before. This guy, who seemed fairly normal the night before was acting strangely. There was a pair of massive shoes in the middle of the breakfast room for some reason. The guy explained they were the shoes of a man who had the biggest feet in Britain some years earlier and he was from Stratford. Why did he have them? Who knows, he never said. He took the orders for breakfast, firstly orange juice and cereal. As he brought it he said 'three years, eighty days, ten hours and twenty minutes' and he left in silence. Then he brought the full English breakfast and said 'three years, eighty days, ten hours and thirty minutes'. Then finally he brought the toast and coffee 'three years, eighty days, ten hours and fifty minutes'. He then walked silently away leaving my dad and uncles in silence wondering what was going on. He looked like he was going to kill himself by all accounts. They headed back over to the Green Dragon and my dad asked Ray 'what the hell was he going on about?' Ray said that he normally wouldn't send people there, but as they were desperate the night before it was best he could think of. But what about the counting up of time? That was because the guy had lost his wife 'three years, eighty days, ten hours blah blah blah ago' and he couldn't forget it. Had she died? No, he just lost her, she had gone. I think she just left because he was a nutter. On top of that, Liverpool losing, a nightmare journey, getting mooned at by a big hairy Scouse arse, it couldn't get any worse. Or could it? They headed back to North Wales where my Uncle Len owned a guesthouse in Betws-y-Coed in the Snowdonia National Park. They would stay there and drink their sorrows away and head home on the Sunday afternoon.

Well the Sunday was glorious so they decided to stay for a few jars by the river. After a few, one of the lads ended up on a big rock in the middle of the river. My dad shouted to him 'how do you get across there?' and was dutifully supplied with directions to the stepping-stones that led from the riverbank. So my dad went to join him, pint in hand. You are probably already ahead of me here but just hold on. He made it safely to the large rock in the middle of the river. They are now added to the sites that tourists must see. The area sees millions of tourists each year but it is not exactly famous for the sight of two Scousers on a rock in the middle of the river drinking brown bitters (that northern mans tipple again). They didn't mind being the focus of the attention and dutifully posed for photographs raising a glass to the masses. Someone shouted to my dad 'how do you get across there?' Instead of just shouting directions he made the mistake of standing up and trying to point it out. A patch of green moss underfoot caught him out and he went arse over tit, and in no time at all he is at the bottom of the river bed gasping for air. He only needed to stand up, it was only knee deep so he wasn't going to drown. There are probably pictures on walls in Tokyo of that very moment as he reckons every Japanese tourist in Britain at that time took a photograph. Being at least a mile away from the hotel, he had to do the walk of shame through the village. I am proud of him though as he tells me he never spilt a drop of his pint, see it's not all bad. That was a further excuse to stay in Wales on the ale all day, his trousers had to dry out before he could come home.

—⚏—

The following year, we headed home after beating our rivals Everton in the Cup Final following the Hillsborough disaster. We had our Stratford journey as per Cup Final routine, a little more subdued than normal obviously, but we were getting on with things. After an emotionally charged 120 minutes Liverpool won the cup and they were to have a parade on the Sunday to show the cup off. The parade would also include the Everton team bus, as it was an occasion for Merseyside to be proud. Having rallied around each other to support the city following the disastrous events of the 15th April, it was right to have a joint lap of honour whoever was victorious. Well we had our victory lap before them. Our mini bus full of sweaty smelly men, flags flying, scarves fluttering and people old enough to know better doing moonies out the window. We took to the route directly before the buses to the cheers of the masses. If you are never going to be in an open top bus through lack of talent, you might as well hijack the parade!

As you will see once again, the football is not the 'be all and end all' of things. It was the conduit for friendship and belonging and a lifetime of memories. For my memories replace your own. They are hopefully as funny and entertaining to you as mine are to me. I was recently recounting these memories with Zil, my dad and Tommy the Butcher and whilst the brain might not be as quick on some things, on these points we were crystal clear.

Sunshine in May on Cup Final day. Has a lovely ring to it don't you think, everyone should sample at least one. Me, I am luckier than most but then again, also greedier than most.

If you want to win the cup then you better hurry up cos we are Liverpool FC!

—⁓—

6

Inside a disaster

There by the grace of god!

As I look out of my window today across the cliffs of the Island I can see the Mountains in Cumbria, which reminds me that England is really not that far away. It is a million miles away from the England of seventeen years ago though. Today is the 15th of April 2006, and it has been a very long seventeen years since the worst day of my life. The 15th April 1989 was FA Cup semi-final day and as the spring sunshine flooded the streets of Liverpool no one could have predicted what the next 24 hours would bring. Today it's a beautiful sunny day, which bears a remarkable similarity to that Cup semi-final day. A clear sunny day to travel across the Pennines to Sheffield was certainly a rarity; usually driving conditions ranged from blizzards to dense fog. So that day God (if you are a believer) was smiling on the travelling faithful and it was going to be a great day.

I am writing this on the anniversary of the Hillsborough disaster and today Sheffield Wednesday have delayed kick off by 15 minutes as a mark of respect. The disaster is always marked by the time that the referee stopped the game, 3.06pm. From the press reports, the minute silence is immaculately observed, which always seems to be the case, as the fans understand that it really could have been them. Speaking from experience, it really could have been me or any of my travelling companions, friends or even work colleagues.

For seventeen years I have carried a myriad of emotions that have surfaced at different times in my life. I have been angry, grieving, relieved and appreciative of what life gives. As I look to my right, I see pictures of Steven Gerrard with the Champions League trophy in Istanbul, and me and Zil sharing that glorious night. In front of me I see pictures of my beautiful wife who gave me the best day of my life on the day she married me. I see pictures of my nephews Daniel and Joshua (Our Kev's boys) and Daniel complete with his cheeky smile, is in his Liverpool kit. You may be thinking 'so what? That is just normal life'. That's the point; I am really grateful for my normal life and that of my younger brother. Two yards the other way and one of us may not have come home. This is why I feel guilty, relieved and angry in no particular order. Another 96 people should be sharing my views, but they would be views of their own lives, whatever life held for them. Unfortunately they had no choice as their lives were stolen away in a wholly avoidable tragedy.

I can remember it like it was yesterday. My memory just needs a touch of prompting nowadays as I have put it away in my brain in order to ensure that it doesn't consume my life and make me a victim too. Little did I know that this day was going to change my life forever and affect many of the relationships that I held dear at that time. People changed and some changed forever and silently drifted away. There were more than 96 victims, 96 families and friends of the deceased were affected forever. All in such a public domain, full of lies and mistruths which tainted their thoughts of their loved ones' final moments. Some people have a lot to answer for and how they sleep at night is really beyond me.

As we were seasoned travellers, this was just a normal day out for us. Tickets were sorted out with no problem and I had a car full of the usual suspects. It was going to be a great day out with the company I kept. We never saw trouble, always had a great laugh and looked forward to our away trips more than our home games. Today's travelling companions were Our Kev, Zil, Brian and Big Chris. Picking Kev up was easy as we still shared a bedroom in my mum and dad's house in north Liverpool. You have to remember I was still only 23 and Our Kev only 20 years old. Girls were not really on the scene at that point. Our consuming passion was for the Mighty Red Men and most of our money was spent following them around England. The other boys lived just outside the City of Liverpool; Brian in the upmarket area of Maghull, where we aspired to live, and Zil and Big Chris in the leafy countryside of Aughton, just outside the market town of Ormskirk. By the time I got to Aughton in my Ford Escort (1.6 GLX by the way- as that was really important then), it was a beautiful day more akin to summer than spring. By eleven o'clock we were on the road to Sheffield with our music blasting and a carload of chatter and as always the craic was mighty. How many conversations can go on between five people? Well today it seemed unending as we all had the Milwall game to buzz about from the previous Wednesday night (as discussed in the Cultural experiences chapter).

We had been to Sheffield on numerous occasions, so I knew the roads like the back of my hand and we planned on being in Sheffield by one o'clock. We had plenty of time. We could get a pint if we could but drink was never my priority as I was driving. M62 to M6 over the Thelwall viaduct on to the M56 through Stockport and on towards Glossop and the Pennines. Funny how on that day, considering the amount of traffic due, someone in their wisdom decided to place road works at the natural bottleneck in the route, bypassing Glossop to go over the Woodhead pass. On the busiest traffic day of the year no one let the travelling supporters know about it. I remember it taking an hour to travel approximately five miles, and by then we were starting to push it time-wise. We were, so it seemed, ahead of most of the match traffic. This was one of the catalysts from the problems that would build later on. When you hear that people arrived late, traffic was one of the major reasons - we were not all in the pub as you may have been led to believe.

As you drive down off the Pennines you head through the steel town of Stocksbridge, this was the marker for Hillsborough, the home of Sheffield Wednesday Football Club. It was a regular venue for Cup semi-finals due to its capacity and the geographical nature of the competing clubs. From Stocksbridge it took about ten minutes until we parked and another ten minute to walk to the ground. That would be okay for us as it was just getting on for two o'clock; we would be there in time for kick off.

As we neared Hillsborough, on the left hand side was the base of a valley and on the right hand side were the steep sides of the valley, with rows of houses climbing up the side to a road at the top. From past experience, parking spaces would be available and as long as we had our crampons with us, the climb up would be easy after our forthcoming victory. It was like parking in San Francisco, wheels locked against the kerb so the car didn't fall backwards. Definitely no more than second gear, especially with a car full of lads. A parking space duly found, it always paid to make sure that everybody knew exactly where we were by memorising the street name, as all the streets look the same. For a quick get away I wanted everyone together at the car quickly, as often we got split up at matches when we were standing on the terraces. The meeting and greeting after the game was always fun though, it could keep us going for quite a while on long journeys home, regaling individual stories and thoughts on what we had seen and heard.

As we walked past a pub I noticed that as it was full they weren't allowing any more people in, which suited me on a day like to day. So that kills the myth that no one drank at all or that we were all rolling drunk. That's for the West Midlands Police, who following the disaster interviewed me and thousands of others. They were only interested in the behaviour of the fans and how much they had drank, not the actions of some of their own kind. This was Thatcher's Britain and we were classed as scum, we were guilty until proved innocent. It was just a normal day, some people drank and some didn't - nothing unusual there. We headed down towards the ground past the dodgy car showrooms and past the slowest chip shop in the world. This was a place where 30 minutes before any game the chips were never ready - not like the chippies behind the Kop where they must feed hundreds if not thousands in the hour up to kick off. I can see it now, as we neared the ground we took a sharp left and we were in Leppings Lane. Ahead of us and to the right was a set of old brick turnstiles.

This is where it started to go wrong. The amount of people trying to get in was far greater than I expected, and there was very little evidence of crowd control outside the ground. The Police horses marshalling the crowd were actually from Merseyside police and outside of the horses there seemed to be little police presence. The crowd was already a heaving mass but there was an opportunity to marshal people back up the hill alongside a wall. The problem was that access to the other stands also seemed to be through the same area. It looked like the whole of Liverpool's travelling support had to enter this way and we were all there at the same time. Whilst accessing the Leppings Lane terrace you also had access to the West Stand, which was directly behind the terraced area. It turned out that 10,000 fans had to enter the ground through just seven turnstiles, that's over 1,400 through each turnstile and the majority in the hour leading up to kick off at 3 o'clock. Simple calculations show that it works out at a minimum of 23 people per minute, which is just impossible to do. From my perspective it looked as if the crowd had not been controlled earlier and as a result the sheer weight of numbers arriving meant there was little chance to gain any element of control.

Everyone has their own view as to what then happened and this is mine and mine alone. The following is an account of how I felt and what I still feel seventeen years after the event. Even now I am starting to bring pictures back I have buried for such a long time, I don't know if I really want to do it.

No; I do <u>want</u> to do it. I don't need to do it because I found my way forward around it years ago, but when confronting the thoughts again, I have raised the visions I didn't ever want to see again. I can now see myself penned against the wall linking the turnstiles, just inches from getting to the turnstile and into the ground. Then, as the body of the crowd moves, I am spinning back into the crowd behind me. I am already losing sight of all my mates and this has really become 'look after number one'. There is no control of the situation at all now and the pressure on my body is unbelievable. I have been in crushes before but never anything as intense as this. People are pleading for a release from the situation but those joining the crowd from the back cannot see what is happening ahead of them. As kick-off nears, the pressure becomes more intense and people are more desperate than ever. Some, to avoid the pressure, are climbing on to the walls surrounding the turnstiles, with ticket in hand and are being beaten back by police. A horse enters into the seething mass of bodies and only adds to the chaos. The people at the front become more at risk as the crush intensifies. I am now pinned next to a big blue wooden gate that is usually an exit gate and I am next to a girl who I work with, who says she is struggling to breathe properly now and she is terrified in the crush. I think that someone is going to die outside the turnstiles. People are pleading for the gate to be opened to relieve the pressure. After what seems like an eternity the gate is opened and the effect is like uncorking a champagne bottle and the bubbles flooding out, forcing people in to the ground. I can see many people still showing their tickets to police and stewards. That's how badly behaved we are.

I still have my full ticket after all these years. Complaints about the management of the crowd outside were met by the normal response of South Yorkshire's finest (Police if you need to ask): 'Shut up or you will be arrested'. It's normally not that nice actually: 'get in before you're nicked', in other words.

Was it the right decision to open the gate? For me it certainly was, otherwise I might not be writing this now. Take it from me, people would certainly have died outside. As it turned out 36 people actually sustained injuries outside in the crush. What I don't understand is what happened next or how it happened.

Looking from the pitch Leppings Lane is a terrace with a large seated area, the West Stand, directly behind and above it. To the right, as you look is the North Stand with a large uncovered triangular terraced standing area filling the gap between the two. As I enter the ground there are three ways to enter the terrace area. Directly in front of me is an alleyway, which I know leads to the sections behind the goal. A second entrance is around the side of the West Stand wall to my right. Finally the third entrance, and the one we are heading for is found by bearing left around the back of the West Stand, walking along the length of the stand to the entrance to the large triangular uncovered terrace. As I had been to the ground on a number of occasions, as recently as the February of the same year, for a league game, I am aware of exactly where I want to go and it is not down the alleyway in front of me. In the league game we had taken our places on the terrace, right behind the goal and right in front of the alleyway exit on to the terrace itself. When the section was full a wooden gate was closed blocking off the alleyway from the terrace and I gather the other end of the alleyway leading back to the turnstiles was closed also. The problem is once you're in you actually can't get out from the middle of the terrace unless you force your way through the crowd to the side and then back to your original position. I had noticed that there was a terrace area to the left between the West Stand and the North Stand on the left-hand side. It provided an elevated area of terrace, albeit an open one, but the experience in February was so poor that it was the much better option. That is where I am heading now.

That was the plan for us all, but after what happened outside all five of us are split up, so I am trying to see where everyone is. People are flooding into the alleyway towards the terrace. I think "that's strange the middle pen must still be empty otherwise it would have been closed off by now".

There are no stewards or police directing people away from the alleyway.

What we now know is that it was an overcrowded terrace. The trouble is that the police knew it was already overcrowded and did nothing about it. The effect was that hundreds of people poured into the already overcrowded section immediately behind the goal, which resulted in the people in this section being forced towards the fences at the front and the sides and being crushed; crushed to death. Due to the problems on the terrace, panic ensued in the alleyway. People who saw the horrific events unfolding in front of them turned to see a wall of people bearing down on them, totally unaware of what was going on outside in the daylight. Needless to say, with nowhere to go, people were trampled to death in the tunnel with no way out. All of this was avoidable.

I am standing at the head of the tunnel and I am perched upon a crowd control barrier, hoisting myself up above the crowds to see if I can spot Our Kev or my mates. At this point I can just see Our Kev and he has seen me, luckily. He tells me 'I was just heading down the tunnel'.

For years I have told him he wasn't heading down the tunnel, because he says I saved him. Nothing of the sort, it was luck. I didn't do anything and I've always believed that he wouldn't have gone down the tunnel willingly because we had discussed it. We had agreed exactly where we were going to stand and it was very clear there was no misunderstanding. With a plan we always ended up together and thankfully it was the same that day. He was maybe getting carried along in the crowd and, as I say it was a stroke of good luck seeing him.

Our Kev is fighting his way across the crowd to get to me, and it's just nice to be back together. With a feeling of relief we start heading towards the area of the terrace we had originally identified. Behind us we leave masses of people in chaos, we're still unaware of what we are going to face when we actually get on to the terrace. It is now three o'clock and I can hear the referee's whistle start the game. We race up the steps on to the terrace two or three steps at a time, relieved that we are inside just in time for kick off.

Like us, others heard the referee's whistle, and in their haste caused a quickening of the crowd to get to the terrace, exacerbating the problems.

As we head up the terrace, we climb the steps up towards the corner and the corrugated side of the North Stand in order to find a good vantage point to see the game. This is not too hard as the area is still thinly popu-lated. I don't know how it's happened but we have quickly picked up our fellow travellers somewhere along the way. As the game has started, we pick our way through the crowd towards an ideal position near the North Stand. I keep shooting glances over my shoulder towards the pitch, as Liverpool have started attacking and they are threatening. Within minutes Peter Beardsley has hit the bar with a thunderous shot. Now though, it is clear there are problems in the centre pen behind the goal. From our vantage point I have now stopped watching the game and my eyes are drawn to the crowd and the unnerving actions of the crowd as a whole. It looks to me as if it is a sea of people desperately trying to stand up, with a wave rippling from front to back and side to side. It appears they have literally no control over their actions and the wave doesn't have a shore to break on. It keeps being forced into the walls and barriers with little or no escape. The people at the front are being crushed and no matter how hard people try they can't stand or take the pressure off the others at the front.

People are trying to escape this terrifying maelstrom. People at the back are being hoisted to safety into the West Stand right behind, with fans leaning down grabbing hands and arms and dragging people up with their sheer strength. Other fans behind are acting as a counter weight so they don't get dragged down into the sea of desperation. Once one gets out, people start flooding upwards. I can see people at the front who can't gain any element of height trying to climb the fences, sometimes they are unwittingly using others as a ladder. These escapees are often not fortunate as many are beaten back by baton wielding police. They seem to be under the impression this is hooliganism and not the desperate act of people trying to save themselves.

I can see the Police control room in the right hand corner of Leppings Lane directly in view above the chaos behind the goal. They are looking straight across into the desperate mass, as we are now. People in the outer pens, standing on the same level, can't see what is going on but with our elevated vantage point it is only too clear. As more people are coming over the barriers the referee has blown the whistle and stopped the game. It is 3.06pm.

This is a time that now lives long in our memory. 3.06 pm became the time when we remember the victims of this terrible tragedy. The 15th April 1989 at 3.06pm was just the start of things to come, and the start of years of unanswered questions and heartache for the families of The 96.

As the players are taken off the pitch, the exodus from the terrace gathers pace and people flood on to the playing area. The players aren't even off the pitch and the goalmouth is full of people. It is clear from where I am standing that some of the people on the pitch are not moving and there are other fans desperately trying to get the injured breathing. This is not just one or two fans this is tens, maybe hundreds, of fans carrying injuries. The final injury toll inside the ground was 730 people. What are the police doing? They are forming a barrier across the pitch at the half way line to stop the fans heading to the Kop end where the Nottingham Forest fans are housed. They still look like they think it is hooliganism, for some reason they can't see what is going on yet once again, those in the control tower can. Not all the police are so inactive, now some of them have seen what is happening and are trying to help get people out of the centre sections, it looks like they're fighting a losing battle.

The Forest fans are booing and shouting abuse but they can't see what is really going on. Oh God, this will silence those boos. Some quick thinking fans have ripped the advertising hoardings from their mountings and are starting to use them as makeshift stretchers to ferry the injured away from the carnage to a place where help must be waiting. The fans are carrying the injured the full length of the pitch and through the police ranks to the far corner of the Kop and in front of the fans at that end. They have to go the whole length of the North Stand and that's where my dad is sitting in the front row with a view of the whole disaster being paraded in front of his eyes.

Unfortunately help was not waiting as there were only two ambulances on duty at Hillsborough that day, and one of them was told to remain in position a mile away from the ground. The fire brigade with specialist cutting equipment was not available until far too late. The disaster recovery plan was totally flawed and as a result people died. We put our faith in people in charge of our safety and they let us down that day.

Now this is where my guilt takes over me and haunts me still.

All these people are helping others on the pitch and what do I do? Nothing, nothing at all. I am just standing there and I am watching others desperately try to save lives. Me, and thousands of others, are frozen and watching this disaster unfold in front of our eyes and are powerless to help. I really want to help but I can't, or rather I don't. I am helpless to help. That's the truth but also the truth is that I have got onto the cinder path around the edge of the pitch and now I am heading up the touchline towards the Hillsborough Kop. I am head-ing away from the disaster area and up towards where I know my dad is sitting. Selfishly I am thinking of telling him that my brother and I are safe and tucked away in the corner. My eyes are firmly fixed on the rows of anxious people watching the scenes in front of them; they are frozen. After what seems like an eternity I have spotted my dad and can see immediately the look of relief on his face, which quickly turns to panic as I am on my own. He is looking for Our Kev. His face turns back to relief as I quickly reassure him that my brother and friends are all safe. He later said 'I kept expecting to see one of you on the hoardings that they are carrying past me'. Then selfishly again my thoughts are turning to home where my mum must now be aware of what is going on. We promise each other that we will get in touch with home and let mum know we are all safe. I don't really want to leave but I head back up the touch-line to assure my brother that dad is okay too, and he's relieved. It felt better that only one of us went to find him as long as the other stayed put. Once again I move up the terrace through the silent masses and back to our posi-tion high up in the corner. The same look has spread across Kev's face until he hears that dad is okay. All the lads feel the same as they all know my dad and their thoughts are now turning to others that they know are there. Now, as I look around, I can see the tangled crush barriers in an almost empty pen; the crush barriers have buckled under the sheer weight of bodies.

People don't know what to do next. We are standing staring, not knowing how to react. Normally 90 minutes and maybe extra time then the referee's whistle will signal the end and that is our cue to leave. Now there isn't a cue to leave we are at a loss. Eventually the tannoy system comes to life for the first time in what seems an eternity. The stadium announcer asks everyone to leave the ground in an orderly and safe fashion and that is our cue to leave in near silence. As the terrace empties slowly there is hardly a murmur as we file out of the ground not daring to look at the now desolate terracing. Many people can't bear to leave. It is clear that many people have lost friends or family and grief starts to pour from small groups of fans. Others seem to be searching in disbelief, hope or plain terror of what might be. We are lucky as we head homewards, five of us together as when we arrived, heading back up past the chip shop and up the hill towards the car. As we are leaving the ground the first rumours of deaths start to circulate first in single figures then quickly into the teens. It comes as a shock even though we had seen the disaster unfold. Maybe we don't really want to believe that something that should have been a celebration could leave people dead in such a short space of time.

By the time we get to the car, compose ourselves and put the BBC Radio Sport report on, we are still unprepared for what happens next. We are sitting discussing the events of the afternoon and we are trying to patch together events ourselves and then the presenter says 'that the initial numbers of dead...' and the words hit us hard. That sounds strange when I already know there are deaths, well there is something different between thinking you know something and having it coldly confirmed and so clinically and directly. I may have misheard; I think he just said 'up to eighty fans are feared dead'. No he must mean eight. No, he has said eighty. All of a sudden the mood in the car changes. It is more than

*just quiet, there is confusion and despair. I don't think
we can formulate in our minds what has happened. I just
want to go home and go home right now.*

As we headed off I started to think that the news I
have just heard must be having a devastating effect on
the people at home. Our first priority was to let our
parents know we were safe and unharmed. On the way
out of Sheffield we pulled into a side road where we saw
a phone box. As we were waiting to use the phone box a
lady appeared from one of the houses nearby and told us
to come and use her phone. She wasn't the only one, the
people of Sheffield were trying to help in whatever way
they could.

I must say I have recently seen a web forum on a
Sheffield based site that is so vitriolic I won't repeat some
of the messages on it. Now, in my opinion and many
others I have met over the years, the one thing that comes
out of this horrible disaster was the support of a number
of people in Sheffield on and after the day. There is a
view in certain quarters that everyone on Merseyside
hates Sheffield. That is just not true, there are some
people who hold their own views, with or without
substantiation, about Sheffield and its people. Whether
they had bad experiences I do not know, but most people
look at the people of Sheffield with great respect. There
are some people there who post such messages who do
not deserve the same respect. They have their own views
about Liverpudlian's. Let them have them. There were a
few people at Hillsborough that day who did not behave
themselves but the few became the majority in many
people's eyes. The myths and mistruths spread by the
media took many years to overcome and some of them
will never be undone.

The lady offering us help really did so, she went out of her way and way beyond what we could ever expect. Besides the offer of tea and sympathy she opened up her world to strangers, she probably never really realised how important her actions were to five lost souls from Liverpool. At that moment I remembered that when I was in Heysel Stadium in Brussels for the European Cup Final in 1985, my mum and dad were worried sick that I was a casualty. That time it took me until three o'clock in the morning to let them know I was safe. That was the earliest I could do it in the days before mobile phones. I always remember my mum and dad saying it was the longest night of their lives. This time, at least my dad was aware I was safe and so was Our Kev, but my mum must have been at her wits end. I had promised my dad and he had promised me that we would try our best to get in touch with home at the earliest opportunity. We stood silently in the hall trying to ring home but the phone lines to Liverpool were constantly engaged. If we were thinking rationally at the time we would have realised that all lines to Liverpool would be busy as everyone would be trying to do the same. The penny finally dropped after about ten minutes of trying. Zil had got through to his mum to let her know we were safe, he lived just outside Liverpool and crucially his area dialling code was different. As we still couldn't get in touch with home, Zil asked his mum to ring our mum and see if she had any luck. She promised to keep trying, and then we could at least start our journey home and leave this hell behind us.

As we started the torturous journey home, traffic had started to build as everybody was desperately trying to get away from the scene of the disaster. Not a word was spoken. Everyone was lost in their own place replaying the events of the afternoon. What had started as a glorious day had literally ended up as a disaster. The silence in the car was unbearable as we wound our way over the Woodhead Pass, out of Sheffield and on towards Manchester and ultimately home. We didn't really realise how lucky we were to be actually going home. I struggled to drive all the way home in this silence because concentration was difficult. You take driving for granted but if you don't concentrate you're in trouble. As we headed out of Sheffield, I missed seeing a large pothole in the road and the jolt it sent through the car shook everyone for a moment. I put a tape (no CD's then) into the stereo and turned it back on; we'd turned it off earlier as it had been the purveyor of such bad news. Don't even ask what was on the tape as it's not relevant. I just needed something to break my mind away from replaying the carnage behind the goal. Years later, after a fall out, one of the lads in the car told me he thought I was an inconsiderate bastard for breaking the silence. To which I replied he was an inconsiderate bastard for not thinking about me having to drive home after seeing what we all saw. At least I got them home in one piece.

Regardless of the stereo being on or off I don't remember any conversation in the car all the way back. As always after an away trip we ended up in a bar in the small town of Ormskirk, about five miles north of Liverpool, where a number of the lads lived. A place that was normally bouncing on a Saturday night was deserted at eight o'clock. We walked in and ordered four pints and a coke for me. We were only staying for one drink and then going. Two hours later none of the pints were finished and it was time to go. We had at least started to talk about it, none of it made sense and no one knew what our future held now, this was what we did, we followed football. What happens next?

What really happened next was that everyone needed to go home to see their loved ones. By now, memory serves me that we had all been able to make contact to reassure everyone, and my mum especially, as to the fact that my dad was safe as well as us. Thinking back now it was probably selfish to stay out and not go right home but we just didn't think. We had to try and deal with what we had seen. As Kev and I dropped the lad's at home, there was the briefest of goodbyes and promises to call, and then we headed off down the A59 to Liverpool. With a mile to go, all of a sudden the headlights on the car went and then the instrument panel went dead and the engine cut out. Just before Aintree racecourse (the home of the Grand National) we ground to a halt. A turn of the key and nothing, then again and all we heard was a click. There was no juice in the car. That was all we needed. Kev and I managed to push it to the side of the road and called the AA 'We'll be out in about an hour'. Yeah cheers! If ever an hour felt like an eternity this was it. We wanted to be home, not stuck in a car in the cool of the spring night, so close to home. I said to Kev he might as well go home, but he wanted to stay, no point going home on his own. We had to go together. We had the sense to ring my mum again. She had worried enough that day - no need for anymore. Well that pothole got me didn't it! It had dislodged a piece of metal from something attached to the radiator and it had burnt through the alternator cable. The AA man juiced us up enough to get us the mile home. At the door, a rather relieved mum (that's an understatement) met us with a big hug and broken smile of relief. Where was my dad? He still wasn't home. At about one in the morning he walked in ashen faced. His coach had to stay in Sheffield as one of the passengers was missing and no one wanted to leave in case he was traumatised and eventually returned to where the coach was. Eventually at 11 pm they left Sheffield. The passenger was never to find his way home, God bless him. He was gone! The coach had to leave a son who had travelled with his father. Left alone, to the start of years of grief.

When I hear tales like that, I feel so relieved we were all back together. I couldn't get any feelings other than relief but I immediately felt the loss of the others. The days ahead would bring answers to all my questions. How many died? Who were they? Did I know them? Did I get them their ticket? These were all questions that couldn't be answered at 1am following the worst day of my life. That was for tomorrow and I was lucky to see tomorrow.

—⁓—

Two years on in the summer of 1991 as I lay flat blinking into the operating theatre light of St Paul's Eye Hospital in Liverpool, the physical effects of Hillsborough had manifested themselves from within the mental effects of the disaster. As the surgeon prepared himself for the procedure my mind kept flitting back to 'that day'. Following two years of sleepless nights, stress had taken its toll on my body. My eyelids had cysts within them and had become noticeably hard and misshapen. The surgeon explained that due to a lack of sleep the tear ducts within the eye hadn't been doing their natural job and had resulted in infections in three out of four of my eyelids. Since the disaster my sleep patterns could be described as irregular at best and non-existent at worst. I would go to sleep exhausted and if I didn't drop off immediately a first inconsequential thought would lead to a second, then a third, and in no time at all I would be replaying the pictures from the 15th of April in vivid Technicolor. I would be going to work on so little sleep it was hard to function, good job I could hide behind a computer screen all day.

As the nurse dropped a solution carefully into my right eye, the world around me became blurred, with the eye deadened by the solution the surgeon then injected local anaesthetic into both lids. I felt like he had stabbed me never mind a pinprick - it was more like a javelin rammed in my eye. Thankfully it took effect quickly and the surgeon went to work on the eye, with a patch on the other eye I was blissfully unaware of what he was doing. I could feel some pulling and scratching but no pain and then the sickly sweet smell of burning flesh. It turned out that the operation involved slicing along the eyelid, scraping the cyst out and cauterised (hence the burning flesh) the lid shut. With a dressing and an eye patch I left the hospital to return the following week for my left eye, which only required action on one eyelid.

As I felt a little sorry for myself recovering at home thanks to a recommendation of 48 hours rest I realised I was actually one of the lucky ones, I was effectively a bystander, what would the effects have been like if I was caught within the central pens.

—◊◊◊—

Sometimes I realise how lucky I am and then there are sometimes when I really realise how lucky I am. Today is one of those days, Liverpool are playing Blackburn and in two days time it will be the nineteenth anniversary of the Hillsborough Disaster. I am sitting in my living room tuned to Sky Sports and the teams are gathered around the centre circle. They will observe a minute silence in memory of the 96 who perished at Hillsborough in 1989. The referee blows his whistle and silence engulfs Anfield and my living room in the Isle of Man. It's my chance to remember on my own and pay my respects. Then through the window comes the sound of Charlie my son and my wife Nikki giggling in the garden, Nikki is keeping him out the way so I can watch in peace. The sound of my family laughing makes me really realise how lucky I am. There by the grace of God. It was actually two years since I last wrote those words at the beginning of this chapter. Nineteen years on and it still doesn't go away

—◁◁◁—

7

A return to normal

As I woke up on Sunday the 16th of April I thought things would never be normal again, but it's incredible how things move on. If I'd had two hours sleep I would be amazed, and then it was exhaustion that made me sleep. The nightmares had started already. *Our Kev hadn't seen me and he had gone down the tunnel, then there were empty seats in the car on the way home.* Things I knew not to be true, irrational yes, but so real, my tired mind was playing tricks on me, and cruel tricks at that.

Staring into a morning cup of tea is not a normal pastime but that was what I was doing. The three of us (me, dad and Our Kev) had all returned home. We were lucky, but we didn't feel that lucky. None of us were speaking to each other. We were all alone, wrapped in our own thoughts. At Anfield, Peter Robinson, the then Club Secretary, decided to open the ground for fans who had headed there out of a sense of longing to be close to the Club. I can't explain why so I won't even try, but I had that same longing as well and I headed to Anfield with Our Kev and my mum as company, God bless her. Flowers in hand, respect in my heart, and a sense of despair, the pull of the Kop dragged me up Everton Valley and towards the ground. The Anfield pilgrimage was altogether something different that day.

As we walked around the back of the Kop, the sun shone, bouncing off the broken glass in the back of the Kop windows. We moved silently through the car park and up to the Anfield Road end where the gates were open. We walked silently along the cinder path and just past the half way line on to the lush green grass and headed towards the Kop goalmouth. I had longed to do this for years, head towards the Kop with a red shirt on my back, bearing down on the goal before I burst the net with a stunning right foot. Bearing down on the goal now, it was not the whites of the keeper's eyes I could see, but a beautiful array of flowers, bouquets, scarves, teddy bears and personal football shirts. Seemingly positioned as a piece of art but not by artists - these had been placed carefully by people who cared. Individual scarves hung from the crossbar or were tied to the netting. Messages of hope and despair in equal proportion flapped gently in the breeze. Reading the messages was all too much to take, and I headed up on to the Kop. Instinctively I headed to 'our spec' where we would all stand for every home game, and as I did so, others followed. Immediately I started to think 'who would I see again?' All these people that I knew every other Saturday but didn't really know at all. I wondered what had become of them less than 24 hours earlier.

I gently tied my scarf around the barrier that marked my position, hung my head and could no longer hold back the tears. Our Kev joined me and as we hugged each other, we sobbed our hearts out. The enormity of it all hit us - we were the lucky ones. Writing this now I can see the scene clearly before me, the trickle of people was now a stream and others had followed me on to the Kop and stood or sat in silent contemplation. We were the people who didn't yet know if any of the victims were known to us. For others, this journey would be an exercise in dealing with their grief in the days to come. As I lent over the barrier and wiped my eyes, the flowers filling the six yard box started to cover the lines of lime. By the end of the week the carpet of flowers was to cover one half of the pitch and include football shirts from many football clubs throughout the land. Our neighbours Everton where hugely represented as it was an event that transcended the football rivalry and affected the city as a whole. Even many Manchester United fans, for years sworn enemies, should never be forgotten the way they reacted to the tragedy. Barring the mindless minorities, many football fans know that it could quite easily have been them.

After what seemed like hours we left the ground in silence and headed past the queues that were now forming outside the ground and back down the hill to home. The week to come was both heartening and disconcerting. Heartening as one by one all my friends and contacts who I got tickets for got in touch. Each and everyone had their own story to tell. Some had lucky escapes. One of the guys from work came home with no shoes on as they were ripped of his feet in the crush as he battled to get out. Alex, a girl from work who I had seen outside the ground in the crush, told me she was lucky to be here as she was crushed outside the ground and on the verge of passing out as the gate opened. I was working for the local council at the time and the management were very understanding with people who had been there and offered as much support as possible.

As the week wore on and the reality of what happened started to hit home, the vultures in the media started to peddle their lies and mistruths. Lies, is not too strong a word for what was printed in the Daily Star and The Sun in particular. The story that The Sun printed was entitled 'The Truth', their version of the truth was to say that Liverpool fans picked the pockets and urinated on the dead and dying bodies. How disgraceful if true but how reprehensible to report it if it never actually happened, and it didn't happen. In a detailed Government report Lord Justice Taylor found no evidence whatsoever. The Daily Star immediately withdrew the allegations following the uproar on Merseyside but The Sun never did. Months later they admitted the story was false but the damage was done, Kelvin McKenzie actually rang Kenny Dalglish to ask what he could do to make things better. Dalglish told him to print a story entitled 'The Lies!' McKenzie refused saying he couldn't do that so King Kenny put the phone down on him, and The Sun has been paying the price for years. In the initial uproar that followed the scandalous reports, the paper was boycotted on the streets of Liverpool and copies finding their way on to the streets were ripped and burned. To this day there is no major circulation of that paper in Merseyside. It was one of Merseyside's working classes daily reads, along with the Daily Mirror. Now it is still reviled in Liverpool, and rightly so and McKenzie is still peddling his version of events all these years on. Can you begin to imagine how you would feel if you were one of the bereaved families?

The talk in the press was whether Liverpool would play on in the FA Cup or even finish the league season. The stench of death still surrounded football and Mr Personality, Graham Kelly, who was Chief Executive of the Football Association at the time, was debating the future. 95 people (Tony Bland the 96th victim died in 1993 following legal battles to switch off his life support) no longer had a future. If they started playing again would you go? Would you ever go again? What would it feel like? That decision was delayed due to the period of mourning that had to be endured first. The Club and the players were in no fit state to play any games. To their credit, all were consumed with supporting the bereaved families and injured. The actions of many of the first team squad are to be admired and every funeral had a player or representative present, and if a particular player had been the fan's favourite, the club would do their best to make sure they were present. The player's lounge at Anfield was open house to the families and the likes of Ronnie Whelan, Steve McMahon and John Aldridge are reportedly still in touch with many families today. Dalglish himself was going to as many as four funerals every day. Craig Johnson even flew all the way around the world to support the Club and fans, having retired and returned home to Australia just two years earlier.

And me too. I had the unenviable duty of attending a funeral. Gary Philip Jones, eighteen years of age. That's what he will always be known as on the memorial at Anfield on the roll call of the dead. It is called annually at the memorial service and in all the books you read. To me though, he was little Gary from up the street. The Jones's lived fifty yards up the street and I knew them all.

I was mates with Gary's older brother Ste in my younger years, and had been a regular visitor in the Jones household over the years. As we had grown up, we started to move in different circles and only met when we saw each other in the street. It's the sort of thing that happens as you go to different schools then start working. I would see his sisters more than Ste and in particular Cathy who I would often see out and about in town. I still do at times, even though it is maybe every two or three years. The Jones family was very much like ours, good and honest and not befitting the tragedy that befell them.

Gary went the match that sunny afternoon and didn't come home and it ripped the family heart out.

As I sat silently in the packed church there was nothing I could say to make it better. I paid my respects and left silently without the family ever knowing I was there. I went for them, for Gary, and for me. It was the first time I remember popular music at a funeral and the Danny Wilson (a popular band from Scotland) song, Mary's Prayer, played in the church as one of Gary's favourite songs. I never realised it had religious connotations until I heard the line *'say ten hail Mary's leave a light on in heaven for me'*. I still hear it regularly today on local radio and I always think of Gary and his family, I hope he rested in peace and left the light on.

The cover up started immediately and for me to go into detail here is not appropriate, but needless to say justice is still waiting to be done over eighteen years later. No one has ever been brought to account and the lies and the insinuations still carry too much weight. If you need to see more about the disaster I would recommend you look up the following website **www.contrast.org/**

hillsborough or watch Hillsborough, the docu drama written by that wonderful writer Jimmy McGovern. The drama was fully supported by the families group and it tells the story better than any one person ever could.

The weeks that followed are a bit of a blur and normality ... well I didn't know what normal looked like anymore. On the Saturday following the disaster we attended a service of remembrance. A service for all faiths, for all people. With my brothers and friends we listened, amongst the throngs outside the Kop, to the service relayed from inside the ground. With a carpet of flowers inside and the Kop bedecked in tokens of respect and grief, space was very limited and we stood outside in silence. At exactly 3.06 the moment the game was stopped, a minute's silence, immaculately observed, was held. We could hear the birds singing, the slight breeze rustling discarded papers and the flags flying at half mast at the back of the kop. No one said anything. There was nothing left to say, it was all too soon.

The following day we headed across the Pennines once more to a service held at the Cathedral by the people of Sheffield as they had suffered too. Some people have nothing good to say about Sheffield following the way the local papers and football club behaved over the years. But for me, normal people helped thousands of us with the support they showed through opening their homes up to us, the survivors. Normal people cared and helped others and they do not deserve to be tarnished by the actions of others and neither do we. We went across to pay our respects and visit the ground, and this started to close the chapter for me. Leaving the scene on the day itself was not the way I wanted to leave it. The visit proved to be cathartic for me. As we headed out of

Sheffield on the same route we had taken the previous week, we delivered flowers and chocolates to the lovely lady who had kindly let us use her phone. Slightly bewildered and ever so thankful, she graciously accepted our gifts with a tear in her eye, and we headed back on to the Pennine range and back home.

As the weeks dragged on, the return to football was always going to happen, both for me and for Liverpool. We didn't know any other way, and once the funerals had been completed, the focus turned to the day that Liverpool could take to the pitch again. This would be up in Glasgow against Celtic, who had kindly offered Liverpool the opportunity to return to playing ways prior to their return to league action against Everton, and the replayed game against Nottingham Forest. Celtic was what everybody needed and an estimated 10,000 Liverpool fans headed up to Scotland on a Sunday afternoon. The ones that travelled were ready. Others were not and couldn't face the return to football yet. My mum has always asked me 'have you got your ticket?' She asks it religiously and I always had it firmly grasped or stashed away in a pocket. This day normal match routine was out the window and the thought of returning to a packed stadium must have been playing on my mind. I totally forgot and when we got to the coach, we had to drive home and get the tickets, making the coach departure by seconds for the journey up north. Once seated in the coach, albeit rather flushed and sweating profusely on an early May day, it was like normal service had been resumed. The talk was about who was going to play? How were they going to play? And an air of excitement, obviously tempered a little, about going to Celtic Park. The long journey north was worth it.

By the time we boarded the coach home, we had been released from the previous three weeks of despair and desolation, and we found a sense of optimism on which to build our future. Liverpool had won comfortably against a Celtic team that had played just twenty four hours earlier, Dalglish made an appearance to the deafening roars of 60,000 Celts and Scousers, and the welcome was way beyond warm. The Celtic fans welcomed us as their own, scarves were swapped, we sang each other's songs, with the most moving being *"You'll never walk alone"* and we all stood as one, side by side. Celtic have never been forgotten for that and will always hold a place in my heart for the way we were treated. A day of trepidation turned into a day where we could move on and that's just what we did.

The first competitive game was against (of all people) our local rivals Everton. The Evertonians had been magnificent in the aftermath of the disaster. This is what makes today's bitterness between supporters seem so senseless. As I write this, a small boy in Liverpool, just eleven years old, Rhys Jones was shot dead on his way home from football practice. A passionate Evertonian who would wear no other clothes than football kits and Everton gear, Rhys was killed by a bullet fired by another teenager and his only crime was to be in the wrong place at the wrong time, on his way home from football practice. Liverpool fans will mourn his lost youth to support their neighbours and it's at times like this that our city becomes one again.

That night, thousands of scarves which had been left on the pitch in the days following the disaster, were joined end to end to link Anfield to Goodison Park as the two teams met. It was named the 'chain of Hope'. An impeccably observed moment of silence was followed by booming chants of "Merseyside" to show the nation the community spirit that is rarely seen in modern day life. The match held little significance but it was a return to what we knew. The lost were not forgotten but the present went on to create a future.

Then came the largest leap of faith. A return to the Semi Final stage of the FA Cup. Liverpool had decided to play on in the competition as a tribute to the fans that had lost their lives. The overwhelming majority of people had agreed it was the right thing to do. Now people wanted Liverpool to go on and win it. Thousands of Liverpool fans headed to Old Trafford to take on Nottingham Forest again. This time Liverpool got the bigger Stretford end and Forest the smaller Scoreboard end. That was fine by me as the scoreboard paddock very much resembled the Leppings Lane end of Hillsborough. There was only one team who was going to win that day and it was Liverpool who were carried through to the final on a wind of emotion and deafening noise as the Scousers roared their team to victory. Even the Forest fans seemed resigned to the fact that it was unwinnable for them. Liverpool reached a final that was to be more appropriate than could ever be imagined, against our neighbours Everton.

The season will show that Liverpool ended up winning the FA Cup Final and losing the league in the 90th minute on an amazing night against Arsenal. To me that didn't matter - my life had changed. I can't honestly say it was for the better or worse I was just different.

The old adage "life must go on" is true no matter what anyone says and people do move on, some quicker than others. It is an individual thing and for me I was moving on, I had realised I was lucky. I took this as a sign that I should never take anything for granted. I was going to live my life for today, with one eye on the future of course, but nothing was going to stop me. I was no longer thinking "when I am 25 I will do this" then "when I am 30 I will do this". I had been waiting for people to do things, now there would be no waiting. I was going for it. Heysel and Hillsborough were personal warnings to me. My philosophy on life changed that day in Sheffield. Life doesn't wait for you, it passes you by or it is stolen away, I realised you are never in control of your own destiny. My advice to anyone starting out in life would be to make the most of what you have and follow your dreams.

—〰—

8

The European Experience

As we stepped on to the dock in Calais at 6am on a warm summer's morning, we were embarking on a journey that would reinvent my life and would be a cathartic experience. It was a trip that was to allow me to emerge from the shadow of Hillsborough and give me a new beginning, complete with a stronger outlook on life. I was going to enjoy life and experience things that I had put off or been too tentative to do. I was no longer waiting for others, I was just going to do things and if people wanted to join me, the more the merrier! If I had to go on my own, so be it. As it turned out, the only time I ever had to go on my own anywhere of any distance was Barnsley (well it was Istanbul really, but Barnsley was a close second). Barnsley was memorable as it ended in a riot after they had a third man sent off. It was a dodgy old departure from the car park behind the away end at Oakwell that day I can tell you. Anyway forget Barnsley, I was heading across the channel for the wonders of Europe.

I had seen how quickly life could be taken away. It scared me that I was only 23. Life had only just begun and there was so much to do in the big wide world outside of Liverpool and football. I had already had two close experiences of how things could be taken away in seconds.

1989 was the turning point when football became *one* of the things I loved and not just the only thing. I had always thought that everything could wait until I had followed the Reds around the country for a few more years. But things can't wait, actually they don't wait or won't wait, you have to seize the day. *Carpe diem*. Now football had to fit in with other things such as music and travel, and lots of travel at that. Football often goes hand in hand with the music scene in Liverpool as many of the football faces are the music faces too. They were to be seen watching the Reds at Anfield or Echo and the Bunnymen at the Royal Court. Today you can still roll up at an Echo and the Bunnymen concert some 25 years on and see faces from the Kop, maybe a little withered and worn, often balding and wearing glasses, but it's them still. The same passions exist but they fit in with other bits of life such as wives and families.

The great European trip was by Inter Rail, which was a train ticket that cost £145, a fortune in those days. Ticket in hand you could travel around the European rail network in standard class for not a penny more. Not a penny more if we bunked into first class or sleeping compartments but that was not always possible with eagle-eyed guards and moaning old French women who would grass us up. The £145 turned into a bargain when compared to the fact it cost £55 to get from Liverpool to Dover by train. At least, unlike some, we didn't have to jump in the toilet every time a guard came by!

My faithful travelling companions were Our Kev and Zil. I think it was the first time we had actually really enjoyed ourselves since that fateful day in mid April (without any degree of guilt at least). This was, after all, a new beginning. We were going to places we had never been, there were no old memories and the experiences would all be fresh. The continent was ours to see and to do what we pleased. The original plan was for seven mates to do it all together. I remember sitting on a coach on the way to Middlesbrough in February discussing it and everyone was well up for it. We were all between 18 and 23 and life was great, lucky to have a job and enjoy each other's company. It was to take us to the next step, away from the beaches of Spain and the likes of Lloret de Mar and Watney's red barrel. Heading to Teeside on a miserable day, our mood was spiced up with thoughts of Paris, Rome and Monte Carlo.

What happened to the other four? Hillsborough happened and I don't think they could face being reminded during that summer. You were reminded by simply being in the company of others who had witnessed those terrible events. The decision not to go was something that was never even spoken about. It was their decision and one that I and the other two lads fully appreciated and respected. Everyone needed a little space to deal with things in their own way.

As always, it was left up to me to organise everything. For this trip, this initially consisted of booking the trains from Liverpool to Dover, ferry tickets from Dover to Calais and the Inter rail tickets. That was it. No comfortable hotels booked, no one picking us up at the airport and taking us to our hotel, no one speaking English to give us the heads up about where we were. This was a voyage of discovery and it was really exciting. I also bought a European phrasebook, the Rough Guide to Europe and the Thomas Cook European railway timetable (which was to become our bible during the three weeks we were away). The phrasebook told us how to order a meal in a restaurant, order theatre tickets and how to get medicine at a pharmacy. In reality we could order a meal in pigeon English, we weren't going the theatre, and we could get headache and tablets for the wildies (travellers tummy, Delhi belly you get the picture) off the shelf and read the price ourselves in Francs or Lira or whatever currency. This was in a time before the euro had arrived and every border we crossed, we had the nightmare of changing our money. Travellers cheques were base currency and then we would be ripped off at varying degrees in order to get hold of hard cash for the land we were travelling through. It was tough as we only stayed in each country for a short time and we had to judge how much to change. Some countries could really stitch us up as it cost £5 for a small beer. Switzerland was particularly expensive I recall.

Using the phrasebook generally resulted in us ordering a bowl of wet socks that we needed to dry on our hosts' bare buttocks prior to covering with tomato sauce. The English abroad. We might as well give up. On a number of occasions we reverted to speaking our version of someone else's language. We just shouted English at people very slowly (CAN YOUUUU TELL MEEEEE WHICH WAYYY TO DE ARKKK DE TRIUMFFFFFF PLEEESE). No wonder the Parisians took the piss out of us and wouldn't speak English. It was amazing though how many people could speak better English than three Scouse lads. Now I feel very ignorant when abroad and somewhat ashamed, I would love to be able to converse properly with someone in their own language, but then again if they can speak the master language why bother! To my shame I am far too lazy to learn, as Del Boy would say, "Mange-tout Rodney, mange-tout".

Now the Thomas Cook European timetable was a masterpiece. Forget Dickens and Shakespeare this is *the* must have book. I had already travelled all around Europe by the time I even set foot on our first train out of Liverpool, all from the comfort of my living room. It was great if you wanted to go from Paris to Rome in one night, you would know every station in between and how long the connections where. You knew whether you could get food, sleeping accommodation, if it was fast or if it was slow. You knew which ghost town in the middle of Italy you would be arriving at around three o'clock in the morning. It was so helpful in planning our route it was unbelievable. Years later, all the skills I had learned on this trip stood me in good stead for that magnificent journey to Istanbul. The Thomas Cook guide had all the railway schedules from Norway to Nottingham and York to Yugoslavia. We figured out that we could go to sleep in Nice and wakeup in Rome, or stay awake all night from Geneva to Amsterdam, whatever took our fancy. The beauty was that we just turned up, wrote our journey details on our ticket and headed to pastures new, how exciting! So prior to leaving suburban Liverpool we had our European adventure sort of mapped out. Something like this: Liverpool to Paris, Paris to the South of France, on to Rome, Switzerland, and finally Amsterdam, and that was just for the first two weeks. At that point Zil was to leave us and head home and me and Our Kev would head on wherever. Me and Kev had jobs in the local council and Zil worked in a Bank. We had great leave entitlement and the benefits of flexi time. He didn't.

Rome was to be the highlight of the trip for us. Following years of stories from my dad and his generation about their escapades in the Italian capital in 1977, when Liverpool won the European Cup for the first time, we just had to go! A football match was also on the itinerary as the Italian league was still in its final weeks. We were originally planning to watch one of the mighty Milan clubs but our schedule did not allow it. As luck would have it we were destined to watch our Italian football in Rome.

A change of scenery called for a change in haircut for me, a holiday haircut of the worst kind. I decided to change from the fashionable flick (of a kind) to having it short and spiky. I had graduated from the pudding bowl as soon as I could run away from the scissors. I had moved effortlessly on from sitting on the leather boards at the barbers so it didn't break the poor barbers back bending that far down. That was when a haircut cost virtually nothing and you talked about football with your dad and the barber who obviously had to follow the Reds (Evertonian barbers were never to be trusted). Nowadays you have to talk about the latest pop sensation whilst listening to Radio One thump away with some teenager chewing his gum to the beat (how old am I? I am turning into my dad). Then you say 'How much? For a haircut? You're having a laugh'. It will be back to the pudding bowl before you know it, life always goes full circle. You begin life pissing yourself uncontrollably and you end up doing the same thing 90 years later.

Anyway, back to the haircut. After work on the Friday with an early finish, it was straight to the barbers.

On a whim I said 'Do something different', but the barber must have heard 'Make me look like a prick for my holidays'. I looked like Fido Dido looking over that big wall. You could see me from miles away, looking like a big long bog brush. The pictures are still under lock and key to this day. The funny thing was, as it grew I ended up liking it and it took me another fifteen years, just prior to my wedding, to change it.

At least it got the holiday off to a start with a great deal of laughter, obviously at my expense. Meeting Zil at Lime Street train station must have been one of the highlights of his year. What was he laughing at? He looked like the Cuprinol man (from the wood stain advert, with hair like a wooden James Dean quiff). I wasn't bothered really, I was on my hols and dreaming about trundling across Europe on my favourite mode of transport. We loved going to the match on the train, you could get up and move about and we didn't get stuck in traffic jams, and we could have a drink if we liked.

As the train pulled out of Lime Street, I was in total control. I had the timetable and the guidebook and I knew where we were going. I seem to remember the other two just turned up and followed what I said. That's all well and good if you have good travelling companions and they were great, they never moaned and let me do everything for them. It got a bit tiresome and I made them do things themselves, but often they did it so badly, I ended up taking over anyway. Deep down I love it, you know, organising stuff, I should have been a travel agent, my dad always says.

In the heat wave of 1989 with the elegance of Paris, pretentiousness of Cannes, warmth of Nice and the sheer unadulterated show of wealth in Monte Carlo behind us we went buzzing into Italy. We were on our way towards the Eternal City of Rome. As we boarded the overnight train from Nice, we dreamed of the Vatican, the Coliseum, the Spanish Steps and La Dolce Vita. Well, we would have dreamt if we had got any sleep, but as always we arrived at our destination knackered. If you want to know more about our time in France you will have to buy my next book as it is too long a story to tell here.

There was so much to look forward to. Like Paris, it was one of *the* classical cities to visit. Rome had always held a fascination with me, as my dad had travelled there in 1977 to watch the Mighty Reds win their first European Cup. I was only eleven at the time and I hung on every word of his stories of his escapades in the Eternal City. Even as an eleven year old, my dreams centred on doing the same when I was older. I never realised it would be thirty years before I'd have stories about European glory that I could tell my kids. But when I did, my story beat my dad's hands down.

Times were tough in the 70s in Liverpool and there wasn't a lot of money around, especially for luxuries such as following the Mighty Reds around. 1977 was a classic football year and Liverpool had got to the FA Cup Final the Saturday before the European Cup Final was to be played. The FA Cup Final was a dear enough do, but when they had beaten FC Zurich in the Semi Final of the European Cup, all eyes turned to Rome. People begged, stole and borrowed to raise the funds to go. I am proud to say that my dad only needed two of the three and stealing was the odd one out. He begged my Mum and borrowed from my Auntie and Uncle, who being classed as better off could lend him the money to get to Rome with his mates (including my Uncle Len, the money lender). He only borrowed it on the grounds that the money would be paid back and paid back very quickly. On this occasion though, the overwhelming need to be there made him swallow his pride accept the help from my Uncle Len. Oh and how glad he was that he did. He has been living off Rome '77 ever since, and I bet it seems like only yesterday to him. It was only the second time that he had been out of the UK. The first was a year earlier when he went to Belgium to watch the Reds win the UEFA Cup against Brugge. I was surprised he was allowed to go abroad again after that. He got so bladdered on the boat home from Belgium that he nearly took the return trip back from Dover, as he was looking for the ships captain to thank him for being a safe driver. In 1977, a holiday on the Costa's was still a fairly unique experience, never mind going to Australia or the States for a couple of weeks. For a lot of the male population of Liverpool, travel abroad was only there for following your football team (Red or Blue). Remember, in less than thirty years, the world has become a much smaller place and within 24 hours and for under £600 you can be in Australia. If you went to Australia 30 years ago you stayed.

So, back to my dad and 1977. He was in one of the elite groups who actually flew to Italy, others took far more tortuous routes to get there. The train was a popular option for many. The train left Liverpool on Monday evening at 7pm travelling via Dover then ferry on to Belgium, Germany, Switzerland and Italy arriving in Rome on Wednesday morning. Normally it would go straight through France but because of strikes in France (what's new eh?) the train had to go via Belgium and Germany. A long journey, which was made horrendous by lack of heating, appalling sanitary conditions, no drinking water and no food. The stinking and hungry hordes arrived in Rome on the Wednesday and despite their travel troubles they turned the town RED. From the Coliseum to the Vatican, the Scouse legions breathed in the Roman experience and turned the stadium into a travelling Kop. Can you tell I was brought up on the legend of Rome?

What made this show of strength and passion so unbelievable was that the Reds had just lost the FA Cup Final the previous Saturday to Man United, so it would have been understandable if the fans were subdued. No chance. This was an occasion and as I was told in no uncertain terms by one of the lads nearly thirty years later, 'We were made to do this'. Call it cocky, call it conceited but we honestly believe we are destined for occasions such as Rome and Istanbul. When the team took to the pitch at the Olympic stadium that night in Rome, what they found stunned them. They were expecting 9,000 fans and in front of them were an esti-mated 25,000. Just as in Istanbul all those years later when we got 20,000 tickets and took 45,000 fans. The Kop in full voice on foreign soil, waiving masses of flags and scarves, singing themselves hoarse as their heroes entered the modern day Coliseum. There was no way they would lose and as it turned out, they were carried on a wave of red and white to their first European Cup. It was to be the first sign of English domination of the competition. If you ever see pictures of Rome in 1977, you will see there were about 20,000 red and white

chequered flags in the Liverpool end. I was really looking forward to getting one when my dad got back. No
chance. He spent all his money on ale and seeing the
Pope. There is a picture of him and his mates getting a
pony and trap ride in Rome, how weird is that? How
expensive is that?

If your dad was in Rome, you were definitely a
celebrity in school and your celebrity status went up
when you went to see the Cup come home. Who thought
celebrity came with the introduction of Big Brother? I
was one all those years ago. My dad was a hero for me.
He had been all the way to Rome, spoke Italian and ate
the local food. He was an explorer pushing the boundaries on the continent. Well he went all the way to Rome
at least! He didn't speak a word of Italian, but he was
amazed that all the little kids in the streets and even a
parrot they came across could speak fluent Italian. Now
without using the words 'foreign muck' he wasn't too
taken with the food. It started out well in the first restaurant he came to as he recognised that spaghetti was on
the menu and he liked spaghetti on toast (Heinz
Spaghetti that is). He ordered and ate that, well he didn't
really as when it came it didn't look the same as 'our
spaghetti'. According to my dad it looked and tasted like
rope so he wouldn't eat it, and he wasn't the only one.
My Uncle Len wouldn't either, so sitting in the corner
was my Uncle Dave who became the human dustbin for
the next three days. In three days in Rome my dad ate
two packets of biscuits, and he didn't even drink copious
amounts of beer as he wanted to savour the whole experience (not the spaghetti experience, the winning the cup
in Rome experience) and he didn't have enough money
to buy lots of beer. He certainly was clear headed enough

to remember that Rome was a wonderful place and the sights he had seen were amazing. So much so, that from me being a wide eyed eleven year old to being a wide-eyed twenty three year old, Rome was never in question when planning our travelling itinerary in the months previous. All roads (or tracks) had to lead to Rome.

—w—

It can be a long old night on a train when you get virtually no sleep at all, and that's just what happened again. By the time we rolled into Rome, if I had slept in total for an hour I would be amazed. Once the sun rose over the rolling fields of Italy, there was little chance of sleeping any longer. The sun had risen by about 6am and there was still a good two or three hours to go until we got to Rome. I was looking out of the window and aching for my first sight of Rome.

I was thinking about the story of Romulus and Remus, children who were raised by dogs in the seven hills on which the City of Rome is built. They were left by the River Tiber to starve by their mother and a she-wolf rescued them. Years later Mars (Roman God of war) told them to build a city, which they dutifully did. Legend has it that the two boys fell out and Romulus killed Remus and named the city after himself. What sort of brother was he I hear you ask? Now, Romulus and Remus would be called feral children and Channel 4 would be doing a documentary about them, not naming cities after them. Romulus ended up killing his brother, sounds like some Brookside plot doesn't it. Now don't get the idea that I was well educated, it was just one of those little things picked up in school that stays with you for life. I can still picture the illustrations in the worn book, children wrapped in blankets and surrounded by wolves. The wolf was to become the symbol of the City of Rome, similar to the Liver Bird representing our great City of Liverpool. Further similarities exist with the respective creatures dominating the football club crests of Liverpool and Roma. Rome was always going to be one of the highlights of the European tour, especially as we were going to watch Roma play at home at the Olympic Stadium, as the Italian football season had not finished yet.

All that was still to come as there was so much to look forward to in Rome and the excitement was building. The best thing about this type of holiday was that we never got bored, there was always something new and exciting around the corner. Every day was thrilling and every other day we seemed to be arriving somewhere new and exciting, there was no chance of getting bored.

There I was desperately looking out of the window for the Coliseum and the Vatican, and all I could see was Edge Hill (the railway sidings just outside Lime Street station in Liverpool). It was exactly the same, just railway sidings and depressing tower blocks, not what I was hoping to see. As the train lurched to a halt, we were out of the door in seconds. One of things we had learned was that the first people to get to the Tourist information offices tended to get the better accommodation and would be away from the station in minutes. Otherwise you would queue up for hours and end up with a rubbish room. As usual, it was left to me to sort stuff out, I was off like a shot storming up the platform like Linford Christie (without the lunch box), leaving my bag with the others in order not to slow me down. I was one of the first there and true to form I sorted out a decent Pensione

(B&B to you), which I was told was ten minutes walk away from the railway station near the famous Villa Borghese. I was so quick that the other two were still ambling onto the concourse looking for me, swinging my bag between them like two girls.

We trotted out of the station and, as always in Italy, the station was a wonder to behold, not like UK stations which were like 1960 planners' dreams gone wrong. Just think of London Euston station (a soulless space if ever you saw one) and you will know what I mean. These places were not soulless; they were classical buildings that you would expect to be home to a museum not a railway station. From the tired rail tracks that lead the train into the station to the classical architecture that greeted you as you stepped on to the station concourse, it couldn't have been anymore different. Like two different cities, or more like two different worlds.

The streets of Rome ooze class. The Italians think they are a really classy race and with good reason for most of the time. It's strange, even the ugliest Italian man thinks he is sex on legs, but obviously they are not all that they think they are. The classic look (crisply laundered shirt, belt as big as your head and perfect creases in their trouser legs with a quality pair of brogues) was the look of Rome. Even the tramps seem to be in a different class than the London version. Other than the tramps Gucci and Armani were the uniform (yeah, like I would know). The women had their own classic look, high heels, slender legs, low cut top and slim waist, well that was the hookers, but the normal women carried themselves with such an air of authority and grace they definitely turned our heads, even the old birds just had something about them.

The walk to the hotel was as promised and completed in less than ten minutes and located in a decent district that was fairly central to all the attractions. As we entered the Pensione, things didn't look too promising though. The floors were marble but nothing else promised a decent hotel. Nervously we entered, and we found a little gem of a place and it only cost us 35 grand for the night, lucky it was 35,000 lire and not pounds (it still worked out at about £5 each). The Lire was probably the most difficult currency to use as everything seemed so bloody dear and prices seemed to change every day. Inflation in Italy was rife and the Romans could always take advantage of an Englishman's inability to work out the currency. If you ever questioned a price the vendor would all of a sudden be unable to understand or speak English. That must be why every time I have been the Coliseum it has cost me at least £5 for a bottle of water.

The room was great, light and airy, which for most of our travels was a novelty. The decoration was a little unusual as the whole room was decorated in some sort of Italian tartan. It must have been the tartan of the McDel Piero clan. It was a really bright yellow with an interwoven tartan of all the colours that had no right to go with yellow, if you suffered from migraines you would be in trouble. The window opened onto the street outside and, even though it was a quiet neighbourhood, the sounds of the city assaulted our senses. Rome is a cacophony of sounds, car horns, street delivery men and the babble of excited locals issuing Italian greetings in their own excitable way. Italians greeting each other is an amazing sight, if ever there was a nation who spoke with their bodies it is them. The expressions tend to be emotional, impulsive and often volatile. Shoulders shrugged, arms stretched out and faces contorted. An Italian must surely be the world's best gurner, just picture Luca Vialli with a horse's collar around his neck, or Gianfranco Zola, no need for the collar, he is the Italian Peter Beardsley. Sorry boys, great feet, shame about the boat race! As a keen observer of people's body language, I could watch Italians all day long. They fascinate me. I could never really tell whether they were angry, sad or deliriously happy. Some other races could give them a run for their money (Arab races for instance). Only the Italians have the race won hands down.

—⁂—

After an hour's snooze and a quick clean up we headed onto the streets below to get close to the Romans and their unfamiliar ways. It was hot, damn hot, and Rome is a city to be seen so the days ahead were bound to be fairly gruelling. There are must-sees for a visit to Rome, and if it was going to be the only time we went, there was definitely a pecking order for the lads. The Coliseum, the Vatican, the Trevi Fountain and the Spanish Steps in that order. One thing that originally eclipsed all those sights was the Olympic Stadium, scene of Liverpool's greatest triumph, home to Roma and Lazio, the city's rival teams. More importantly, it was going to be where the World Cup Final would be played in 1990 (a year away but at least we would have been there). Rome was the seat of power and learning and we still put visiting a football ground before the other sites of historical importance. *That was before we started sightseeing.*

If you have ever been to the Coliseum, you may well understand what my thoughts are about the place. From the outside, it looks what it is: decaying, an extremely old building that has no particular use. Inside, it comes alive. You walk in and know it is centuries old (it actually opened in 80A.D.), but two hours later you have lived your life in the Coliseum during the times of the Lions and the Christians. The place comes alive with every passing minute you stay there, your mind runs riot with what happened in this place. Every nook and cranny has a story to tell and I found myself sitting there for hours astounded by the feelings that washed over me. Even though it was really hot, parts of the site had a real chill to them especially in the bowels of the building where the dungeons and cells used to house the sacrificial Christians, or in the antechambers holding the Gladiators waiting their turn on the stage that was Rome. Fighting in front of the Roman Emperors was not only a duty but also a real honour. The bowels of the Coliseum would also hold the lions that would be brought out to entertain the glitterati of Roman society. Years later, I was watching Russell Crowe in the film 'Gladiator', and it is supposed to be a really close representation of Roman life. As I sat there It took me back to that hot June day in 1989 and I realised my imagination had been brought to the silver screen. Maybe I should have given Russell a ring. I could have been sitting pretty in Hollywood! You never know they may make a film of this book yet and Russell might get to play my dad with Brad Pitt playing me!!

We did the old mooch around the tour groups (who had all paid to hear the guides), until the guide clocked us. Not too difficult as we were not wearing lederhosen or Hawaiian shirts, sporting flashy cameras and saying 'awesome' after every sentence uttered by the disinterested Italian guide in broken English (in a manner that was clearly designed to annoy instead of inform). The guides have this amazing feeling of superiority to anybody and everybody, and didn't take too kindly to us listening in for free. Good job they didn't listen to anybody and only talked their own form of nonsense, otherwise they may have heard the dissenting Scouse voices piping up and calling them a 'stuck up prick' or asking if they had any 'shit flavoured Cornettos'. Security staff (one old woman with half her teeth missing and a man with one eye higher than the other) were called at one point and we quickly went missing to the other side of the Coliseum. Even if we had tried to leave, I don't think we could. It was like trying to leave Caesar's Palace in Las Vegas, we just couldn't get out and all the signs for exit lied sending us off to a part of the building further away from the exit. At least here, unlike Vegas, we wouldn't lose our shirts before we got out of the building.

One thing we did find out, before we were so rudely identified as interlopers, was that during the opening celebrations (which lasted approximately 100 days) they actually flooded the bottom of the Coliseum and built galleons, which would recreate the great sea battles of the past for the pleasure of the Emperor and his clingons. The sea wasn't that far away (about seven miles I think) but to think they went to all that trouble to entertain the elite it was quite obscene. Think about that now as an undertaking and then think back that this was some two thousand years ago. It's akin to trying to rebuild the pyramids, you just wouldn't bother starting, unless you are in Las Vegas (and then it's all polystyrene or something).

The amazing thing about the Coliseum is that it stands right next to one of the main arterial roads in Rome, flooded with traffic all day and all night long, with the modern car belching out fumes to batter the building senseless. If it's still there in a hundred years it will be amazing! The bonus was that there was a metro station right across the road from it, exactly what a building dating back to just after Jesus was around really needs. The metro was fine and just like any other subway system in the world's great cities. That's right, it was full of freaks and robbers, but the freaks were scarier here as they couldn't abuse us in English and really got quite upset, as we didn't understand the vitriolic abuse they were dishing out. Some people are so sensitive aren't they? It was on the way to the Coliseum that we had our very first international mugging attempt. Amsterdam and New York were to follow within a very short period of time.

Even for boys from a city renowned for its crime, it came as quite a shock. Liverpool's reputation is not totally unfair, the reputation that preceded football fans in particular was that they robbed their way around Europe and there is plenty of evidence to substantiate the claim. The scally movement and designer clad youths on the terraces started with stealing trips surrounding Liverpool's games in Europe in the 70s and 80s. The reputation unfortunately tarnishes the majority of good honest people in my city including me.

Back to the Metro. Zil was standing there just minding his own business trying to figure out the Metro map, which to him was always a chore and he never mastered until he had actually finished using the Metro. Whichever city we were in Paris, Rome or even London it was always much easier for me to take charge, at least we got where we wanted to go in a decent time. So there he is trying to figure out which way the Vatican was and, all of a sudden, he felt a movement in his trouser pocket. It was not the sort of movement you usually felt in those regions. Some cheeky get had his hand in his pocket trying to get at his cash. Lucky for Zil it was the wrong pocket, as being the daddy on the trip I was looking after his cash. As quickly as Zil could try and get at the guys hand, it was out of his pocket and before he could say 'Fuck off you cheeky bastard', the guy was moving out of the doors and abusing us as if it was our fault. Gob smacked, we had to check we had seen what we thought we had, as the slime ball scurried through the crowds and away from view. Now, after watching years of 'Cops, Robbers and Videotape' on reality TV, I realise it was all a ploy. Try your hand as the train is coming to a stop, the doors will open and you can make your get away. If you get caught, be brazen and shout very loudly making the complaint yourself as people will never think its your fault, then look at the people you are directing your abuse at and make your getaway. Nowadays, it seems like they teach it in places such as Albania, Bulgaria and Romania (if the aforementioned TV programme is to be believed) and export the art to the gold paved streets of London. It is certainly a skill and one I have seen prac-tised on a number of occasions at football matches. 'Dippers around' was a shout often heard around the throngs trying to get in or out of games. That's one of the reasons I never carried a wallet. This thief had his hand in Zil's trouser pocket, what a cheek! It took Zil quite some time to recover from being touched up down below. Below ground in the subway that is.

Another reason to hang around inside the Coliseum, besides annoying the local guides, was that it was roasting hot outside. Being fresh off a train with only a couple of hours sleep, the heat would take its toll early in the afternoon. At least in the nooks and crannies we could cool down prior to a swift walk down to the Forum. The Forum was the main thoroughfare of early Rome, a sort of downtown in the days of the great and the good, a place where you could even see Caesar. The Forum leads from the Coliseum, down to the Piazza Venezzia and to the giant Victor Emmanuelle monument. Considering it was centuries old, it was in better nick than some of the shops round our way. At least it didn't have any corrugated blinds to protect it. Let's see if some of our buildings are standing in two thousand years time. I do exaggerate somewhat as the Forum is in ruins and is a place where you need to imagine what used to happen there. All I could picture was 'Up Pompeii', a seventies comedy film with Frankie Howard (oohhh no missus!!!). Absolute classic comedy! A story of a well to do Roman's manservant (Frankie Howard), a mix of camp men, buxom women and double entendres in every line of every scene. It recreated the feel far better than 'I Claudius' or 'The Borgia's' ever did in my view. Lets face, it Rome was a den of inequity which would make even the most broadminded individual wince. It's good to see that swinger's parties are bringing it all back again.

All this sightseeing was tiring to say the least. It was the height of the summer and all the energy we had when we left Lime Street Station was starting to disappear. There seem to be more resting than activity these days. If we walked more than two hundred yards without a sit down it was an achievement. Afternoon siestas would have been the order of the day if we could have actually guaranteed it that we would wake up at a normal time after just an hours snooze. The general rule though is sleep through from the afternoon and through the evening wake up at three in the morning, freezing cold with a bit of kebab stuck to your face. Hold on, am I getting confused with a Friday night now? The afternoon siesta left us feeling drained generally. Power nap my arse! Due to the issues with afternoon naps, we would endeavour to fight the tiredness and pray for a second wind. Nowadays we would be more likely to find a bar and have a pint, but in those days, I was more or less teetotal after falling out with alcohol after numerous vomiting incidents. As we trailed through the traffic laden streets, we often came across classic little piazzas hidden down alleyways. These hidden gems were either deserted or heaving, nothing in between. Italy is full of these surprises. Try going to Venice, as there are so many hidden between the canals it's amazing. In Rome, one such piazza contains the world famous Trevi fountain (three coins in a fountain and all that). On a side note, if I had all the money I have ever thrown into a fountain to bring me luck and make me return, first of all I would be rich and secondly I would be rich enough to return. I have finally sussed it out. It's a scam, somebody makes rich pickings from fountains. Tell you what, you wouldn't find any cash at the bottom of a Scouse fountain, it would probably hit some scally on the back of a neck before it made a splash. It's exactly the same with golf balls. 'Do you want to buy any lake balls?' is the shout on any golf course with a water hazard. Should be more like do you want to 'buy any stolen golf balls', as any little dreg with wet undies can tell you that they are fully aware they are trespassing and stealing my property. Do I sound like a man who loses golf balls in water on a regular basis?

As we neared the Trevi Fountain, I was really hoping that there were no shell suits wading through the water collecting their drinks money for the evening ahead. The Trevi Fountain is legendary, the most beautiful fountain in the world, a scene of romance and beauty and, last but definitely not least, the place where thousands of Reds fans washed when they arrived in Rome following the train trek across the alps in 1977. They would have been cleaner if they had been mucking out Hannibal's elephants. The fountain probably needed fumigating after that. After numerous false alarms we came upon the Trevi fountain in a Piazza down a tiny alleyway in which you couldn't actually pass anyone coming the other way. The alley, as usual, stank of piss, show me one that doesn't and I will show you a hotel corridor, then again maybe they are just the same. As you walk out the alley it opens out into a Piazza, which is totally dominated by the fountain attached to one whole side. It was actually dominated by scaffolding, couldn't see the bloody fountain for scaffolding poles and protective sheeting. All that messing around to find it and it was crap, it was probably the biggest let down of the whole trip. We had to make do with buying a postcard to see how it should have looked.

We trudged away from the fountain, tired and disappointed, and headed back to the gaff for a freshen up before an evening on the tiles taking in "La Dolce Vita". La Dolce Vita literally translates as "the sweet life" and means the good life full of pleasure and indulgence. Sounds great to me! Rome is synonymous with the sweet life following the film of the same name directed by the famous Italian Film Director Fellini in 1960. It is a phrase that transcends the Italian language. Nothing more reeks of La Dolce Vita than a night on the prowl in the centre of Rome and the delights of the Spanish Steps. The freshen-up was usually a quick swill and a change of T-shirt. It often took the three of us less than half an hour in total. We weren't dirty or anything but we don't stand on ceremony and we didn't have enough cash to party all night long to impress the local chicks. As it turns out, we had absolutely no chance at the Spanish steps as it was teaming with all the local lotharios sharking in to anything female with a pulse. Usually the American girls were fair game, they believe any old crap. I know, I have tried it often enough in the States. I have been related to the Beatles on a number of occasions. With the size of my nose I always pass for Ringo's nephew. Some Romans are slime balls though, you could actually see them lining up the conquest and preparing for the kill. Dodgy hairstyles, shirt open to the naval, medallion shining in the moonlight and single red rose in hand. I guess it's cheaper than treating a bird to a full night out with chips and curry sauce, cab ride home in the hope of a fun size Mars bar moment (your lucks in). Which one is going to work? It's got to be the Roman approach every time.

The Spanish Steps were a people watching heaven. As our cash was tight, a drink from the local Spar and a position at an appropriate place on the steps and we were sorted. At night it was still seventy degrees and more than comfortable. Who could go back to normal life after this? The problem was that once all the girls had been targeted and probably been defrocked some-where close to the steps, the lotharios would turn their attention to anything with a pulse. 'Piss off you slimy get' may not have been fully understood but the feeling behind our outburst certainly was, there was no chance of an Italian stallion entering our stable.

Once again, as the evening wore on, tiredness would creep up behind us and suddenly we'd need to sleep really badly. As we headed from the Spanish Steps towards our hotel, we tracked the map towards our destination, only to find Rome's red light district in our way. I was amazed Rome had a red light district as Italian men didn't think they ever had to pay for it, they could get it for free on the Spanish Steps, all for the price of a red rose. They couldn't get this on the Spanish Steps, men with tits and knobs, Pre op transsexuals I believe is the correct modern term. They were beautiful looking until you looked below the waist. This seemed to be an Italian thing as we found an identical "scene" just a few days later in Milan (or as they like to say it on Football Italia Meeeeelannn). As I said before though they will shag anything. Well that woke us up, no way that we were going to fall asleep around here, homeward bound (hotel that is) and tomorrow we were to have an audience with the Pope himself.

—◊◊◊—

Refreshed by a good nights sleep and a hearty continental breakfast with croissants and milky Coffee (oh yes a quality breakfast), we headed out into the glorious day that awaited. Today we were off to see his Holiness the Pope (John Paul the Second). You're not still believing that are you? We were not invited to see the Pope, as we were as it was clearly stated in my youth, "Proddy Dogs". That was Protestants in faith to the normal world, but to kids in Liverpool we were a "Proddy dog" and they were a "Cat lick".

When I was growing up, religion didn't matter in any way at all to me. I grew up in a multi-faith school. Multi-Faith really meant two real faiths then the odd weirdo like a Jehovah's Witness. There was only one of them I knew, and she nearly died because her mum and dad wouldn't let her have a blood transfusion - how nuts is that? Liverpool was only a multi cultural melting pot in the south of the city and then only in certain parts. North Liverpool was certainly an alien place for others who weren't the same. I don't know if it was something that was actively discouraged but non-white people didn't live where I did, unless they were Chinese and ran the chippy. I didn't think of it as racist, it was just the way it was. Anyway, I was a fully paid up member of the Protestant Church, done my time through being confirmed, taking Communion and going to the Adventurers (a church group for the Yooofff of the parish). Religious pursuits was just something I did to fill in time. I had stopped really believing when I was thirteen and my Granddad died. He was a great man and he died aged 67 doing someone's garden of all things. To him it was just a normal day helping someone out. He was a really kind generous man and at my age I probably never realised he was not in the best of health and that his death was possibly not that premature considering his health. He had actually been ill since he was 56 but to me it was all very sudden. What got me was the lack of warning for me as a thirteen year old. Why, if God was so great, did he take him away when there were all sorts of robbers and evil people still here, surely God should look after good people? No one really gave me a satisfactory answer and I think I decided it was all bollocks. Either God didn't exist or he had his priorities wrong. But there was still a slight doubt and I was half expecting him to come good for me and send me a sign. That sign might have been at Hillsborough all those years after my Granddad died. Maybe I didn't see it as that, as I was already lost to the religion. I admire people who retain their faith and still believe, as my mum still does, but it was not and is still not for me. I was too inquisitive and there were too many questions left without answers.

To me the Vatican was only a tourist attraction, at least until we stepped into St Peters Square and it all changed. We walked up from our hotel in the early morning, partly to save the metro fare and secondly to see Rome coming to life. I may have said before, a city coming to life is one of the great things in life to see. The sun was climbing high in the sky and the heat of the summer was intensifying by the minute. We slapped on the sun cream and we were away. Not that I had much skin left that wasn't covered by my tracksuit bottoms and oversized T-shirts. I looked like an Albino who had used 'Just for Men' (hair dye) over a prolonged period. That sun wasn't getting at me. Someone must have been looking over us and guiding us to the Vatican because if the crazy Romans could knock us down they certainly would. Any foot on the tarmac and we were fair game for the Roman Michael Schumachers. Don't think a red light was going to stop them; we were as much a target on a Zebra crossing as anywhere else, perhaps more so. Road rage was invented in Italy, there was a non-stop abuse of other car drivers, passengers and pedestrians, and anyone was fair game as far as they were concerned. *DON'T ever* get a taxi! That was another reason why we were walking. They had no respect for their own life so why would they give a monkey's about yours? It was a mistake walking though, besides running the gauntlet of the insane drivers, it was getting hotter by the minute and we were walking up hill (unbeknown to us) and it was bloody miles from our hotel. It only looked an inch on the map, it can't be that far, can it? There was a Metro stop close by, why didn't we use our common sense? We saved about 50p each, penny pinchers!

As you dodge the cars around the tree lined boulevards you eventually come to the River Tiber, which splits Rome in two. This is where legend has it that Romulus and Remus were cast adrift in a wicker basket by their mother. Well the River must have been safer than the roads, the boys wouldn't have stood a chance.

St Peter's Square changed everything. As you enter via a boulevard the whole square (it's more like a circle really) opens up ahead of you. The Piazza ahead of the Vatican buildings was like an ant's nest with the worker ants heading to worship. It was quite interesting being there as a non-Catholic as I didn't get swallowed up in the whole awe of the place from a religious perspective. I took it in as a people watching experience of the highest calibre, people with the ultimate belief in their God and who were totally captivated by it all. I got to thinking that most of the people in front of me actually treated their visit as a pilgrimage. As a protestant, non-practising even though I was, I felt a tinge of jealousy as the Catholics have Rome, the Muslims have Mecca, and we Protestants just had big cold cathedrals. You also had to think though that the poor believers paid every penny it took to both create and maintain the levels of opulence of the Catholic Church in Rome.

The buildings that make up the Vatican City (yes, it's a city in its own right) are quite outstanding, and the creators, artists and sculptors did an amazing job. As you walk around the cavernous buildings you gaze in wonder and silence at the unbelievable standard of artwork and amount of gold before your eyes. Unbelievably, people still damage wonderful works of art, so certain precious items are cased in plastic but still look amazing. One particular statue attracted me, a figure of Jesus lying in Mary's arms after he was taken down from the cross. I was touched and mesmerised by the sight of this. I even bought a replica, which I took home for my sister in law Jeanette (a practising Catholic). It was greeted as one of the best presents she had ever received. At that point, weeks later and back in England, I fully appreciated how lucky I was to have visited the Vatican. I have met many people over the years who held it as a lifetime ambition and there I was at 23 years of age being lucky enough to do it. The one thing I would say is that I always respect others' cultures and beliefs and try and understand them. It is too easy to just abuse and disrespect others due to a lack of your own knowledge. Religion is the easiest thing to dismiss and provides the greatest cause for division in the world today, whether it be Protestant, Christian, Jewish or Muslim, religion has a lot to answer for. It also provides an easy shield for people who wish to terrorise others and fracture society. This is not something new, it has happened for centuries.

—∾∿∾—

The following day we worshipped at our own shrine, the one of the local football club. We were over that initial fear of going to another game following Hillsborough and looked forward to sampling the wonders of Serie A. It was the league that had attracted Liverpool's finest in recent years in the likes of Souness and Rush. Rush went to Juventus, seemingly as an appeasement to the Italian Club following the Heysel disaster. In my opinion Rush was a world star and would score goals anywhere in the world. If he had been English, the world would have been at his feet and the world cups of 1986 and 1990 may have really meant football came home. Rush was a far better goal scorer than Lineker, and Lineker was brilliant for England. Would the two of them have been able to play together? Maybe not, Lineker would not have even got a game. However, the boy from small town Wales couldn't hack it in the goldfish bowl of Italian Football. He didn't seem to speak the language, but then he never really mastered English so Italian was a tough ask - he was no Ray Wilkins or David Platt. Thankfully, after a season, Rushie came home and played his part in the Cup win following Hillsborough and his two goals against Everton went down in Liverpool legend.

Italian football was a little like the Quickstep. Slow, slow, quick, quick, slow, with a few more slows for good measure. If ever a football league needed a highlights programme it was the Italian League. Ninety minutes could be purgatory but it was not going to put us off the experience, which it certainly is. You don't get many neutrals in an Italian football ground. The game we had chosen was Roma at home, but against who? Who cared! It was Roma at home in the Olympic stadium, the venue for the following years World Cup Final. It didn't get much better than that. As it turned out they were playing Atalanta (who were from Bergamo, near Milan in the north). They had a couple of minor internationals playing for them, top players in Sweden or somewhere like that.

We didn't learn our lesson from the day before and once again headed out into the heat on foot and to the Olympic stadium. We headed out straight from breakfast onto the sunny Roman boulevards, it was already 70 degrees at ten in the morning. Football in the middle of June was a novel experience. We were used to football in lashing down rain, the only times I remember it being sunny was on Cup Final day or the first day of the season. Every other match day was wet and windy. Today the skies were blue and, while already hot, it would be getting hotter, there was nothing more certain. As we headed north and out of the city centre it wasn't long before the Olympic stadium came into view. It was still some distance off but the huge silver disc dominated the sky. The nearer we got, the more excited we became. I felt like I did the first time I saw Wembley all those years earlier as a young lad. The classic sight is standing at the bottom of Wembley Way but truth be told it was many years before I stood at the bottom of Wembley Way. We used to approach from Wembley High Street, and Wembley Central in particular. When I got to the ground, I always liked to walked back down Wembley Way away from the ground, just a hundred yards or so maybe, in order to take in a little more of the atmosphere. The real excitement for us used to be seeing Wembley from the train as you headed in to London from the North West. It was always a good sign if we saw Wembley on the way to games in an FA cup run. The great thing as we got to Wembley was the throng of people on the concourses around the ground. What would it be like here? Would there be hot dog sellers who didn't wash their hands? Would there be ticket touts spivving off the decent fan? Would there be loads of scrapping to avoid? Would we get ripped off buying Roma merchandise?

None of the above concerned us as when we got to the stadium as it was bloody well closed! We were met by perimeter security fencing denying us access just a hundred yards away from our shrine. It was closed for renovation for the World Cup Final the following year. We were gutted we had come all this way in the heat and one of the highlights of our trip was snatched away. All was not lost though, as some kindly soul took pity on us and told us that Roma were still playing but at the much smaller Flaminio stadium, which was not too far away. The big question now was if it was much smaller would we get a ticket? The Good Samaritan pointed us in the direction of a ticket office not too far from the stadium. We did get inside the Olympic Stadium, the original one that is which is right next door to the modern giant. It was a much smaller stadium with numerous athletically posed marble statues (Genitalia prominently displayed as with all Roman statues) surrounding a running track and stone standing areas. A classic sports stadium based on Roman times I expected. We eventually got to the ticket booth and, from my very limited understanding of Italian, I could see they were still selling tickets. Well there was a queue, people giving money and getting tickets in exchange (don't have to be a linguistic expert do you?). There were signs up showing locations in the ground with tickets available and with tickets remaining.

The North Stand (Curva Nord) behind the goal looked a good bet, cheapest tickets and standing with the locals, we were Romans for the afternoon (well only a fool would be in the minority with the away fans).

Up to this part of the trip, I had done virtually all the talking where pigeon French and Italian was called for, and I had made a point of rubbing it in at every opportunity. Today though, Zil suddenly announced out of the blue that he would get the tickets. Well I nearly fell over and Our Kev took a step back and thought 'stupid get', there was no way he was volunteering to make himself look a tosser. I regained my composure and let Zil head to the ticket counter. Before he even got to the queue he was back with us. 'What do I have to say because they might only talk Italian' No shit Sherlock, but at least he had learnt something from our journey so far. Out came the translation book with all the phrases he may need, you know, things like 'which way is it to the local clinic for people with genital warts', and 'Can I have three tickets for today's match' are never in such books. So after a few minutes, I arrived at the correct phrase in perfect Italian for 'hello, I would like three tickets for today's game in the North Stand'.

For those of you who read Italian it went something like this 'ciao tre bigliaterri ....Curva nord'. So we practised it a number of times so Zil was happy with it before he joined the queue, I made him repeat it to me a number of times until I swear he was half Italian, he was word perfect. So off he trots to the back of the queue and I can see him repeating it over and over again. As he neared the front of the queue he called me over and proceeded to say 'ciao tre bigliaterri ....Curva nord'. I was so proud of him, it nearly brought a tear to my eye, my bi-lingual mate. I decided to stay with him in his hour of glory, he got to the front of the queue, puffed his chest out and before he even got the word 'ciao' out, do you know what the woman behind the counter did? She only spoke to him didn't she, in Italian! Zil wasn't expecting that at all, he started sweating and shaking and reverted to the Englishman's last chance when dealing with foreigners, he started shouting at her in slow English and stuck three fingers in her face. 'CAN I HAVE THREE TICKETS FOR THE MATCH LUV' As she disgracefully babbled away in Italian once more, we pointed on a little map at the desk exactly where we wanted to stand behind the goal in the North stand. Unbelievably she passed over three tickets and we passed an unbelievable amount of Lire back (all in all it was still only about seven quid each), still not used to the exchange rate. Zil was gutted, he had blown his chance, wasted his time learning Italian when all he needed to do was to point, lift three fingers and give the right amount of cash. I call it the McDonalds language, anywhere in the world you can walk in put the right amount of fingers up, tender the right cash and know the local words for 'would you like to max that?'

So three hours to go before kick off, what do you do in the middle of nowhere without a single pub to be fed and watered in? We went and watched the Roma Handball team play. They had their own little indoor stadium close by and it was free so we couldn't refuse. It also got us out of the midday sun, which was a bonus. With high energy, great excitement and plenty of goals it was enough to keep anyone entertained or so you would think. After an hour the score was something like twenty all. It lost its attraction and the Scouse lads were getting fidgety. It was becoming like a game of basketball, which bores the arse off most people. You score, they score, you score, they score, blah, blah, blah and every so often some eight foot fella with size twenty feet misses a sitter and the Yanks go mad. It will never replace football and handball will never replace anything really, it's just a game you would make up in the school playground and be bored with after two playtimes. So I did what you would expect any intrepid traveller to do, I went to sleep on the seats to catch up on my kip. Half an hour power snooze and I was ready for the afternoon ahead. We headed out into the bright sunshine and with less than an hour to kick off, proceeded into the ground to find our spec. All was fairly amiable as we headed around the back of the terrace to our designated area. In the alley-way leading to our standing area there was a guy standing selling drinks from a large bin full of ice - water, coke, sprite you know the sort. I didn't think anymore of it just that it was a great way of keeping drinks cold.

That was until we stepped inside the terrace behind the goal. As we went in, we were directed left towards a fence at the far left hand side of the goal. There we found a space about half way up and right next to the fence, it was a great place to stand. No it wasn't! Couldn't have picked a worse spot, we were right next to the away fans and there was definitely more action to see off the pitch than on it. As it turned out, this was the last game of the season and that's the type of game we got, nothing to play for and a poor exhibition game. This didn't stop the home fans who had their own way of ending the season in style, which looked like it was going to be to lynch every one of the away fans from Bergamo. They had about as much support as Torquay at Carlisle on a

Wednesday night in the LDV Vans Trophy (or whatever they call it now). To be fair, they had around a hundred fans hemmed in by about a hundred Italian Policemen. It seemed a bit over the top at first until you saw what the away fans were trying to do and what the Roma fans were trying to do to them. They needed protecting .... from themselves at least. You can picture them if you remember the poll tax riots in Trafalgar Square, tousled or dread locked hair, hadn't washed for a week and drugged to the eyeballs, so much so that they feared no one and felt no pain. The hundred or so Atalanta fans spent the whole of the first half hurling abuse and coins, and hurling it in our general direction, but we were OK as there was a big fence, about fifty empty seats and a line of police between us. This didn't seem to discourage them as they constantly pushed their luck with the police lines. To be fair to the mad men of the north, there was severe provocation by the Roman Hordes. The drinks man had his bin of ice removed from him and the ice now became a horrendous weapon. Even in the heat, the ice was still of a substantial size and when it found its target the wounds seemed to be quite severe. A number of the Atalanta fans were sporting bloodied heads as half time approached. Zil turned to me and muttered the immortal words 'this is great mate' Just as a coin smashed him in the middle of the forehead, seemingly thrown by one of the half-men half-ape away fans, who were now foaming at the mouth and incandescent with rage.

At this point, the halftime whistle went for the action on the pitch, funny thing was it also signalled an end to the action on the terraces. The Atalanta fans sat down and talked amongst themselves, the policemen took off their riot helmets and lit up cigarettes and chatted amiably to the once abusive hoards they were protecting. The Romans did the old pie, Bovril and having a piss half time ritual, so familiar to us in England. You must be joking! They went outside to try and get at the Atalanta fans from the back of their stand. We took the opportunity of the empty terrace to find a more suitable and safer area from where we could watch the second half. As the second half started, the Roma fans filed back in to take their places and resume hostilities, which they did with a vengeance, and having somehow got out of the stadium, and back in again, they had armed themselves with all manner of missiles. Within seconds of the referee's whistle, the barrage of missiles from both sides of the away fans pounded into them. The police? They just stepped aside and let it happen. The Atalanta fans, or at least those that were not maimed in the missile barrage, went ballistic. They tried to break out of the cordon of police and the police finally lost their patience, drew their riot sticks and beat the living daylights out of the fans, I don't think a single fan escaped a bit of their version of Italian justice. Well that was it, the men from the north were a shadow of their former selves and couldn't even muster interest when their team pulled a late goal back. In all the excitement Roma had actually won 2-1. Did we get what we expected? No. We got so much more but of the wrong stuff. Before our eyes the sheer level of violence and the length of it was something I had never seen in England. The English disease has been an Italian disease for years but somewhat glossed over by the dwarfs of UEFA in Switzerland. England got deservedly hauled over the coals for hooliganism, but Italy escaped for years until a motor scooter (yes a motor scooter) was hurled from an upper tier of the San Siro stadium during an Inter and AC Milan game, then UEFA had to take action as it was in their prestigious Champions League in front of millions of viewers. Add industrial fireworks and flares raining down on the AC Milan goal and they had to take action against Inter.

The end of the game produced yet more unbelievable sights. The Roman fans seemed hell-bent on a pitch invasion, and a thirty foot wire mesh behind each goal was going to stop only a few of the hardened supporters. The Referee's whistle signalled a dash for the tunnel from all the players, who must have known what was coming, as the last five minutes of the match took place entirely in front of the players tunnel. Atalanta showed no interest in equalising, the players at least wanted to head back north in one piece. With the players gone, the pitch was a magnet for the Romans and the daredevils amongst them were on top of the mesh in seconds, climbing up it like monkeys. Once on top of the mesh, they proceeded to climb down the other side before dragging the netting down with a combined show of strength in order to allow easier access for their fellow supporters to enter the playing arena en masse. Before it turned into a riot we took the opportunity to skulk away from the ground and head into the centre of Rome and north ourselves. We were definitely not travelling to Bergamo with the Atalanta boys you could be assured of that, as long as we avoided their football special home we would be quite satisfied.

We headed back in to the city centre. Thankfully, due to a fast exit from the ground, we left the Romans to rape and pillage their own stadium and jumped on a bus. The bus was packed to the rafters and it bounced all the way to the bus terminus in the centre of the city. The Roma fans, departing with us, gesticulated wildly as the bus passed through the streets at breakneck speed. In the 90 degree heat, it was not the most pleasant journey I had ever undertaken, and it was a blessed relief to come to a journeys end. We draped ourselves over one of Rome's many fountains, with the fine mist produced by the fountain a beautiful relief from the heat of the late afternoon. Just a few hours more and we would be leaving the Italian capital and heading north to the industrial powerhouse of Italy and the streets of Milan.

Leaving Rome at 10 O'clock at night, I had the chance to reflect on the days' events as we trundled north to the relative peace of Milan. The Roman experience would live long in the memory, but it was not glorious like my dads. The football was both disturbing and disappointing. We were looking into the English football fans past but the hooligan future of Italian football. England was to move on, thank goodness, and watching football was to change for the better. The sheer violence and hatred on display was to be thankfully a thing of the past for us.

Rome lived up to all our expectations and so much more. The rest of Europe flew by in a number of train journeys and border crossings. We rattled through Switzerland, Holland, Belgium and France again and with each country came a new experience and an energy that was to change me. I was refreshed and re-energised and my demons had been exorcised (or at least started to be). Life began again, and life would be great for us all. My head was clear and I could now begin my new life in earnest.

—ᴡ—

9

POSH and Proud

'Port Outward Starboard Home' (POSH) is a great motto for a seafaring society, proud of their ocean going heritage. Why then is it the motto of a city on the farthest edge of Lincolnshire, miles away from the sea? It's beyond me, it is one of life's little mysteries.

Another of life's little mysteries is how I ended up swapping a comfortable life in the local City Council in Liverpool for a role behind the scenes at a professional football club (albeit in the lower reaches of the football league, it *was* still professional). As you will see 'professional' was often a term I would use very loosely, due to some of the things I witnessed. A better description might be stolen from outfits such as Gerry Cottle's and Billy Smart's, it was a circus most of the time. Whilst not lifting the lid on the insides of football, like a Panorama investigation or a Premier league investigation run by a senior ex-copper, I can show you how the inside of football is a total contradiction to the glossy show of a Saturday or Sunday afternoon, Friday night, Monday night, 4am in the morning on Thursday, whatever the TV executives decree really.

I *honestly* used to believe in the beautiful game, where right was right, wrong was wrong, good teams overcame bad and people actually cared. I discovered that's a load of bollocks and my love of the game became tainted, battered and bruised. That the things I saw at a lower level are not multiplied at the highest level is something I find difficult to believe, especially if you agree that where there is money there are always liars and cheats. You only have to look anywhere in society to see that where money rules, so do cheats and robbers. Behind the closed door of a football club should have been intriguing and delightful. Instead it was hugely disappointing and disconcerting. Stay with me though - there were some exciting and wonderful moments in my three years of being POSH.

The POSH are Peterborough United and the local team of the City of Peterborough. Peterborough is small for a city but qualifies as one due to a fairly impressive cathedral, which dominates the town and is only challenged by a rather large (for its time) shopping centre. Situated on the river Nene (so not wholly landlocked), the city is the first major stop outside of London as the trains hurtle up north to the outposts of Leeds, York, Newcastle and then on to Scotland. Thanks to its location less than an hour north of London, it was starting to become part of the London commuter belt and investors were taking advantage of lower house prices and great business initiatives. Major employers such as Thomas Cook, Pearl Assurance and Norwich Union were all basing themselves in a place where it was easier and cheaper to do business with a cheaper cost base to employ staff. The local population was expanding like mad, which made it a great time to be in the place and a wonderful opportunity for the local football club to expand its client base.

Well, you would think so, but the club never quite got it right, on or off the pitch, in order to serve this new potential customer base. Peterborough was a new town and with it came problems. The city was divided by a ring road, which whilst giving great access to the city, formed a physical and mental barrier. It was like another of the planners' dreams of the 1960's, where massive housing estates very quickly became soulless, lifeless and the ideal environment for crime and deprivation. Just think of any housing estates with high-rise flats, and then ask yourself if there was anything good about them. Peterborough wasn't quite that bad because it lacked the high-rise flats. It had nice little houses with greenery and the countryside not far away. It did become soulless because the town planners designed small communities that were all the same. With easy access to the ring road the suburbs were identical, hundreds of houses built around a pub, a Chinese takeaway and a Spar convenience store. You could go to three or four of these areas and you couldn't tell which one you were in. There was a lack of community spirit and a real suspicion of outsiders.

I went down well with the locals with my strong Scouse accent. Hands went to their wallets and purses very quickly; the look of horror on some peoples' faces was really quite upsetting. Before anyone thinks this is about 'Everybody hates Scousers' it's not. Glaswegians, Geordies, and Northerners in general were all mistrusted and made to feel like real outsiders. I stayed in Peterborough for three years, had quite a number of good friends, but few of them were locally born and bred. Most were outsiders like me. Just so you don't think I am really paranoid, the first experience of this was probably the one that put me on guard for the rest of my time there.

I learned to accept it and after that it never really hurt or affected me that much. You can't change everybody's perceptions can you? Part of my job was to bank money from the soccer schools I ran for the club and, as we were extremely successful with the amount of children we coached, we would often deposit large sums of cash and cheques on a daily basis. After the first month, following daily visits to the same branch, generally seeing the same cashiers day in, day out, I had deposited approximately £10,000 in cash. One day I had to cash a cheque on the football club's cheque book made out to cash for £100. The senior cashier wouldn't pay it, claiming she didn't know who I was and that as I wasn't local, she was suspicious. She told me to go away and get proof from the club that I worked for them. Bollocks! I had paid her £10,000 in a month into the club account, the cheeky cow. When it came to taking over the business a number of years later, I moved the account to a local competitor. The woman, who was now a branch manager, called me in to save my business for her bank. Her face was an absolute picture when I recounted the story and told her I couldn't keep my account with her because I didn't really know who she was and I couldn't really trust her with my own business accounts. There you go love, stick that right up your self righteous arse. As you can see it probably did annoy me a little, how small minded people could be. They would rather believe the mistruths and lies in papers such as The Sun than see for themselves. Scouse, Mancunian, Geordie, Irish or Scottish, we have all been there. Some (not all) people in southern and middle England really need to consider spending time above Watford Gap. A word of warning to them though; Watford Gap is miles north of Watford.

Now I don't wish to bang on and sound like the Merseyside Tourist Board but why not visit the North West and see for yourself - don't believe the lies. I used to tell the people I knew in Peterborough to go and visit but they would always respond by saying they didn't want to get mugged or they valued their car wheels. If I have heard the one about stealing their hubcaps once, I have heard it a million times. I laugh along as indignation only adds fuel to the fire, and laughing along confuses people and usually stops them in their tracks. Use the jokes yourself and it confuses them more. Just remember Frank 'It's the way I tell em' Carson who built a career on Irish jokes (he was from Belfast for Christ sake), or Stan 'the Germans bombed our chippy' Boardman from Liverpool who made his living out of Scouse jokes. Laugh at yourself; it's the first line of defence, or attack. Do you know what? Those people who took my advice and took that giant leap of faith, and made their way to the end of the M62 motorway, actually loved it! They were bowled over by how friendly people were and what a wonderful place it was to visit with so many great things to see and do. They couldn't believe they had swallowed the lies for all that time. Go tell your friends!!!!

By the way, I am a realist and not so naive that I don't know there is a reason why Liverpool has a reputation. There are robbers and scallies there, and they are responsible for some of the things that are said, but there are people like that everywhere. Peterborough had its own element, you probably know your own as you read this. What perpetuated the Liverpool myth was the actions of certain members of the darling London press who, at every chance, compounded the image. Long after

Manchester had outstripped Liverpool, as the car crime capital of the UK the perception was that Liverpool was still the capital of crime. It is actually well down the list of top hot spots.

—⁓—

So how did I end up in Peterborough? It was by accident really. My cousin Tony had landed himself a job at Peterborough United as part of the Youth Development set up, but because they had so little money, he had to pay his own way to be there. Tony had been running his own soccer schools, TWS (Tony Williams Soccer schools) successfully in Northern Ireland for a number of years, crossing the political divide by having Catholic and Protestant children playing alongside each other. I had hardly seen Tony since we were in our early twenties as he had left the Liverpool area to go and study some sports qualification or other. Actually, we had made a pact to go to see every Liverpool game together and he broke it after about eight games to move to Cheltenham to study. That's when I met Zil so it must have been 1986, Liverpool's Double winning season. He left Liverpool and I stayed in the Council and followed the Reds. He got his sports degree and went to work for Norwich City and run TWS in Norfolk and Wales prior to going to Ireland. Norwich was a bit of a bonus for us as, each time we went to watch the Reds there, Tony would get us into the Canaries lounge for a pint, a bit of scran (food to you) and a catch up before and after the game.

I had the great pleasure of going on a tour of Florida with the cream of TWS a few years before I got to Peterborough. From his soccer schools, Tony would pick the cream of the crop and mould them in development centres before taking them to tour English league clubs or play in European Junior football Competitions. The Florida trip was a further (yes 3000 miles further) variation on this theme.

I ended up in a warm and sunny Florida for two weeks in April and had a wonderful time. I was only a gofer really, but felt part of something so removed from my normal life, that it was quite exhilarating. The TWS kids stayed in home stays with the American families who were hosting the tournaments, and the coaches and myself dossed five to a room in hotels. It was all a bit hit and miss but great fun. I didn't even know where I would be staying when I arrived in Florida. Two hours before flying from Gatwick to Orlando, I still hadn't heard from Tony for at least a couple of weeks. When I got there, I rang home and he had left a message with my dad saying what flight they were arriving on. I had to wait hours at Orlando Airport for Tony to arrive. The flights he said he would be on came and went and the airlines wouldn't give me any information as to who was on them. Then at about 10.00pm, some seven hours after my arrival, forty kids waltzed through arrivals with Tony acting like the Pied Piper. They had missed the flight connection in New York and they had to take a roundabout route to get to Orlando six hours late. Nothing ran smoothly and they had flown by the seat of their pants. This was a sign of things to come. The two week tour took in Orlando, Sarasota on the Gulf Coast and Fort Lauderdale just above Miami. The kids were brilliant, and though mainly Irish they included a number of Welsh kids who were in the original soccer schools prior to Tony's move to Belfast.

Many of the kids playing football on this trip actually ended up at Peterborough in the Youth Development scheme. They played in the representative teams right the way through to the youth Team ranks. There were even a number of them who ended up as professionals.

Three months prior to the trip, I had split up with my first long term girlfriend, who I had been foolish enough to get engaged to years before I was ready. The trip to Florida turned out to be a blessing and helped me move on from the ruins of that relationship. When I came home, I had a real spring in my step I just didn't care anymore. I had just spent two weeks in the company of kids who were on a trip of a lifetime and their normal life on the streets of Belfast or Londonderry (or free Derry if you prefer) was much tougher than my comfortable life. These kids without their football would have just been caught up in the sectarian abuses that blighted their communities.

The kids did take some liberties with the families they were staying with though. Once they found that the families were all rich beyond their wildest dreams, living in mansions, they started making up sob stories. Such as the story of a little boy who would walk to school in West Belfast in his bare feet because his mum couldn't afford shoes. Well that got him a pair of new shoes and a pair of training shoes. Each day they would roll up with gifts of one sort or another, Gameboys which had not made it big in the UK at the time (unless you had some money) was the goal of many a boy. When I left Florida, little did I realise that I would see many of these boys again as they headed through their football careers, I treated it as my trip of a lifetime, which it was, but more was to come.

The next time I saw Tony, it was at a family party, you know the sort, your Nan's 70th birthday and you show willing until about ten o'clock when you can scoot off to the nearest nightclub. Well we had a great night and ended up at one of the biggest clubs around, The Paradox near Aintree racecourse, which was one of those clubs that was famous for a couple of years and wouldn't let the dregs in. I had heard on the family grapevine that Tony had got this great new job at Peterborough United and now it was time to tell me how good his new job was. Peterborough had just been promoted to the 1st division (now the Championship, used to be the 2nd division, call it what you will it was the one below the Premiership). We caught up on our time in Florida and my travel following the Reds during our time apart and my thoughts on looking for a new job. I thought nothing of it until the phone rang a couple of months later.

It was our Tony. 'How do you fancy a new job running soccer schools for me?' he asked. I was stunned. 'But I know nothing about soccer schools' to which he responded 'You will learn fast mate. It's working in football Keith, you can't turn it down'. We talked for an age and the upshot was that I would drive down to Peterborough and spend the day with him, watch a match and then I could make a decision. Nothing ventured, nothing gained! So I arranged to travel down the following week to see the 1st division outfit in action. Well, a lot happens in a week in football and they'd been relegated by the time I made my visit. They had gone up via the play-offs the previous season and, although the division was too tough for them, one of their highlights of the season was a defeat of Liverpool in the Cup (Milk, Carling, Coca Cola variety or just the plain old League Cup, take your pick). Guess what? I was there, and Liverpool were awful and the noise that was created by the London Road crowd was deafening. At least I knew the way and here I was heading down the A1 to Peterborough again, but this time with a view to joining a professional football club. Yes me, on the other side of the Directors door!

I drove to Peterborough and had a whirlwind day, meeting the great and the good from Manager to Chairman and to top it all, sat right behind the home team dug out to watch the match. I was sitting watching the game, secure in the knowledge that a five-year contract was mine if I wanted it. All I had to decide was whether I wanted it. I had been here before, the big question was do I leave Liverpool? I had been to London and been offered jobs on three separate occasions, but I had always bottled it and stayed at home, with my comfortable secure life. I couldn't turn this down could I? The answer was no. I was leaving my friends and family but I had a great opportunity that may never come again. Working at a football club was beyond my wildest dreams. I had made my decision on the three hour drive north which was to become a regular occurrence over the next three years. Within four weeks I had given in my resignation after ten years at Liverpool Council (job for life), left home for the first time (at the age of 28 about time too I hear you say) and left my friends and family in misty eyed farewells. I think if it hadn't been so quick, I might have bottled it again and life could have been so different.

I was going to run the administration side of the biggest soccer schools operation in the country at that time, Posh Soccer. Forget your Bobby Charlton Soccer Schools or Ian St John football courses, Posh Soccer gave more kids the opportunity to learn to play football. The aim of Posh Soccer was to give every kid the chance to have fun, boys, girls, kids who could play or kids who had never kicked a ball in their lives, able bodied and kids with disabilities. Based at Peterborough United Football Club, Posh Soccer's tentacles were eventually to cover as far West as Banbury in Oxford-shire, as far North as the south of Yorkshire, as far East as Ipswich and as far South as the outskirts of London. In its heyday, we were speaking to over half a million kids and coaching up to 100,000 kids per year. Here I was, coming from a comfortable job in Liverpool nine to five clockwatching, to a life of twelve hour days and loving every minute of it.

Tony was the mastermind of it all and could honestly see Posh Soccer Schools running nationwide. The prob-lem was he could only see expansion and not consolida-tion of what we had. We were too busy building new franchises, leaving no time to look after the existing franchises we already had on board. All the promises we made to the new franchises couldn't be maintained and ultimately they lost faith in us and it all started to fall apart.

Posh Soccer started as a way for Peterborough United to support its Youth Development policy. Their Youth Development Officer Kit Carson (sounds like a cowboy doesn't he?) was famous in the world of football youth development and was responsible for many of the play-ers that had progressed through the Norwich City ranks in the early 80s, the likes of Lee Power, Tim Sherwood, Ruel Fox and Andy Townsend owed Kit something. It was Kit who made the Cockney Andy Townsend (now ITV football pundit) realise his Irish roots and play so many times for the Republic of Ireland, even Lee Power who played for the Republic a record number of times was as Cockney as pie and mash. Lee sounds as if he is born within the sound of Bow Bells and says 'awight' more often than Michael Barrymore. Kit tries to convince everyone they have Irish roots and could play for Ireland, and often he is right - I think Jack Charlton owed him a lot. The funny thing is, not one of them has an Irish accent, Kit, Andy Townsend or Lee Power. Tim Sherwood at the time was captaining Blackburn and heading towards the title, but it didn't stop him ending up in my office for a cup of tea with Kit.

I got on great with Kit, and still do, and one of the big reasons was that he shares a love of Liverpool and all things associated with Liverpool. Great city, great people and a great football club (Liverpool not Everton). He held my attention the first time he ever talked to me about why he loved Liverpool FC because he had been lucky enough to watch them train at first hand. He contacted Liverpool when Bob Paisley was in charge and asked if he could observe the team training. Amazingly he was granted permission to. Bob Paisley greeted him on the first day and told him quite sternly that he could observe but should only speak when spoken to. For a month, Kit kept this up and it must have killed him as he travelled with the team, on the legendary bus to Melwood for training, and shared lunch with the team. On his last day, Paisley approached him and personally thanked him for how he had behaved and said he was welcome at any time. Now, not many people can claim that on their CV. Kit learned so much from Liverpool; about how they conducted themselves, how no-one should get in the way of your work, their training methods and the way they built team spirit. These things flowed throughout the Youth Development structure at Peterborough, and I was amazed and grateful to be part of it.

The motto of Posh Soccer (the soccer schools part of the Youth Development area) was 'Football is Fun'. It is too, or at least it should be. The idea was that the kids should have a great laugh with all their mates and make new friends along the way. We employed mainly young local lads with loads of energy who loved giving something back to the kids. The kids loved the lads who worked for us and that bred our success. The sound of laughter was synonymous with the sound of footballs being kicked around. Behind the fun though, the kids learned some important lessons in every session. Each session was designed to ensure kids warmed up properly, learned some new skills (passing, shooting or easy tricks) and then had a little match to put their learning into practice. We used this as a mini World Cup and the kids loved it. We also incorporated an American penalty shoot out and the time would fly by.

Behind the fun, the main aim was to improve the Youth Development side of Peterborough United, and the soccer schools were the cheapest and most effective way of doing so. Talent identification as a by-product was a massive bonus and within a couple of years Peterborough United's youth policy was booming. When I joined, the focus was moving towards the talent development area, as that was where the better coaching staff felt more gainfully employed, working with the better kids was the buzz. What we had to be careful of was, that by taking that course of action, we were actually putting the business at risk. My view was that the good kids would still come as they wanted to be with their mates and I was proved right. We still got the better kids coming. Do you remember your world beater mates dropping you because you were crap? No. I don't either.

The soccer schools worked on a number of different levels in order to maximise income and identify good kids and provide an outlet for the better kids to improve. Most Soccer Schools operators only worked during school holidays and that's where the money was made. Posh Soccer worked five days a week, Saturday mornings and every day of every school holiday. We ran football sessions for kids from the age of 5 to 14 with the biggest take up under the age of 12. To maximise our energy and income we would utilise our time wisely. We would run hour long sessions after school in one of the local towns or city suburbs at designated primary schools for the duration of a term (usually a six week period). After that we would run a Soccer Studio in the same town or area but open it up to all the other kids in the area from other schools. Then to finish the night, we would run a second Soccer Studio at an area a short distance away in order to extend our catchment area and our income stream. We would often run up to six separate sessions a night and up to thirty a week. The skill was to make best use of the time we spent coaching between 3pm and 8 o'clock at night. This was our bread and butter work and it probably sounds great, and would be if it were true that you only worked between 3pm and 8pm. Behind every After School or Soccer Studio session, there was an enormous amount of promotional work to ensure good attendance at all these sessions. As a thanks to schools for letting us speak to children or run courses, we would provide free school coaching sessions during PE lessons and develop teachers to coach kids. We had four full time staff and about twenty part time staff, who were mainly students and fairly flexible, and at £5 an hour (which was good in the mid nineties), financially beneficial to all. We would charge £1.50 a session and have no more than twelve kids to every coach. So it was quality regardless of quantity.

The holidays were really busy, as we would provide Soccer Schools varying in length from one day to three days in length, depending upon the holiday and opportunity available to us. Summer Holidays often allowed us to offer longer courses. Cost wise, it was £10 for a day or £25 for three days. This was cheap childcare for many parents. We offered them well looked after kids by qualified and caring staff. In my three years in charge, I only remember a handful of complaints, and usually they were from parents whose child had misbehaved and another child had taken the law into their own hands and given their kid a clump. We were forerunners in having our staff checked and vetted, and we also took our child protection and safety concerns very seriously. Now these things are common and mandatory practice but we did it very much off our own backs.

The build up to the holiday period was extremely busy with promotional work and every one of us would be out on the road speaking to morning assemblies or individual classes at schools the length and breadth of the East of England. In a school, the job was to go in and get the kids excited about the football schools and make sure they got a brochure to take home to mum and dad (or whoever looked after them). We had to make sure they would get home and be buzzing so much that no one could say no and still have an easy life from their child. Our standard presentation often mentioned Shearer, Beckham and Fowler, Penalty Shoot Outs, world cup matches, prizes, certificates and loads of fun. We always guaranteed that every kid got a certificate of participation and as many as possible won medals.

After being there a year, I brokered a deal with the Club, which allowed us to offer a free match ticket for every child who attended and for parents to purchase a half price ticket to come with them. A stroke of genius – two bums on seats that would not normally be there, one paying money in to the club coffers but both paying money in at the snack bars, money in the club shop and buying a programme, a must for every kid at a match. In my last season at POSH we issued 20,000 tickets and this was at a time when the average attendance was under 5,000 at each home league game. We were certainly doing our bit to raise the profile of Peterborough United in its Community and outside also. We were actually running Soccer Schools a hundred yards from Leicester City's ground and in the middle of Ipswich and Norwich (this was to get us into trouble with the FA though). Years before Milton Keynes Dons ditched Wimbledon we were booming in the land of the roundabouts.

We had all this great stuff going on at the kids level and things were booming, so what could go wrong? Well, we were undermined at every turn by people within the club, petty jealousies became vicious vendettas. The problem was that whilst the first team were poor the youth teams were great. We had kids travelling all over Europe and winning trophies while the first team were steadily sliding down the divisions. We were creating the players of the future, but the future couldn't get here quick enough, and the club kept wasting their time and money on ordinary players who didn't give a monkey's about who or where they played, as long as they got paid. The players often didn't even live in Peterborough, that was the level of their commitment – they didn't even bother getting their own place. My lads were more famous in Peterborough than half of the players who showed little or no interest in being seen around town. The funny bit is, to an under ten I was a professional footballer because I had the tracksuit on, (it was in the pre ale gut days) so I might have at least looked the part. We were the lifeblood of the club but people kept trying to cut off our blood supply. Everything was such hard work, even though we were bringing in tens of thousands of pounds a year to fund the youth policy.

From the money we made, we would buy kits for the representative squads, fund trips abroad for the representative squads, pay my coaching staff to support the representative squads and spend the vast majority of my spare time supporting the glorious future of the Posh. I was working over 70 hours a week for £12,000 a year, I am not moaning because it was the greatest thing that I have ever done, but the Posh got us on the cheap, big time!

The Club, it seemed to me, were terrified of being successful because it brought so much hard work with it and there were too many people who had comfy lives that were being changed if we moved up a gear. From the ticket office to the boardroom, there was a lack of will to push the boat out. Instead of supporting the youth set up and giving them the financial muscle to attain greatness, we had to go cap in hand to local business to support the kids. What did the local businesses get in return?

They got short thrift and treated like dirt, they were questioned as to their motive for their support, which undermined our relationships with the people who gave us the much needed financial support. My sponsors kept coming back time and time again to support us, but they would never support the main club. That says a lot doesn't it?

I always remember a quote aimed at Peter Swales at Man City. Whilst he was not named the quote 'There is a cancer within' was aimed directly at him. Whilst he was running the club, City would do nothing and go nowhere. Why? He was a megalomaniac and wanted to be in total control of everything from the kit washing to picking the first team. It was all about reflected glory. He wanted to be Malcolm Allison's mate and John Bond's for that matter too. He could never be in the background and was always interfering. Peterborough had their own people who wouldn't stop meddling, anything that was good was undermined if they were not involved in it. Overall, the attitude at the club was that they didn't want to get to the big time, it was all too much like hard work. I remember we drew Aston Villa in the League Cup and the ground sold out with a gate of 15,000, even after getting beat 6-0 away. They complained like mad, 'Too bloody busy'. They would rather have 5,000 in the third Division than be knocking on the Premier League door. It was not everybody at the club, but there were enough to undermine the footballing side of things, much of it, as is always the case in life, was driven by jealousy, of either money or opportunity. That night I was thinking that this is what it was all about –Aston Villa, massive team, great support, Big Ron Atkinson in charge (complete with enough bling that I had to wear shades) and led out by Paul McGrath (a man mountain). I wanted this every week it was so exciting. But others - No!

The jealousy drove people to be difficult and create obstructions, and it is no wonder that ten years on from my arrival they were still languishing in the bottom division of English football. Small football clubs are often run like family concerns with people wanting to be the big fish in a little pond. It's amazing the feeling of power some people have coursing through their veins when they walk in the Directors entrance. The people who made the club actually tick on a match day did it for the love of the Club and were often treated appallingly by the people in charge. Football Clubs contain a number of small cliques, some powerful, some not so and they are bitter because of it and finally some people who can't see they are being exploited. There seemed to be a little clique for whom nothing was too much bother, possibly in return for goods and services, they gained privileged access that the man in the street could only dream of. The money-go-round centred round these people, men with supposed financial clout, but you never saw any of it. They talked of money but not all of them actually put any into the club, they just lived off it. Golf days, corporate events, all the same faces propping up the bar with the sycophantic support of the men at the top. Smiling assassins many of them, and when the club was really struggling financially, they were nowhere to be seen. The men who put money behind the Community Scheme and myself were treated with disdain by the men in charge. It got so bad that many of them would never give money to the main club but would support the youth policy wholeheartedly.

For a more focused explanation of lower league football politics, take a look at Ian Ridley's Floodlit Dreams[1], a story about him taking over a failing non-league football club and starting to turn it around. See the lies and deceit he is faced with, all those characters I can relate to, as that is life in the lower divisions, maybe even it's life in the Premiership when you listen to some of the shenanigans at Liverpool in 2008.

I am deliberately not giving names as I don't see that serves any purpose and I am not trying to score points, just point out what its like. For Peterborough United you can read any local club in the land.

The one thing Peterborough did have was reputedly the best youth policy outside of the Premier League and I am proud to say I played a small part in making it tick, and even paying for much of it though my Soccer Schools. In 1993 Peterborough recruited Kit Carson who was already a guy with a big reputation after running the Youth Development programme at Norwich City.

Well Kit brought his whole operation and 25 school-boys from Norwich with him to start the Posh Youth Policy. The Club didn't know what had hit it, the kids were playing the likes of West Ham, Man United and Tottenham and beating then regularly. Players would come to Posh because of Kit, often shunning Man United and the likes and allegedly big signing on fees. Kit's philosophy is all about making the kids special, special players, yes, but more so, special people who were a credit to the club, Kit, but most of all themselves and their family. They dressed professionally, shirt and tie, no jewellery, were always well mannered, and acted as ambassadors of the football club. In their time at the club, all players will have been all over Europe, representing and winning trophies for the Posh. The club trophy cabinet was full of the kids' trophies. They were the pride of the city and the supporters. Supporters would take an extra interest in the kids and were, on the whole, extremely supportive. Some of the local leagues at times could have their moments and stir up trouble in the local press, usually when their best player went to represent Posh instead of the local junior club. There was a lot of mud thrown saying it wasn't in the kid's best interests, but it was, I can guarantee that. The flack was often thrown by parents whose children were not good enough to stay with the club, generally the kids knew it but the parents would not accept it. At the age of sixteen, when the apprenticeships were handed out, the kids were clever enough (and man enough) to know the decision if it was a no. Those boys who were not good enough for a contract still went on to do great things in the world of football.

The Soccer Schools were a great place for the boys who didn't make it to learn a new trade and become a football coach. That was how my partner in running the Schools got involved. Gaffa (also known as John Morling) was a cockney urchin (in the nicest way), from the East End of London, and he is a top lad. He is your proverbial naughty little boy and he is over 30 now, a proper little character and only 4 foot 8 (well really 5 foot 4). Gaffa played for Kit as a kid but was never going to be big enough in stature, though his heart more than made up for it. He went on to work for TWS and then ultimately became the Head Coach at Posh Soccer Schools at the tender age of 21. Gaffa would organise the sessions, what to do and where to do them, keep all the coaches in line, and ensure the delivery of the Soccer Schools as a product, was of a very high standard. It was all about fun, and that is Gaffa for you too. Be careful when he is around, you never know what may end up in your bed or even your shoe for that matter. As a career after football, I don't think you could beat it.

Gaffa could have the most fun with the kids who were never going to make it, all playing for fun, he was in his element. Gaffa could switch from the fun side to become more serious and coach the Academy boys to a very high standard. To show you how good he was, he was actually the 2nd youngest person ever to have received the full FA coaching badge. The youngest became an England Manger, namely Graham Taylor. He even missed my wedding so he could go on a Premier League coaching course, even though he was still at Posh, three divisions below at the time. He is now working for The Republic of Ireland running the Youth Development Programme for the under 16 age group and coaching teams up to the under 19 age bracket.

Many of the coaches who worked for us, had either been on our books or were still playing as Youth team members. It was great for us, and the kids loved it when a lad coaching for us would make his debut in the first team the following Saturday. I am proud to say that both Simon Davies (Tottenham, Everton and now Fulham and Wales) and Matthew "Mushy" Etherington (Tottenham and West Ham, for whom he ripped Liverpool to bits in a Cup Final) both coached for me and Gaffa, amongst a host of others. They also both made their debut against Liverpool, I have never seen Mushy admit this, but he was a big Liverpool fan and

I took him to his first game when Liverpool were up the road from Peterborough at Nott's Forest.

From my days at Posh I was lucky to see lads grow up, such as Davies and Etherington, but also Adam Drury (Captain of Norwich City) and Luke Steele who went to Manchester United at 16 and then on to West Brom. Luke ended up breaking me in two during the Barnsley Cup run of 2008, when he signed on loan for Barnsley the day before they played Liverpool at Anfield in the 5th round of the FA Cup. One training session and not knowing the names of all your players may be a handicap, but he produced a magnificent performance to deny the Reds, and set up a last minute winner in front of the Kop. I was listening via the Internet and didn't know whether to laugh or cry, I was immensely proud that it was his heroics that denied me a potential trip to the new Wembley. Luke made it to Wembley after helping the Tykes beat Chelsea in the next round, earning a semi final trip, and himself a contract with them at the end of the season. The final was one step too far, but I was following him all the way. Nikki and I met him a couple of years earlier when he was with United and he was telling us of the likes of Barthez and Ferguson talking to him in training. Didn't want to tell him I couldn't stand United as he was still trying to forge his career with them.

There are far too many to list here, but looking at the Sunday papers I will often see the old boys' names in print. Old boys, they are only in their early twenties most of them. There are others who didn't quite make it due to injury or the wrong move at the wrong time, and those who just didn't get a chance after progressing to the Professional ranks. One lad deserves a mention –

Dave Billington, Dave was a cracking lad, really professional, and he was a credit to everyone who knew him, and two hours before he made his professional debut at London Road he was in my house having beans on toast as a pre match meal. My dad was amazed, down for the weekend, he was sat in my house with a mere slip of a lad who two hours later was wearing the blue of Posh and bossing the game like a seasoned pro. No surprise that after a handful of appearances he moved for over £500,000 (a lot in those days) to the then Premier league team Sheffield Wednesday. Disappointingly, devastatingly for Dave, his professional career ended before it really began, with a knee injury, which at the last count had accounted for twelve operations. Dave ended up playing in the minor leagues for the likes of Banbury Town and Oxford City. It is a fine line between making it and not, and luck plays the biggest part of all.

There are people up and down the country running youth schemes, who cut their teeth as coaches for Posh Soccer, thanks to Gaffa and myself, (mainly Gaffa to be honest) but I paid them! Some of them have even turned up in America, coaching with our Tony. Following his departure from Peterborough, Tony ended up carving a successful coaching career in the US. All underpinned by the Posh Soccer structures (well why change a successful formula?). He now coaches in Pennsylvania and is still trying to identify talented kids and change peoples' lives, well he changed mine so thanks mate!

—⅏—

I learned a lot of lessons at Peterborough, which stand me in good stead today. I learnt that it is a skill to meet people on their level and if you do, you have a much better chance of influencing them in whatever way you need. Whether it's to sell them something, get sponsorship money or just simply get along. From the millionaire to the bin man, people are different and need to be treated so. Treat them as individuals, listen to them and you get more back. I would get stopped all the time, spot me a mile off in the club tracksuit, everybody wanted to talk about the Posh, what was happening, who we were signing, who was sick in a taxi on Friday night before the match, who butted who in training. I couldn't even shop in Tesco's, it used to take me an hour for a basketful. I didn't want to be rude and it also made me feel important, next best thing to being famous I'd say.

I was well established at Peterborough, it was a long-term plan, it was even mooted that I had the potential to be the Club Secretary if things changed upstairs at the Club. Well that change wasn't forthcoming and before I knew it I was actually facing the cold streets of the Lincolnshire city. Without a word of warning we were made redundant, and all in a very underhand way. The Soccer Schools were going from strength to strength so how could that have happened? Numbers were better than ever, money was flooding in, the Club's standing in the community was higher than it had ever been, and here we were faced with the unemployment queue.

Tony moved on from the Club after spending less time with Posh Soccer and concentrating on the development of the better players. The lack of time earning money and more time spent developing the future wasn't appreciated upstairs, they wanted everything at once. Didn't they understand you had to speculate to accumulate? This was the first sign that everything was not well with the financial side of the club, which was to ultimately blow up when Barry Fry was trying to buy the club. There was penny pinching aplenty, and this was part of it. When the Soccer Schools were set up, the Club were promised that they would make £50,000 profit a year, which they did, and then some. But the money went out of the Soccer School accounts and paid for all the Youth Development work too. The only thing it didn't pay was Kit's wages. So they were running Development teams for quality children from 5 years of age through to 16 years of age. Playing every Sunday, home and away, incurring travel costs, kids were travelling from across the country and Ireland, so costs were high, even though they all slept at the Club itself on a Saturday night prior to games. Throw in the European tours every holiday break and you have a costly little outfit to operate. That's why Posh Soccer was great as it funded the Youth Policy to a main degree and helped sustain arguably the best Youth Policy outside of the Premiership.

So when they told me we had not made £50,000 a year profit, I wasn't surprised, we were £9,000 in debit over three years which was, in my book, pretty good. We had covered our wages, paid all our costs and funded the youth policy. What a result. To those in charge, it was an excuse to say it was a loss making organisation and had lost £159,000 over three years, which as you will see is not actually correct - you can't lose money you never had. Further investigation into the accounts showed transfers out to the main Club of which I was unaware. That was the problem of not controlling our own finances, the Club always did. We were well and truly stitched up. The worst thing was that they folded the Soccer Schools business when I was away on holiday for a week, knowing I was the only one who knew anything about the Company profit and loss. This was also the week after I had secured them a grant from the Football League for £125,000, which they needed to finish the new Stand, which was fast becoming a white elephant.

The football league grant was withheld for a number of reasons to do with the club, which they had to address in Lytham St Anne's. One of them, which may seem to be a bit petty, was that we were operating our Community Programme outside of our jurisdiction. Well there was no point in denying it, we were running a Soccer School right next to Leicester City's ground, and we had operations in the centres of Norwich and Ipswich. I had to appear before the League and justify our position, which was 'Well they were not running anything, so children were actually missing out'. The Clubs were moaning but not doing anything in their own community, whose fault is that? I had to promise we would be good boys and operate only within one hour of Peterborough and not in the immediate vicinity of any other football club. That put Leicester, Norwich and Ipswich out of the picture. Anywhere in between was fair game though. As it happened my promises were easy to keep as the Posh Soccer empire started to implode following Tony's departure. Promises that were made couldn't be kept, people got frustrated and we went our separate ways. As we came out of the hearing, I drove the Chief Executive to Preston Train Station so he could go back to Peterborough and I went on to Liverpool for a week's well deserved holiday following a long summer season. His parting words were 'You played a fucking blinder there son, I won't forget that'. What part of that did he forget when he made me redundant the following week?

Not just me, but the three other lads who worked with me as well.

It was underhand, no other words for it, and I knew it would happen one day, I had seen it done to others, why would I be any different? My life was in a spin, what would I do now? Redundancy pay? You're having a laugh. A weeks pay for every year of service, hardly a great pay off was it after three years. I rang my girlfriend at the time back in Liverpool, having just been away for the week, I said I might be coming home a little earlier than thought, to which she went quiet. Then proceeded to say 'Well I have been thinking and I think its time....' I finished the line for her and put the phone down. Redundant and dumped inn one day yippee doo! Not the best day in my life.

Well I hadn't spent all this time away and learnt so much to not be able to stand up for myself. After a good old session with Kit where we looked at my options (remember he was still there and safe). The best one was for me to make the Club an offer and play them at their own game. I went to the Chief Executive and offered that I would take over Posh Soccer and run it as my business but still run it for the club as their community programme. Nobody would know what they did to me, I didn't sign a secrecy act or anything just gave my word and mine was worth something. In exchange for keeping kids coming in through the door, I needed to retain the status the Club gave us. We would get Club wear such as tracksuits and T-shirts at cost, the office we worked out of rent free, access to the ground as normal and tickets for the matches as before. They knew this made sense as they made a fortune on tea bars and Club Shop when we had the kids in. I would also run the Junior Supporters Club

(Junior Posh) for them as I had previously until the end of the subscription period. Finally I would also carry on with Match day activities to control the kids we brought in, only reasonable, as I didn't want to get the kids there under false pretences and not have them looked after by my lads. That would also allow me to keep doing the ground tours. I was king of the ground tour. I knew more useless information about the Posh than was possible to know, down to how many light bulbs in a floodlight and how powerful (how sad), kids loved it.

The club accepted my proposal (they never signed up to it until my last official day though, so they made me sweat), well it saved face for them, didn't cost them any money as they didn't pay any wages, and they could get rid of me at the drop of a hat, what was the risk? The risk was that they wouldn't make any money out of me and that's exactly what happened, they never made a penny. I had to be more mercenary now and concentrate on making money for myself. We didn't pay any money to the Youth Policy as we couldn't afford to, I allowed Kit to use my coaching staff and especially Gaffa as needed, and Gaffa helped me out by looking out for me when I wasn't there.

I still knew I couldn't trust them, and I looked for a way out. Even though it was supposed to be a secret, everybody knew what they had done to us. One of the dads of one of the Youth Team Players had heard the story and went out of his way to help me. I had known Graham Bowater in all my time at Posh, great fella looked after his family and fully supported what we were doing. He was a big believer in Kit and his way. "Little Bo" was in the youth team, and had been through the ranks in my time there. "Big Bo" was "Little Bo's" dad (obviously) and was well to do, drove a good car, was respectable, well educated and smart. No disrespect to anyone, but amongst the parents he was the one people looked to. He worked for the Prudential as a Regional manger and he offered me the opportunity if I wanted to speak to someone up north. If I was not going to be at Posh, there was no point living down there away from my real home if I was going to be stitched up. So looking after myself on a return trip north to Liverpool, I took an hour to meet up with a local guy who offered me the opportunity to become a Financial Adviser with the Prudential. So after sorting myself out, I offered the club the whole Soccer Schools package back in better shape and as a going concern. Did I jump too soon? Maybe I did, but I would have always got a push when they saw how much money was being made.

On my last day at the club, the Football Club changed hands, Barry Fry, who was supposed to be buying it never did. The debts they uncovered allegedly came to £2.5m so it put him off somewhat. The fanfare was that he bought the Club but he actually didn't until years later. The club was bought by a lovely old fella called Peter Boizot who was *Mr Peterborough*! He was into the Arts and had, years earlier, been the owner of one of the first Pizza chains in the country, Pizza Express, and made his money when he sold it. He became a champion of all things Peterborough, and the when the club needed bailing out, he did so. He offered me the opportunity to stay but I had made my mind up that I was getting out on my terms. I had a new career and could go back to my love (not the bird, she dumped me remember). I could go back to watching the Reds. My dream was always to see the Reds at London Road and I could sort everybody out, never quite got there though. Big Ron (Atkinson) from the Swan and Paul McGrath was the nearest I got to big time football.

My time at Peterborough taught me so much. The value of family and friends became important to me. Learning whom you can and can't trust was a crucial lesson, and I finally understood that my own ability actually outstripped what I thought it was. I had broken the hold that the City of Liverpool had over me, and the future was ultimately to be away from it. I became much more confident and assertive in my time there and it gave me a great story to tell you.

Admittedly I did fall out of love with the beautiful game, but the passion always comes back and the longer you are away from it the more you miss it. What Peterborough did to me was to change me as a person, not always for the better, but I learnt so much and it has helped me be more focused and assertive in my recent career. It has also made me make sure that I would never treat someone the way I was treated. If I sound a little bitter well maybe I am, but these people played with my life and ultimately changed it. Bitterness doesn't become me though ask anyone who knows me. Now I wouldn't want to change anything in life but I always wondered what would have happened if the right people were in place above me. The bitterness of my departure has waned over the years and I always loved to go back and the Posh's score is the first one I look for after Liverpool each Saturday.

[1.] Ridley, I. (2006) *Floodlit Dreams: How to save a football club.* Simon & Schuster UK Ltd

10

'We had dreams
and songs to sing'

Tuesday 24th of May 2005

6.30am Thessaloniki Train Station - northern Greece

The first bars of "Ring of fire" (de de de de de de de der) ring out across the concourse, the Red Army (as The Times like to call us) are ready to move. They can't even speak English, they have spent that much time in the local bars following their flight from the UK. "Ring of fire" is all they can muster, anything with words is far too difficult.

It's not like being in Greece on your holiday where everyone speaks English. On the taxi ride from the airport last night, the only words of English were 'football' as the driver careered past Haraklion's stadium, and 'twenty euro's' as he ripped me off; I was too tired to argue as I hit the Hotel Vergina (work the jokes out yourself - I will get told off by my wife).

With the sun coming up over northern Greece at 7.30am, I wondered, how did I get here? Well it certainly wasn't easy but this is how my story goes.

It all started that wonderful night when little Luis Garcia's goal beat the multi millionaires of Chelsea, controlled by 'The Moaning One'. Probably the most nervous 86 minutes of my life (92 if you count added time). That 'sick to the bottom of your stomach' feeling, replaced by sheer relief and the unadulterated joy, all within minutes. What a feeling! I just wanted to speak to everyone at the same time. I was buzzing that much I woke up to watch the highlights at 3am. Funny thing was I couldn't even be at Anfield as I was working 400 miles away in Jersey.

I could get used to this writing lark, eating croissants as I look out on the sun-drenched plains of Northern Greece.

Following six minutes of extra time and the relief that the final whistle brought, all thoughts turned to Istanbul. How to get there? Who to go with? Getting time off work? I never thought getting a ticket would be so difficult, but that's a story in itself.

You want to see the problem the guard is having checking tickets. He can't wake three drunken Scousers up, but he is trying his hardest. In England he would have well given up but in Greece it is his train!

Anyway, back to the tickets. Whilst waiting for ticket info, which seemed like an eternity, I was trying to build my trip, who to go with and how to get there from Liverpool, whilst also checking out other possibilities on the internet. After checking on numerous occasions the ticket details were posted, my heart sank. You had to have been to eight European games initially; How many? Here is the point - living in the Isle of Man makes it difficult enough to get to weekend games, but expensive and time consuming getting to midweek European games. With a family life and work life to balance it is almost impossible. I could prove only three on the fancard (Liverpool's way of identifying which games people went to) so maybe there would be a slim chance. The fancard is designed to reward loyalty of fans who have attended games rather than have a free for all, it stops any Tom, Dick and Harry getting a ticket. With only 20,000 tickets, the official trips all needed to meet the ticket criteria in order to be provided with a legitimate ticket, so it looked like I would have to look at something a little different for my travel.

Still confident of obtaining a ticket from somewhere I rang around all my contacts from my years following the Reds. Surely one would pop up somewhere? It seemed that lots of people had been offered tickets but no one actually had one, or at least one to spare. Checking on the Internet, the ticket firms were offering tickets at £350 with other peoples names on them and e bay wasn't any cheaper. The message from Liverpool FC and UEFA was that security checks would be under-taken, but as it turned out the fact was that the tickets from the club didn't even have a name on it. If you were unlucky you might get refused entry with an Internet ticket, so Liverpool Football Club was the only answer.

As the tickets got snapped up then so did all the flights and packages to Istanbul. All the daytime flights and one night package were gone near enough right away. I had to do something fast to secure a ticket to travel, as there would be no point having a match ticket if I couldn't get to Istanbul. I started spending hours on the Internet checking out Turkish related travel sites and in particu-lar the 'Turkey Travel Planner' which gave an enormous amount of information. I could see at my fingertips how to get to and from Istanbul, by train, plane, boat and car. I checked numerous flight destinations including Ankara, Dalaman and Izmir in Turkey, Istanbul was already £900 a flight, Bulgaria, from Sofia and Bourgas (a popular route as it linked up with a ferry to Istanbul, which it transpired no longer ran, so I was glad I didn't take that option), Romania with Bucharest and finally Greece and flights to Thessaloniki.

The guard is upset again, feet on seats this time from the drunken Scouser. The guard looks like Robert Kilroy-Silk chewing a wasp. Well one hour gone fourteen more to Istanbul (or it would be, but I am taking a detour on the way to break up the journey).

I am going to the Greek/Turkish border and then heading for Erdine, which is a medieval town from the Ottoman Empire, in northern Turkey. From my research I know I can get a coach to Istanbul from there and it will take about two and a half hours, compared to over seven hours by train.

The drunken Scousers are at it again, foreign money at the best of times is not good when you are English, but when you can't see straight.... The waiter has given up on getting his money for a sandwich but the drunk is going to pay him if it kills him. The waiter is having none of it and the drunk gets a free sandwich and a severe helping of euro confusion.

I finally chose Thessaloniki in northern Greece, as it had a direct rail link with Istanbul (all fifteen hours of a direct rail link) and it was only £230 to fly to compared to remaining day trips for £490. Remember I still had to get off the Island and that wouldn't be cheap, especially with only seven days to go and counting. With one week to go I had no ticket, no flight and no accommodation.

All my contacts were coming up with nothing, but tickets were still on sale at LFC. The criteria was now down to six games on a fancard and if it went to five I would be quid's in off my dads fancard. I threw my hat in the ring and booked my flight to Greece. No going back now.

My lack of Greek is causing problems in making myself understood with the guard, so I try the old English abroad trick, shout louder but more slowly - it seems to work a little.

The whole trainload of passengers now have to surrender their passports prior to the border station at Pythion, I am now causing an enormous amount of confusion by not wanting to go straight to Istanbul. I didn't know whether I have to get off at Pythion and get another train, or stay on this train. I understand that I now need to get my passport back and stay on the train further up the Greek frontier, to Castenas where I can supposedly walk across the border. The police are useless. I'm actually getting off the train and another passenger is making me get back on again (see the lack of language causes so much trouble). The locals are spot on and are going to make sure that I get my stop.

I am giving the guard the eye to see if this is my stop, he is looking back like I am a piece of shit. He motions for me to stay seated. At this stop I am expecting the goatherd and his flock to get on. The passenger look has now changed from cosmopolitan to peasant, and yes, I class the Reds fans as cosmopolitan, but they have all gone at Pythion. I am on my own now.

Back to the ticket story, I managed to get one of the last few tickets available and on the Friday morning. Five days and counting. All I had to do was collect my North

Stand ticket, which was worth all of £15 - I know, for a Champions League final! 'Our Kev' was called into action again, he needed his ID, proof of his address, proof of my dads address and he could get the ticket for me and just post it to the Island and jobs a good un.

Once the ticket was collected I had found out that Parcelforce would guarantee its arrival on Saturday on the Isle of Man, I could now organise all my travel from the Island. Being an intelligent International business-man I worked out that all that trekking to Jersey for work would pay off and that my air miles would get me to Gatwick and back for £30. Now I had a ticket it was plain sailing and for much less than the cost of a day trip.

WRONG!!!!

How wrong could I be! It all went pear shaped. Instead of falling into place it was falling apart. It was now Friday afternoon 3.30pm and I logged onto ba.com to book my flights. Monday afternoon 14.35 IOM to Gatwick would link nicely to the Thessaloniki flight at 17.35. The site wouldn't accept the booking, and now it didn't even show any flights on Monday. I rang BA who politely informed me that all flights booked with air miles had to be done three days in advance and not, as in my case, two days and 23 hours. There will still be seats available though. I went back into the web site to book it and it was now showing at over £300 return. With Nikki going away first thing on Saturday morning following the final I had her kind permission to look on the cheaper side and come home on the Saturday. The website and prices were now blurring into one, so with fresh eyes on Saturday morning I would book it.

At least the ticket was in safe hands, it was with Parcelforce and on the way so I could book any flight from Sunday afternoon onwards. I was only waiting for Kevin to ring with the details of postage, which he duly did. It's a good job I was sitting down because they had charged £56 for their next day service. At least it was guaranteed. It was a price worth paying as I had been willing to pay up to £300 for my ticket. It might be the last time I get the chance to go to a European Champions League final. However, it wasn't in the safest of hands as I thought. Saturday morning came and I was watching the letterbox waiting for my golden ticket to fall on the mat. I waited and waited and waited but nothing came. At midday in the Isle of Man you know the post has gone. Trying the post office was no good on a Saturday afternoon - there was no one there, and Sunday would be the same. What was I going to do?

Sorry to interrupt again but this mad old fella is pointing out Turkey through the window and the town of Erdine, my destination, is in sight. The train is arriving at Castenas and my fellow passengers are making sure I know I have to get off, even if it is all a bit manic. I am looking for the stop, and all I can see is a concrete shelter in the middle of a field. This is Castenas train station. In the middle of a field with a track that leads to who knows where. The only other passenger who has alighted is already on her way as quick as a Greek 100 metre champion avoiding a dope test. I will head towards what looks like a town, whilst just over my shoulder I can see gun towers on what I gather is the Turkish side of the border. As I walk towards the town I start to pass old camouflaged shelters, this sight serves to remind me that this is not the friendliest of borders and there is not a lot of love lost between the two countries.

The only things I pass on the track are dogs lazing in the heat of the afternoon, and it is hot, damned hot. I have just been on an air-conditioned train for seven hours, so I can really feel it. I have just stumbled across what I think is the main street of the town, and it is totally deserted and all the restaurants and shops are closed for siesta time, or whatever its called in Greece. It is now baking hot so I am creaming up, suntan cream that is, because my wife has told me I need to so I don't get burnt to a cinder. It was good advice. This skin sees little uv rays in the Isle of Man so I frazzle easily. As I finish writing this, I am looking like the singing detective after a particularly bad case of sunburn during TT week, where you guessed it, I didn't cream up, sorry love. I look left and right, and to my right about 500 yards ahead is what I gather is the border post.

What am I expecting? A hard time to be fair, a real grilling and an in depth bag search. None of that though, it is quite easy really and a lot easier than I thought it would be, nothing like Midnight Express, and, as you will see later, I think I have picked a good point to cross. First of all there is a Greek police border post where I have to produce my passport to a young policeman. He speaks good English, but he's an Olympiakos fan who remembers Stevie G's goal four minutes from time, so with a big smile he says 'Forza Milan' and points to the border road. If you never been to a border such as this, let me tell you that you don't know where to go or what to do, and just hope you do it right, as all the guards have sub machine guns. The soldiers are pointing the way with their guns, I am somewhat unnerved as they are now behind me, what if they are really bored and fancy target practice, and who could blame them, what is to stop them? Practice on a poor unsuspecting Scouser?

I am now walking straight ahead out of Greece and into Turkey. I have this strange feeling that I am being watched every step of the way. Not so long ago these were very hostile neighbours and the scars are still on the landscape, numerous trenches, bunkers with sandbags and camouflaged buildings dotted all around. The camouflaged sub machine gun-toting guards are taking little interest in me. Call me weird but I feel a little disappointed. There looks to be a walk of about a half-mile ahead. Stood proudly ahead is a huge Greek flag and a trench of water, somewhat like a ford. I gather it is there to stop people driving through the border at high speed. The water looks more like the Salt Lake in Salt Lake City Utah, which I had been thoroughly unimpressed with many years ago. The water is filthy, stinks and has an abundance of creatures living in, on and around. I hasten my step so I don't catch anything before I have even had a kebab. There it is, right ahead. Turkey, with a big red banner which reads 'Welcome to Turkey'. Well it could say anything, like 'go home you Scouse git', my Turkish is pretty appalling as you will see.

Now I have to report to the Turkish police, who appear surly, I think I have just woken him up (well there is only one policeman). I know, I will try my best Turkish, hello and thank you etc all from my page of Turkish phrases. He is not arsed I might as well not bother. He wanted to see my match ticket, stamped my passport with a visa and told me to bugger off. Well he never said anything actually, I had to work out that it was time to go. *This was easy as he just started ignoring me and talking to anybody else but me. Didn't want to go and be shot in the back though, do you know what I mean? It happens, or have you not seen what happens in 'Midnight Express'?*

Now I have to get to the town, 'Taxi!!!' Or should I say 'Taksi', (see they make things easy to understand in some ways, and they are yellow as well, so a mix between English and American). One is waiting so I offer him 10 euro's to take me to the town centre, which, though not far, I think is a good offer. The driver's eyes light up. Now having paid for my coach trip to Istanbul I realise why, he must think it is Christmas, Turkey is really cheap. I try my Turkish out on the driver who is more than willing for me to give it a go, (no wonder after what I am paying him). His car rattles and shakes like Shaking Stevens at his best. He is now asking me to shut the door again, first go is a little weak so he wants me to try again so I give it a good old slam and the car nearly falls to bits, the driver is bottling it and he makes it clear I am not to try again. He laughs weakly and gestures no more door closing and drives on into town. Erdine is strange, we are passing peasants with horses and carts riding through the streets, with all manner of items loaded on the back. This is not what I was expecting. They are seemingly malnourished and I can see all their ribs, and that's just the horses, I can't see the people for the rags that they're wearing.

My 1st class tourist view of Erdine is that it is strange, but then again I am only used to visiting developed countries. I must stand out like a sore thumb, shorts, pasty legs and English, what a combination. Finding a hotel is not a problem, right in the centre of town is the Efe hotel.

I make sure that I check the room out first (been caught out before- never pay until you see), it is clean and has a shower, TV and air conditioning and only 35 euro's - just the job. I think I will head into town with my camera and a pocketful of cash, well about £12 worth. I think I will take a walk through the Bazaar, which seems to go on for ages and is just like a wedding buffet, the same three or four things just repeated the length of the indoor bazaar. Should be called bizarre, as it's full of crap and its bizarre that someone would buy any of it. There seems to be copious amounts of tea drinking going on, the Turks love their tea. Little men and boys are running around with a silver plate with tea glasses, delivering tea to men, and only men may I tell you, sitting on chairs watching life go by. I don't think I got served once by a woman in all my time in Turkey, they are very much hidden away.

I was walking around the town looking at the giant mosques with the call to prayer ringing in my ears, when I too had a calling, but of my stomach not religion. I had seen on the internet that in order to find decent restaurants you had to head towards the river, so that's what I did now, or tried to. From the centre of town I couldn't see the river, so I am now following great crowds of people, in what I thought might be the general direction. Wrong direction! I am heading into the suburbs, which are not exactly classy. It is fairly scruffy and dirty and the wind is starting to build up due to an approaching storm and it is creating dust storms, and the dust has a knack of getting right in my eyes whichever direction I turn. The skies have now blackened and thunder is clapping, and for once it is not to the tune of "Ring of fire". It is fairly urgent now to find a restaurant, from a 'keeping dry' point of view as well as having something to eat.

I am doing an about turn and heading back towards the centre of town, but this time I am going to take a lower road that seems to head downwards, well that's where you would expect water isn't it. It is either going to take me to the river or the shelter of the town. After about ten minutes I have found a road that I recognise from my taxi ride, it's actually the knackered old horses that I recognise first, at what looks like a horses parking garage! So I am on my way across the Ottoman Bridge to a most likely looking restaurant. It looks quite good from the outside. Once they know that I am English I get the guided tour of the restaurant and meet everyone from the chefs to the waiters, I am a star, or an oddity (take your pick). They speak a little English, which helps greatly, 'football and 'Liverpooooool' is what I call a little English. They are giving me a guided tour of the food and the only thing I actually recognise is Doner Kebab, which in England I always thought was rank so keep away from.

The waiter patiently explained how I would receive this delicacy. I assumed it would be in pitta bread like in England, well it was far better, bread on the bottom, Doner on top, Chilli sauce (I think) and yoghurt on the side, and as promised it was lovely, all washed down by the first beer of the day. Meanwhile outside it is lashing down, with thunder and lightning thrown in free. Another waiter comes in who speaks really good English - he should do he's married to a girl from Kent. He just told me that one of his best friends is big Dave from Liverpool whose wife is Sylvia. He even shows me his mobile, which stated Dave Red Nose. I have a good old *natter with the waiter about the football and Turkey in general, he gives me advice about Istanbul and how to get there. I thank my waiter for the Turkish hospitality and then pay my bill, a grand total of £3. It was reputedly the best restaurant in town, it must have been because it cost nearly as much as my coach trip to Istanbul.*

I head back up in to town to get provisions for the coach tomorrow morning, dodging showers as I go. The town is still really busy as night approaches. I am on my way back to the hotel to ring home and give a security report to Nikki. I decide to go out again at about 9.00pm to find a bar for a beer to help me sleep (it's a good excuse isn't it?). The town is still really busy but I can't find a likely venue for solitary drinking so back to the hotel bar, which is where I meet the barman Farti. Yes that's his real name and it was a good job I only found this out as I was heading to bed, otherwise I would never have kept a straight face.

Two hours later Farti now knows how to say and make slippery nipples, and an Englishman's missionary work is done, and with free beers for my lessons. Farti also knows that his English is a million times better than my Turkish, but at least he has taught me how to say Tesekkular (Pronounced Tesh hekkular) without it sounding like testicular, which as you know is just bollocks.

Wednesday 25th Of May 2005

Today's the day. I wake up early to head to Istanbul and a glorious night, fingers crossed. It's 8 am and I am walking through the streets of Erdine to an executive mini bus, which will take me into the heart of Istanbul. If I only I could remember the way from last night. I finally find it but it's gone already - 8am on the button. It's going to be Ok though because there is another one at 9.30 if I can't get one before with another company. The great thing is there are three or four companies who do the route. Yesterday I had a somewhat painful conversation with another company and I know there is a bus due at 8.30 with RADAR coach lines. I have just walked into the ticket office and I am buying a ticket from a guy with, wait for it, a Man Utd shirt on who thinks that Liverpool will win 2-1, he's obviously not a real Man Utd fan then. Cost - 14 Turkish Lira, about £4, he is directing me towards a mini bus with Servis written on the back. Servis actually means that this mini bus is going to take me to the autobahn to meet the actual Istanbul coach. Well I hope that's what it means, remember me and my Turkish language problems. The driver seems to be picking up everybody he knows, there is a mix of businessmen, gabby women with headscarves on, a couple of freaks and one Scouser, me. Boy do I look out of place and they all know it, lots of looking and laughing. Paranoid? Not me.

It is really well organised actually and the mini bus takes me to a big coach station right next to the motorway and all I have to do now is find the bus to Istanbul. Let me see, it must be this one, the one with the big Liverpool flag in the back window. Oh I feel at home again. As I step on to the coach I see, secured at the back, a little bastion of Scouseness, well four lads who are extremely welcoming especially as I am actually Scouse. They say that they have met lots of Reds on the way via

Bulgaria, but few of them are actually Scousers. I have had an easy journey compared to these boys. They have been to Sofia in Bulgaria via Prague, then driven to the border, where they were ordered to leave their hire car at the border. They then had to go through six checkpoints at the border, which took three and a half-hours and then a four hour drive to Erdine. They are quite jealous seeing I have come the easy way!! They got in real late and stayed in the Tuna Hotel, next to my Effing Hotel (well Efe is close enough), near the Anal Hotel and the KockBank (all true bar Effing).

This coach is ten times better than any National Express. For your £4 you get your transfers to the coach, free coffee, free piece of chocolate cake, free water and free aftershave (well some type of lotion the men seemed to be putting on their hands and face). The Turks were splashing it all over, maybe it was Old Spice. We even have the services of an on board waiter, who should have had some free deodorant, though this seems to be a local trait, as I was to find out on Trams and Metro in Istanbul. Overall the coach is great, the two and a half-hours to Istanbul fly by.

So now on to Istanbul, only 95 kilometres to go, 95 kilometres between me and one of the best nights of my life. Soon I will be meeting up with all the lads who are either there, or on the way as I write. Mongoose sent a text last night saying that Istanbul was rocking to the sound of Liverpool. Zil was in Liverpool airport moaning that the bar was shut and he was delayed. Peter (who was feeling less guilty now I had a ticket) has already landed and is on his way to Taksim Square. I knew Istanbul was rocking last night because it was on every one of fourteen news channels on the hotel

TV and it looked like everyone was having a whale of a time.

'All round the fields of Anfield Road..... We had dreams and songs to sing'

Today we dream…. Today we sing all day … tonight we ride to eternity. Sounds good doesn't it.

It's been worth every penny, every bit of hassle to get here and yes I will go back to getting my flight and ticket arranged but not now. I have a day of enjoyment, sightseeing, beer and camaraderie planned, and then? And then a Cup Final, a Champions League Cup Final. I need a new memory to eradicate my last European Cup Final at Heysel in 1985. Roll on the "Ring of fire", "Poor Scouser Tommy", Benitez's "La Bamba" and finally the most wonderful version of "You'll never walk alone". Can you tell I am excited?

So finally the result of 48 hours travelling - the mystical and magical City of **Istanbul**. I am cultured, so I am off to see the sights and views over the Bospherous. Having just arrived at the huge bus station it's no great problem to actually get to the Blue Mosque which is supposed to be the must see. Istanbul has a good metro and tram system from what I can see. I take the metro to Askeray and then the tram towards the Blue Mosque. It is at this point that the enormity of our following becomes apparent. There are Liverpool fans everywhere and this is the Milan side of the city supposedly. I have decided this is time to start sampling the atmosphere and jump off the tram at the Grand Bazaar and walk the rest. Logic says I have only got to follow the tramlines. The atmosphere is great and the fans are mixing well, when you see any Milan fans that is, the normal scarf swapping *and photograph taking is the order of the day. Istanbul has a buzz about it all of its own. The Turkish music is filtering above the bustle of the main road as I head down to the Blue Mosque, and the crowds are getting heavier. Not many of the Scouse day-trippers will be seeing this and I know now that I have made the right decision to undertake my epic journey.*

Which one's the Blue Mosque? Nikki tells me it's called that because it's Blue inside, well that's no help when I'm looking at two massive mosques, which look very similar outside. Well I am taking pictures of both so I can't go wrong. The rendezvous point for all the Reds is Taksim Square on the Asian side of the city, by all accounts it's a fair taxi ride away, but I am taking my chances and walking through the city, I am going to see some of it as I stroll. I always find that the best way to see and feel a city is to walk it. Within minute of leaving the Mosque I find myself walking through shaded cobbled streets and back in time and through into a giant park advertising Tea Gardens with views over the Bospherous. I was heading the right way as the Bospherous cuts the west and the east and Taksim Square was in the East.

It is a good twenty minute walk through the park, and by the time I reach the tea gardens I am ready for a sit down and a drink, not beer though just yet. I want to enjoy today, and remember as much as possible. I got that one from Bob Paisley when Liverpool won in Rome in 1977. The time doesn't come again and you don't get a second chance. So here I am sitting overlooking the busy Bospherous and feeling pretty chilled out. After all my efforts to get here, now it's time to take it all in. I want to see these places otherwise there is no point coming. There is a lot to see and do in Istanbul; an enormous city of 14 million inhabitants, so people watching is something to revel in. I want to sample the city and riverside prior to Taksim Square which for some reason I feel will have more of a Scouse feel to it.

The walk to Taksim Square is long (very long) and hot (very hot), and I pass Sirkcei train station from where I will depart on Thursday morning so I get my bearings. In the busy port area boats are shuttling across the Bospherous, passengers loading and unloading constantly seemingly without a pause. This is normal city life intermingled with an increasing number of Liverpudlian's. Kebab time! 60p for a kebab that tasted fine, but unfortunately somewhat like a Boots sandwich, which promises greatness but has little filling inside. Well it was keeping the wolf from the door and I was getting ready for Taksim and to meet my mates. The wonder of mobile phones, it makes life so much easier when meeting people.

I head across the bridge over the Bospherous, which takes me from the west to the east. The amazing thing about this busy road bridge is that along the full length of it, on either side of a four lane mass of traffic jockeying noisily for position to move barely yards in minutes, there are hundreds of locals fishing from it. They look as if they are catching sardines, which doesn't seem worth the efforts from 150 foot above the river. I am heading towards Taksim and starting to tire in the afternoon heat and the effects of my journey so far. I don't actually have a map but will plough on in the general direction of where I have been told the square is. Walking inland away from the river into the heart of the Asian city, I ask a local for directions for Taksim and he points up a hill *opposite, complete with a big smile and a shout of Liver-pooooolll. The locals seem to like us, not that much though as he hasn't give me any rope or crampons for the steep climb. Local history says that Sir Edmund Hilary and Sherpa Tensing practised here before their ascent of Everest. There is a snaking red line in front of me in single file, huffing, puffing, sweating and some stragglers left by the kerbside, sitting it out catching their breath. It is allegedly about a kilometre up this hill, and this is indeed what greets me at the top – Taksim Square. When I arrive, it looks like the Pier Head after the Homecoming when we won the UEFA cup in Dortmund. There is red and white everywhere.*

—〰—

People are flooding to the square (by the way it is not really a square as per any normal description) in huge numbers. Flags and banners hang from every vantage point, and hundreds are standing on shop and bar roofs. Noise is booming from the Fan festival site. "Ring of fire" keeps ricocheting around the square and all its arteries. Pockets of noise erupt regularly, fuelled by case after case of Efes lager, the local brew, which by now is warming nicely in the sun. The red and white arteries are spreading from the square with people in all directions and the noise is flowing in and out of these arteries. You could only be inspired by the fervour and passion of the Reds fans, coupled with that unbelievable Scouse self belief. Everywhere you go people are talking of our destiny. How can we do anything other than win?

Beyond the square there is a park, which is rapidly filling up in the afternoon sun, exactly what a Cup Final afternoon should be like. I meet up with Mongoose (don't ask why he is called that because even he doesn't know) and Phil and the Norris Green boys who had stayed on the Tuesday night. Phil, slightly gassed already, surveys the sea of red and white and declares boldly 'we were born to do this' and he passionately believes it. Who could argue? I finally meet Peter who, though exiled in Scotland for many years, always signs his letters with YNWA ("You'll never walk alone" in case you never guessed). He has been my mate for over 20 years now, and we have shared freezing cold nights at Boundary Park Oldham in League cup early rounds and the like, so it was nice to share a sunny afternoon in Istanbul. It's brilliant to see your mates in such a far off place. With Peter was Degsy (Derek to his mum), who I remember came to Chelsea in 1986 when Kenny won the first leg of the double, he crapped himself for 90 minutes. It was hilarious. In the 19 years since, I have only seen him on a handful of occasions but that's what happens. Peter has blagged me a coach ticket so I can get up to the ground with him, which also means that I can leave my bag on the coach with no worries. I have had it glued to me since I left the Island.

A gang to my left are having a whale of a time and just behind them is Ian Nolan of Bolton Wanderers, Steve McMannaman and Robbie Fowler are also rumoured to be in the square, once a red always a red. This group by me have all of a sudden turned their attention to a big hotel close by, which has a gym on the 5th floor with treadmills by the window. There on the treadmill is a guy running like he's something out of Chariots of Fire, high kicking action and waving to the masses, he's having a whale of a time. It's one of their mates who has bunked into the hotel and decided to get in the gym for a laugh.

The trouble the staff have dragging him off the treadmill is hilarious. Within minutes he is back to a hero's reception and a can of warm lager.

As 4 O'clock comes and goes, so do many of the squares inhabitants. Stories abound about how difficult it is to get to the stadium, as there is only one road in for the forty thousand of us. The coach is departing at 5 so Peter and I head away from the square and near to where the pick up point is. At a row of shops and bars there are hundreds of banners and people perched on top the shops. One banner reads 'Super Croat Igor Biscan - Used to be atrocious' (sing that to the tune of Superercalafradgalistic espealidocious –if that's right) harsh but true. McDonalds Golden arches are replaced with banners for the new fast food firm of 'Gerrard and Carragher'. I am scouting for a suitable establishment, or area, for after the game and that's when I see the Gotham City Reds, two guys dressed as Batman and Robin and they are having a whale of a time. The place is buzzing - tonight was surely ours, little did we know of the scale of the drama ahead.

The coach is rocking all the way to the Attaturk Stadium. Big Ethel and little Steve Dooley have positioned themselves at the front of the downstairs section of a double decker coach and Peter and I are sitting right behind the driver. Ethel (by the way he is about 6 foot 8 and built like the brick proverbial) a tray of Efes at his disposal is now in prime position for the young Turkish guide who basically does what he's told to do. That's why we have a Turkish announcement of 'Doonken Fergoosun takes it up the Boom', to the delight of the whole coach. The guide keeps starting "Ring of fire" without any undue influence, he is having the time of his life. Turkish driving leaves a lot to be desired though, it seems to be every man for himself and any gaps are there to be filled with near misses a-plenty. It's like a scene from the film 'Duel' at times, with trucks trying to run cars and coaches into kerbs and verges.

Heading to the Attaturk is a long and seemingly unending test of one's bladder control. As we near the stadium all the local factory workers and families from housing projects/council estates are filling the side of the roads and they are all waving and clapping. They seem to be glad we are here, we seem to be Turkey's choice of team. Quite a few of our perceptions and the garbage peddled by the English media are dispelled immediately. The press seem to be desperate for trouble, it is a much better story than 40,000 northern English men actually respecting the country and the people they visit, well it just won't sell papers will it. The only thing to report on was excellent behaviour from what I saw. Fans are giving the scarves away to local children, along with those ridiculous Carlsberg shocking red wigs. The local kids already look like cup winners, all decked out in scarves and flags.

As we near the stadium a Scouse lad has been knocked over somehow and is in the road desperately trying to get up and get to the stadium. He has a lump on his head akin to something from a Tom and Jerry cartoon. I hope he makes it even with a thumping headache. As we near the stadium, chaos has ensued due to the 'one road in' issue. Taxis, buses and coaches are all trying to get down this two lane road heading towards a stadium on the moon, that's what the Attaturk looks like from our view. It's desolate. As the coaches slow down it's a sign for the biggest piss stop in history with thousands going by the side of the road in the middle of never-ending scrubland. The funniest sight is a girl who is legging it away from her coach to have a leak behind a mound of rubble. Well, none of her coach can see her but another 50 coaches behind can so she didn't quite succeed. People have now started to bale out and walk, not a great idea for after the match when you need to find your coach, but it is only four hours to kick off so they may be worried about getting in.

As I have my world in my bag I am staying with the coach so I can find it afterwards. As we get closer I can see masses of fans at the Fan Festival site behind the North End entrance. Word has reached the coaches that there is no alcohol at the ground. People who have heard in time have trays of beer with them and all of a sudden they are as popular as Jamie Carragher. From the coach park there are numerous hazards to avoid: loose banks of earth, two foot high kerbs and storm drains to name a few. Brian Reade in the Daily Mirror was later to compare the movement of fans to the stadium as almost biblical. Coming down a hillside is a stream of people all wearing red and white, marching through this wasteland towards a promised land, the stream flows on for hour after hour.

As we arrive Pete Wylie and Wah! are taking to the stage at the fan festival site. Wylie is decked out in red and white and has a Bez (Happy Mondays) wannabee behind him. He soon has the crowd rocking with tracks such as 'Better scream', 'Story of the Blues' (he inserts the line the Story of Emlyn Hughes), 'Sinful', 'Come-back' (which was to prove quite apt), 'Heart as big as Liverpool' (obviously) and a version of "You'll never walk alone". For YNWA he invites the crowd to join him on stage, I am sure he didn't mean the entire crowd but that's what he is getting. The Turks in charge are having a fit and are having real trouble getting people off the stage. They are sure it is going to collapse and to be fair I am surprised it doesn't.

The Reds are well ready for this and we have been for years. The common thought is why on earth did they hold it here with such bad road connections, but then again why did they ever hold anything at Wembley. It is quite obvious UEFA never walk in fans' shoes and don't want to, if they did they would get rid of all that phoney opening ceremony crap and let the champions show you the cup. That view is about to change somewhat, apart from the catering which was woefully inadequate, I think this stadium itself is a wonderful venue for a European Cup Final. The ground is a magnificent setting for such an occasion.

At the end of Wylie's set I finally meet Zil, who I have been trying to meet all afternoon. He is on a day trip and has been delayed at Liverpool and taken straight to the stadium when he landed in Istanbul, totally missing Taksim and the city. I have been going to watch the reds with Zil for just on 20 years and he's the one person here in Istanbul who I want to share tonight with. I am so relieved, to have come all this way, after twenty years, and not meet would have been unthinkable. The day I got my ticket I swear he was a happier man than me.

Being in the ground two hours before kick off is not normally something I do, but this was the European Cup Final and the two hours flies by. As the players come out to check the pitch, the Liverpool end is still filling up but more rapidly. It wasn't exactly like Rome in 77 when everyone was waiting for the players to see *the pitch, but the players tonight knew we were going to be special.*

Next time I write in this dairy I hope it will be as a loyal supporter of the five Times European Champions.

Come on you can't do nothing-wrong reds!

—ᴍᴍ—

Thursday 26th of May 2005

The ticket story will certainly have to wait, last night is still so fresh and exciting I don't want to forget anything.

As I said we would, just 24 hours ago in these pages, the Red Army rode into Eternity, with the most unbelievable game of football you could ever see. Three nil down at half time, then three-three, and on to penalties, Dudek saves from Shevchenko and we bring the cup back home. Unbelievable. The Red Army erupts and the red gladiators dance gleefully, if gladiators are allowed to be gleeful. Some of the most unbelievable sights, grown men crying, others hugging, others just quiet in contemplation, then delirious, exuberant, I don't have enough words to describe the overpowering mass of emotion as the players engulf Dudek and signalled a fifth European Cup. The emotion wasn't just confined to one end of the Attaturk Stadium, two-thirds of the ground was bouncing with delight and shaking with relief. Liverpool fans did our Club and our city proud and travelled in vast numbers. There must have been at least 40,000 Liverpool supporters in this oasis in the middle of the Turkish wasteland.

The match itself was the most amazing match ever and created the widest range of emotions I have ever felt in one short period of time. From desolation and disappointment to incredible joy and all within three hours. This is how it went, step by step.

By the time the teams arrived, the Kop was in full voice and rocking the stadium. I won't forget the Milanese, even though they were few in number compared to us. The end they occupied was an array of red, white and black flags and I now know, they were all wearing coloured plastic covers. They were, as most Italian clubs are, extremely well organised and take their lead from designated fans who orchestrate their performance as such. Us though, we do it off the cuff and sing as one often with an uncanny knack, we do it with feeling and passion and love. The Liverpool end was a mass of red and white, hundreds of banners, draped across the empty front rows. Each banner and flag has a story to tell, our local pubs, Jamie Carragher and personal banners such as 'Ian Topping RIP', still remembered by those close who would wish him there. That banner can be clearly seen during the penalty shoot out. I would like to think that brings some form of comfort to his family and friends.

This is what we had come for, or as Phil from Norris Green said, this is what we were made for. **This was our destiny.** The referee blew his whistle and then it all went so horribly wrong. Within a minute Maldini, that legend of the Rossanieri and Italy scored what I believe was his third goal in 18 years, what a time to do that. What was happening to our destiny? Well 89 minutes left so we would just have to change our plan. The problem was that by half time we were three nil down and totally, and

I mean totally ripped to bits. We had a penalty appeal and a Hyppia header that went close, but they had waltzed around our back ten (well it wasn't just the back four) and we had lost Kewell through injury. We were looking at a serious hiding.

Half time was strange. Everyone was totally shell-shocked, there are no other words for it. Our dream was over and we had taken a step too far. Zil wanted to go home, I had a booming headache but thankfully Peter said we were going to win 4-3. He is a nutter! But if the first five minutes of half time was shellshock, during the second five we discussed how it went wrong and what could Rafa do, and for the last five minutes it was 'if they get one you never know' scenario, followed by the most gloriously uplifting version of "You'll never walk alone".

I didn't want to be depressed on my own in the second half so I moved and stood with Zil so I had some company thousands of miles from home, I guess I just didn't want to be alone, and I couldn't have wished for anyone better to be with. Besides, he made me look calm, nerveless and optimistic. He has been with me through the wind and the rain for close on 20 years. Concentrate on damage limitation and limit the embarrassment boys, but if they could just get one, who knows?

With the thankful introduction of Didi Hamann, the Reds looked more solid, although Dudek made a flying save to stop them going four down from a Shevchenko free kick. Then all of a sudden it happened. The fight back of all time began. Stevie G, who has taken some unfair criticism this year, guided a header into the far corner of the Milan net, from a Riise cross, after Gerrard had started the move himself on the edge of his own box, which I think most people won't actually remember.

Initially the goal was greeted with good applause but not great belief, until Gerrard started to raise the crowd. The crowd responded and a cacophony of noise erupted and rippled around the stadium and it seemed to send a shiver through the Milan ranks in the pitch.

The Mighty Reds upped the pace and within two minutes Smicer of all people, so disappointing over the years for such a talent due to injuries and application, struck a well-guided short into the corner of Dida's net. Now the Kop erupted and we believed, our destiny was coming back. Forty thousand throats roared the Reds on for 'one more boys!'. They only obliged four minutes later with a lovely move with Baros putting Gerrard through on goal and he was clipped from behind. PENALTY!!! The referee pointed to the spot and we went wild, but confusion surrounded the Milan area. Was he going to send off their player? Had he given the penalty? Was he saying Gerrard had dived? Well the area cleared and alone with the ball already on the spot was Xabi Alonso. But there was no sending off. Xabi struck it well to the keeper's right but he made a great save, but Xabi followed in to bury the rebound, and we got buried in a mass of bodies. Pandemonium! Three goals in seven minutes, and against the mighty Milan, with one of the world's best defences, amazing!!!!

Milan were all over the place, Liverpool were going for their throats, Riise stung Dida's hands with a rasping drive. Liverpool now controlled the game, playing with three at the back. Traore now looked like he belonged after he was ripped to shreds in the first half. Could Liverpool complete the comeback and score a fourth. As the half wore on Milan started to settle and Liverpool grew visibly tired (well what do you expect after 45 minutes chasing shadows and then a further 30 hauling yourself back in to a game you had no right to still be in). Milan probed with little effect really, and despite a couple of nervous moments Liverpool comfortably settled for extra time, and the pace of Cisse was introduced as a wild card.

As extra time began a rousing version of "You'll never walk alone" rained down from three sides of the ground, the Milanese at one end were extremely quiet. Well they knew how I felt at half time now. Extra time was nervy, but went so quickly it was scary. Liverpool tried to use Cisse's pace but often the final ball was a tired one, from players who were virtually out on their feet. Milan pressed and probed, Carragher, Gerrard, Hyppia, Hamann, in no particular order, made numerous magnificent challenges to foil Milan. Carra went down with cramp in what looked like his whole body, from a stunning blocked challenge. The stretcher came on but Carra wouldn't get on it, even if you chopped his legs off he wouldn't have got on, he was a bit like the Knight in Monty Python's Holy Grail, having all his arms and legs cut off and still wanting to fight. Carra epitomised why we were still in with a chance, passion and heart and the will to win. As he came back on the pitch he immediately made yet another magnificent block. A chorus of 'we all dream of a team of Carraghers' (to the tune of the Beatles Yellow Submarine), echoed around the North End of the Attaturk.

With two minutes to go Milan had THE chance to win the game and to be fair I still can't see how it didn't go in. The lethal Ukrainian Shevchenko headed from six yards out, to which Dudek made a great save low down but the ball went straight back to Shevchenko, this was it, we had fallen with two minutes to go. Then it ballooned over the bar to safety. I couldn't believe he had blasted it over the bar, but he hadn't, somehow Dudek had instinctively put his hands there and the powerful shot came off the top of his hands. The Reds erupted surely we would now get to penalties. Liverpool pushed forward with one last go, we were into added time in extra time and Hamann broke, through to Cisse who forced the ball to Smicer who was brought down. Ideal range for a training ground special, Gerrard, Hamann and Riise combined for one last chance and glory was ahead of us, but the shot cannoned off Cafu to safety and the final whistle blew.

PENALTIES

YNWA rose again from throaty Scouse voices, desperate to play our part to the last. To be honest, I would have accepted not winning after what had happened. I was proud that we had all done ourselves justice all day and all night, if we won it would be unbelievable, but I think I was the most relaxed I had ever been at a penalty shoot out. I think that was how the players felt, it was ours to win but Milan had already blown it, the pressure was all on them.

There was one player who wasn't calm and that was Carra, I saw him gesticulating wildly to Dudek, telling him to do whatever it took to put Milan off, and that's exactly what he did. The big Pole certainly put Milan off to devastating effect. Serghino and Pirlo shots, missed wildly and saved respectively, Hamann and Cisse for Liverpool slotted comfortably. Thommasson stroked his home and then of all people Riise had his effort saved. If there was anyone you would have expected to score it was him, the pressure was back on. Up stepped Kaka who had been instrumental in our first 45 minutes nightmare and he scored easily, now Smicer in his last act in a red shirt, he scored a great penalty and kissed his badge, well he deserved to didn't he? This was going to the wire. If we could score our final penalty we would win. We didn't really think of Shevchenko missing (well you wouldn't would you). He put it down the middle and Dudek got a hand to it. This is where it went into slow motion, as I couldn't tell from the far end whether he had got a hand on it and it went in the net. But the reaction of the players who to a man went running towards the goal signalled the start of the wildest celebrations I have ever seen at a football ground.

As all the players headed to Dudek, one by one they then peeled away and followed Carragher to the fans around the ground, Riise ended up right in front of us shirt off and on his knees, Gerrard in front of his adoring fans, leading a chorus of "Ring of fire". It was sheer unadulterated joy for all, people were still tumbling down the gangways, it was mad. Zil though stood staring ahead, he couldn't believe it, well he asked me at least three times whether we had won, I think he was in a state of shock. I think my feelings will stay with me forever and they are still too difficult to really describe, my joy was mixed with contemplation and thoughts of who I wanted to share this very moment with, Nikki, Kevin, my Dad, my Mum (a rock after Hillsborough), Ian, anyone touched by my fanaticism, the list goes on and on. I knew everyone was thinking of me wherever they were. They all had an eye on Liverpool, but would be so pleased for me, I think you call it reflected glory. In those peoples eyes I won the European Cup as much as the players on the pitch.

Then I thought of me, this was my feeling. It was something I had waited over 20 years to see. It made up for all those long nights in crappy trains, coaches with no TV or toilets, disappointments, but remember following Liverpool is easier than most. This was worth all my troubles to get here. This would banish my thoughts of Heysel, when I was abused in my own city upon my return as if I had killed people, 'I should be ashamed' one woman shouted at me, well if I won the Cup tonight I can understand why people would say that. It's guilt or glory by association. That was always a stain on the character of Liverpool, it will never be erased, but this is what we are truly like. I would like to think that the fans have received as much respect as the team this year for their behaviour and unbelievable support.

The phone networks must have been going crazy, text messages were flying in and out of my trusty handset but I couldn't ring out (well I had no voice left anyway so it didn't matter). As Stevie G lifted the cup and the red tickertape enveloped the team it was a wonderful feeling, then (this is where UEFA get it all wrong) the presentations are not for the fans or the players they are designed to maximise media opportunity. The players were not allowed off the pitch with the Cup. They were chaperoned by an army of stewards, so anyone at the victory parade had a much better view of the cup then me. Well it didn't ruin my night but it would have been lovely to have a close up view of our lads with our cup.

'What we achieve in life will echo in eternity' to quote a wonderful banner in the crowd, how true!!!

The Kop sang and danced until the team finally disappeared down the tunnel. Now to meet Peter again. I had left my bag on Peter's coach, so I headed back with him and Ethel, the chatter and joy as friends met again was an experience in its own right. I called my wonderful wife who had made it so easy to do this and she can't be thanked enough. I am sure I will be paying her back forever (with shoes and handbags) but it was worth it. I started to get the feeling of what it meant at home as well. She was watching with our friends, and as a Turkish celebrity I had to speak to Abi, Nikki's mate, as well. I had just taken her recently to her first game at Anfield and really understood what it all meant. I was lucky to be on a foreign field watching the glory with my own eyes.

As we made our way through the coach park it was absolutely manic, well that's what happens when people get off miles away from the ground and don't know where the coach park is. I was looking to head back to Taksim Square, it was going to be so easy now to stay up all night before my 8.30am train to Thessaloniki. The journey wasn't even going to be that bad now, at half time it looked like it would be the journey from hell. I said my goodbyes to Peter and the lads and headed off to the free buses back to Taksim Square. By the time I finally got to where they were actually leaving from there were none left. There were still hundreds of people waiting for another batch of buses to arrive. So I sat down on a quiet kerb and took it all in. The unused riot police marched past quietly, maybe surprised they had nothing to do. People were milling around, coaches departing with Kopites hanging out of windows and skylights. It was mobile phone time as I caught up on my texts to all manner of mates and started receiving lots from what I could gather was prior to our comeback as the tone was somewhat morose. Some from my wife and the most unbelievable language in them, I didn't even know she knew words like that let alone be able to spell them.

The buses finally arrived at 2.00am, and people boarded in a well ordered and jovial fashion, I think the emotion of the night had now drained most people. I stood next to a girl who had spare programmes and as they had run out at the ground, or had been taken off their rightful owners, she kindly offered one to me to buy. She was getting it for someone at home, but said after a night like that I couldn't go away without one. People at home would just have to read her copy. It only took about an hour to get back to Taksim. To be fair, what was a great place to be in the day, I personally felt now had a little bit of an edge to it. The locals were now pestering us to buy beer and if anything dodgy was going to happen it would be here. I popped down a side street to a bar I had seen in the afternoon. The bar had seats outside and it was still a fairly warm evening, so I got myself a pint and sat outside to take things in. For the first half an hour people were sitting quietly, sharing food, waiting for others, half in a daze it seemed. Then the singing started and never really stopped until, with the sun rising at 7 am, I had to leave for the train station to begin the long trek home. The morning call to prayer had been drowned out by YNWA and numerous other songs.

The camaraderie on these trips is amazing, especially if you are on your own. Within 20 minutes, I went from a table of one to a table of four, and we sung Istanbul to sleep and awake again. People would go to bed and others would replace them and every time a new group walked down the street a number would stay for at least one drink and host of songs. The atmosphere was wonderful and songs that will be aired at Goodison and Old Trafford next season started life in these Turkish streets this early morning, the favourite song went something like this.

We won at Wemberley

We won it in Gay Pareee

In 77 and 84 it was Rome

We've won it 5 times

We've won it 5 times

In Istanbul we won it 5 times

—◦—

At 7am and only a little unsteady, but with great joy in my heart, I took a cab to the station to start my long journey home. I didn't realise how drunk I was until I got the station where I managed to get a ticket and some provisions (pastries, water and Pringles) and I decided to sit on the kerb for five minutes and have breakfast. Someone pulled the kerb away from me and I ended up in the gutter, well it was dry and cleanish so I had breakfast. I met the Fistas (a gang of reds fans) just after I managed to get out of the gutter, and they were to be great travelling companions for the day and night. Roll On Thessaloniki, well it rolled but it wasn't quick. The Fistas it turned out had decorated the train with their flags as it rolled into Istanbul, the evidence via digital camera was quite comical.

On the train back there were quite a few lads who had been on my train coming down, but others who had not and were now in my compartment. All had their own little tales to tell. The ends to which people had travelled to get to Istanbul were quite amazing and now we all had to do it in reverse. Fortunately in my carriage, was Peter from North Wales (but now lives in London) who I had met on my way down. This was to be his last trip as he was emigrating in the summer to Australia with his girlfriend. He had spent the last hour of his trip to Istanbul sleeping by the Bospherous on the side of a bridge. He hadn't seen a proper bed since Sunday night, top effort. The first part of the journey was spent trying to catnap and grab some sleep if possible. It turned out to be impossible as I kept waking myself up humming "Ring of fire" (de de de de de de de der).

It was about seven hours to the Turkish border, at which point our passports were taken from us and we had about a 45 minute wait at the border post, which had a shop and a duty free (of sorts). The Turkish leg wasn't as bad as it sounds, I cat napped for about three hours. But I hadn't had any sleep all night, only beer, not a bad effort I thought. Then we boarded the train again and travelled about another 45 minutes to the Greek border (Pythion) at which point we had to surrender our passports again for inspection. They take your passports away and then come back about an hour later and do a roll call and you hope they still have it. This time we had to change trains and take all our gear. After nearly two hours at the border the Greek train arrived to take us the six and a half-hours to Thessaloniki. Funny thing is that it didn't feel as bad as it sounds.

I am now writing this on my plane from Thessaloniki to Athens, some Greek guy is snorting and sucking back snot like there's no tomorrow, I don't know where he is going to put all that phlegm that he is about to bring up. The flight is only 40 minutes but I have to move so I don't get any greenies on my Bill Shankly T-Shirt. My new seat may give me a good view of Athens as we land, pity my digital camera battery is now exhausted after its use this week. Anyway back to my tale after such a rude interruption.

Well the long trek home was truly on. By the time we reached Thessaloniki it was nearly au revoir for the Fistas and Pete. A few final pints and a plate of mixed kebabs and potato wedges rounded the day off nicely with my travelling companions. The camaraderie of the Reds on the road really shows the true spirit of the football fan, what it should be and generally what it really is, good decent people enjoying life. A number of my companions thoroughly enjoyed and deserved the win. They had been to all Liverpool's European games, bar Deportivo La Caruna I believe. Magnani-mously though they were acknowledging my individual undertaking to make this trip on my own. I had to do it this way and if I had to do it again I certainly would. It is much easier than you think if you like people and share the same passion and dreams as they do. It was never going to be that hard, you only need to take that first step out of the door. I would recommend it to anyone, it is the most amazing experience, you meet great people and you have memories to cherish for the rest of your life.

As I bid farewell to my travelling companions, I slipped into my hotel for what turned out to be little more than a freshen up and a little nap. The alarm went at some ridiculous time, and I had the first decent three hours sleep since Tuesday, and that had to be enough to finish my travels with. From Thessaloniki I took a 40 minute flight to Athens for a connection to London Heathrow. A somewhat tortuous route home but it didn't really matter that much.

I remember exactly where I was when the enormity of Wednesday night hit me. It wasn't behind a goal in the Attaturk, it wasn't in a bar in Taksim Square, and it wasn't any part of my epic train journey. Don't get me wrong I had wonderful feelings in all those places, but my thoughts were always focused on getting to Taksim, getting the train, getting to Greece, catching my train, there was always something I had to aim to do to make it home. Now I was sitting in Athens airport with plenty of time to catch my flight to London and I bought the Friday editions of the Daily Express and Daily Mirror as they were splattered with amazing pictures. To see the effect it had on the people at home, the outpouring of joy in my home city brought tears to my eyes. I am not going to apologise for that, I don't know if anyone noticed but who cared. No one cared on Wednesday night and now was no different. Every bit I read, every photo hit home and affected me deeply. At the game you get so wrapped up and so worn out emotionally that it can drain you and you feel more relief than anything. The effect of the events can become slightly subdued until you revisit them.

Let me explain. I don't get to as many games as I would like, but when the Reds are on TV I kick every ball, shout, swear and kick bins (just ask Nikki), and it gets worse every game. When I go to games I am still really passionate and vocal but for me it is much more bearable. I know I can do as little at the game as at home, I can't affect events on the pitch. Well this is where I am proved wrong and Wednesday night did that. There is now an unbreakable belief that I, as one of 40,000 people, won the European Cup. Ask the mighty Milan, the millionaires of Chelsea, Juventus and Olympiakos, Do we make a difference?

The homecoming pictures, to me at least, show what is great about my city, my home, and my heart. Pete Wylie got it right in his song, Heart as Big as Liverpool, Heart as big as my city' and heart won us the European Cup.

I am now flying over Milan on the way to London from Athens. It's funny, normally when the sun shines silver glistens. I can't see anything glistening and that's because the trophy is shimmering on the banks of the Mersey.

My sojourn was starting to draw to a close, but not that quickly though. Heathrow to Euston in 33 degrees Celsius on the tube is not the best experience after my exhausting week away. But I was heading back to my family in Liverpool who were looking forward to hearing my adventures. Not one Cockney congratulated me on winning the European Cup, and I was still visibly a Liverpool fan. They come a very poor second to the Turks, Evertonians, Geordies, Scots and even no matter how begrudgingly a number of Mancunians. Even my dad in Majorca was feted for his Scouse accent and affiliation by Geordies and Scots (to be fair you do expect it from them though). Cockneys though, nothing - jealous bastards.

The train to Liverpool was something quite different. People were desperate to hear my story once they found out I was actually there. Being the shy and retiring sort, they had trouble coaxing my stories out of me (no chance I talked all the way home). They didn't get the whole story you have just had though. Lime Street Station 'TAXI!!!!' not Taksi anymore. The driver told me how good Liverpool had been the two previous nights before and the place still seemed to be buzzing. Stories of the nightmare returns from John Lennon Airport filled me with great joy in one way, maybe my way home was long and arduous but I had the experience of a lifetime with none of the nightmare delays. He also gave me his copy of that evenings Liverpool Echo which was quite brilliant, ' I can always go and get another lad, have it on me'. Welcome home. Back home everyone wanted to know, my dad returned from holiday on the Saturday morning and finally admitted that he couldn't hold Rome in 1977 above me anymore, until he realised that he has held the European Cup and I haven't. Well he is happy, but Istanbul was spectacular.

Saturday still held more travelling after reading every newspaper and seeing every bit of coverage I could and seeing my nephews who had been to see the team come home was great. Daniel had his blow up European Cup and made me have my photo taken, just like Steven Gerrard! Well nearly. Tom and Matty (mum Jeanette is an Evertonian and usually a bitter one at that, but don't blame the kids eh!) were shouting 'Cisse Cisse' at the tops of their voices as the video of the homecoming came on again and again. Ian, their dad, is a Red and Tom who is only eight has been to two homecomings already, what great memories for ones so young.

My final leg of the journey was by car to Manchester and the last flight to the Isle of Man and home. Planes, trains and automobiles but without the big fat fella (John Candy that is not Jan Molby) and I don't think I am as funny as Steve Martin. Nikki won't agree with that though, she will say I think I am as funny as him. She can't wait to read this as I couldn't get all of it into my text messages (which hardly made any sense). I like to use predictive text (well I don't understand teenage text speak) and don't always check it, so even I didn't know what I was sending at times, especially when I have had a few drinks. The flight was about 45 minutes and as I landed on the Island, I had completed five plane journeys, four train journeys, one coach journey and one car journey, which had covered thousands of miles and taken five days and ten hours. All to hinge on a lone penalty well past midnight in the middle of Turkey. But the experience will stay forever and hopefully now with you after reading my journey.

I never got to finish the ticket fiasco story, but it pales into insignificance now, it doesn't seem to be that important. But needless to say I am still waiting for a refund from Parcelforce for £56. My ticket didn't arrive until an hour before I had to leave for the airport on Monday morning and the relief was tangible. Imagine how much I would be suing them for if I had not got to Istanbul for the night of my life.

MasterCard couldn't even cover it as it was PRICELESS!!!

—◊◊◊—

11

New Beginnings

It's Monday. It must be Dubai! Only joking. Life's not that glamorous, but I am off to Dubai for a couple of days to work, once again expenses paid - that is my hotel and food, not beer (the company I work for are well wise to that abuse). If Istanbul (on that glorious day) was where the west meets the east, Dubai is where the east is invaded by the west in an amazing show of wealth and opulence. Dubai is changing its demographics dramatically from a sleepy creek 40 years ago to an environment that puts Las Vegas in the shade. This is Expat heaven, or for me I am sure it would be hell, nice to visit but give me that little gem in the middle of the Irish Sea any day. The Isle of Man. A green oasis in life's hectic merry-go-round, it's like England twenty years ago (or more) and it's nice to keep it like that. There is little crime to speak of, although even here the drugs menace has reared its ugly head, and with a heavy heart I must say the problems come from the drugs capital of England, my hometown Liverpool. The tentacles of drugs money will not leave any of us alone now.

This looks like my last trip away for a while and that includes the football too. My wife Nikki is nine weeks away from giving birth to the next Kenny Dalglish, or, if it's a girl, Kelly Dalglish. Have a look and you will see what I mean. She is football mad and I can always picture her singing "You'll never walk alone" in Istanbul. Kenny definitely brought her up right. Either of them and I am on the right track. This trip brings home how much it all means. I miss four days of Nikki taking great delight in feeling the baby kicking like Kenny, whilst for me it feels more like it couldn't kick its way out of a paper bag (I can't feel it, a bit like Everton's strikers in the nineties). It's no fun for me being away. I am past that entire going out on the lash while away. My job is responsible and I like to be professional (anyone I work with should not be laughing at this stage), but I miss being at home. I miss Nikki loads and I miss my comfortable wonderful life, *and* it's sometimes difficult to find out how the Reds are getting on. It's weird as travelling often coincides with games in Europe that I have fancied for years, but I suppose that's the price of success. Well, as I said, a little person is now well on the way and must surely come out of the womb with 'sponsored by MasterCard' stamped right across its head, or in my case, probably it's arse. Nikki has said that my duties **WILL** include the cleaning of the wrong end. I don't mind everything that's happening, the cost, the time, the energy, and the devotion to the new life that depends upon you wholly. I am, however, concerned about the first chicken korma nappy (without the chicken that is). I am gagging now at the thought of that sight and as for the smell, let's not even go there. I might get a surgical mask and wear a pair of shades to take the edge off, which would alter the perspective completely. I would only be able to smell my aftershave and the sights would be all in grey.

Writing this book on my laptop helps pass the lonely hours whilst I'm travelling. There is only so much work you can do and I always like to be prepared prior to leaving the office, so on the way somewhere I am only tidying up and preparing myself by reviewing the forthcoming days' materials. See, I told you I was professional, didn't I? I find that the old adage "to fail to prepare is to prepare to fail" usually rings true. I don't like being caught out by a lack of preparation, but also if I don't know something I hold my hand up and find out what I need to know. People know when you haven't got a clue about your chosen specialist field. I do work in a specialist technical field now, and I am pleased to see I'm often referred to as such. If you remember all that time ago at the beginning of the book, what motivates me is the acceptance that goes with being knowledgeable and a source of support to others (not really, I just like getting paid for talking a lot, which would be my chosen subject on Mastermind). Travelling is becoming the main opportunity to get my thoughts down on paper. It's all starting to get a bit manic now as we head towards the birth of the wonder child (I call it that as I wonder how it actually happened, I could swear I was asleep).

Today it may be a bit tougher to write as, on board this Emirates 777 Boeing super-douper all-singing, all-dancing aircraft, there are numerous distractions. They have an entertainment system that's going to make the seven hour flight fly past. "Ice" they call it and maybe because it's that cool. It has over 500 channels of entertainment, which includes videos on demand, films (new releases and old favourites), comedy, sports, drama, arts and music. Then there are the music channels; hits from every year since the fifties, all the latest releases, the essential albums of yesteryear from U2 to the Clash to Frank Sinatra. Then, to round it off, there are classical musicals from the magnificent 'Les Miserables' to Disney's 'The Lion King'. How am I going to choose? The first can of Budweiser will give me time to think. As you might be able to tell, there will always be a part of me that sees myself as a scally from Liverpool who's landed on his feet, and can't believe his luck.

No, I am going to get my writing done, as this may be one of the few chances I get. Everybody I know, especially those with kids, have taken great delight in telling me that my life will not be my own once the little un comes along, so I had better take the chance whilst I have it! One of the lads in work recommended that I go home at night and video my life as it is, because it will never be the same again and you can look at it as the good old days. Well, what I would be videoing at the moment is not really like the good old days, it is one long round of decorating and tidying up. Nikki is in her nesting phase and nothing is ever tidy enough. To be fair, with me around it was never going to be that tidy. I have all my excuses for my untidiness 'I like the house to look lived in' is usually a favourite, 'yes, but not by a gang of gypsies' is often the answer. To be fair that would be unfair to gypsies. I am relaxed (or is it lazy? Take your choice). By the way we have just passed over Frankfurt - just trying to keep you in touch with the life of a travelling writer. Even here on the plane I am unable or unwilling to do housework, I have the crumbs from the complimentary snacks spread all over my lap. The tidying up at home has now taken on immense proportions as I am decorating the house from top to bottom. Suppose it's my own fault in a way. We bought a new build house, you know the sort - the builders use as little paint in the decoration as possible and the same bland colour all the way through. After two years it was starting to look shabby (if you looked closely enough) so to get out of decorating we decided to move house. A bit drastic you might think, but it was my choice not yours. The plan worked absolutely perfectly, Nikki fell pregnant (result, it works!), we found a stunning house where virtually nothing needed doing, not even a lick of paint (it looked like a house on one of those better property programmes), the kitchen was worth 40 grand alone. It was going to cost us a fortune. As you see everything is in the past tense, because it all fell through. We just couldn't sell our house in time, which is unbelievable as it was great (except it needed a lick of paint obviously). Maybe we just got the wrong punters through the door, all lazy bastards like me! Once it fell through the house hunt was off because it was too close to the birth to really look, find and move.

That's fine though, because where we live is great. We only considered moving because the house we saw was so good. We live in a house with a big garden, with grass and plants and stuff, a pergola (for the uninitiated, this is a big wooden thing) with chairs and a patio. All the things I never thought were important as a kid, or even a young man, all of a sudden mean the world to me, but it's also thanks to the wonderful woman I share the place and my life with. She is the inspiration for this book, she gave me belief in myself and shows me understanding, and even laughing at some of the stuff she's read before. She also loved the writing because it's me, so if it never gets published or no one ever buys this book I have still been a great success. It's amazing the feeling I get when

I write it. I don't feel daft with some of the stuff I write, it just comes out right from the heart and I am loving it. All thanks to my beautiful wife and now mother-to-be of my child. It wasn't like that when I met her. I was resigned to being a bachelor after a small number of failed relationships, I say a small number because I don't want you to think of me as a freak that can't hold down a relationship. I was just unlucky and was guilty of maybe some poor choices or maybe being too easy going as I invariably ended up getting stitched up. Well, when I met my wife-to-be I was single, happy and thinking I was going to be like Cliff Richard (not the gay slurs, just a bachelor boy until the day I die). I had given up on the marriage, children and happy family life; it was easier thinking it would never happen than trying to make it happen all the time. When I met Nikki, I was relaxed and confident, so I must have been really attractive and a real catch (well with a name like Salmon what would you expect). To be fair in the previous nine months I'd had a great time. I had travelled loads, spent loads and had loads of fun. That's a lot of loads (sounding too much like Cilla Black for my liking). I had been to the United States twice with mates. Hit the strip in Vegas, drank New York dry, saw the wonder of Niagara Falls, the old people on the boardwalks of the poor man's Vegas in Atlantic City, the sights of Washington and the Grand Canyon, and to top it off, I had also been skiing (or drinking, take your choice) in Italy where I nearly broke both my legs on the last day due to an excess of alcohol and lack of sleep (about 25 hours total sleep in seven days). Top all that off with two-day trips to follow the red men in Europe in Barcelona and Cologne (Bayer Leverkusen really). What an opportune time to mention watching the red men as we are just flying over Istanbul. Istanbul is everywhere now rather like when you buy a red car, or as at present when your wife is pregnant you see loads of red cars or pregnant women, or pregnant women in red cars (how I can tell I don't really know but I am sure it happens). Istanbul could have been the word you never wanted to hear again but now it's the sweetest sound. Just as I have a real passion for following the Reds, I have a real lust for life, and this transfers to my relationships with friends and family, to my travels and my career. I was lucky that I realised early on in life that you should never waste an opportunity and seize every chance of happiness.

Anyway, back to the trips to watch the red men. It was Barcelona at the Nou camp and Bayer Leverkusen in the Bayer arena. Both within a matter of weeks of each other. I went to Barca with Robbie, Mongoose and the omnipresent Zil. He was like dog shit, I couldn't get rid of him. Only messing. I couldn't ask for better company. Friends were vastly important at that time. When I look back, my life was at a crossroads and if I had taken a different path my life wouldn't be as it is now. In October of the previous year I had split up with the girl I moved to the island with, and I was left with a big decision - as The Clash so rightly said 'Should I stay or should I go?' Due to the good mates I had made and the support of family and friends I thought 'don't run away, stay and see what happens'. Nikki is what happened and the rest is history and history in the making. I am going to have my own little dynasty, it was obviously fate. God finally looked after the nice guy, well that's the way I looked at it.

Now I am going to have what I always wanted a wife and family of my own. It's true it is all I ever wanted, but thought I wouldn't get. At 37 a life on the lash following the Reds wasn't a bad second best though. I don't think I would have been that unhappy, but now I am deliriously happy. For the last 10 years, I have been just plain Uncle Keith (or Uncle Keeeefff), now I am going to be "Daddy". Our Ian and Kev are going to get their own back for me visiting their kids, winding them up and then pissing off and leaving them to deal with the aftermath whilst I return to my nice single or married life. I had this great life but missed what I would see as the greatest thing of all, a child. I have thought this since I was in my early twenties when Mike (my best man ultimately) had two young boys and I was as jealous as hell. But he was jealous of my life travelling the world and watching the Reds. Hopefully if you haven't found it already you can see what I mean. Writing this book brings it all together. It softens the blow when you are not watching the Reds, I will have something equally as good to do. Don't shout it too loud but it will probably be better (as long as mini me plays up front for the Mighty Red Men).

The flight was great and seven hours later I emerged from the plane into the oven that is Dubai. This time I had put my foot down and got a decent hotel. Well, if you're travelling half way across the world you don't want a Travelodge do you? I was met at the airport for the first time ever and after the usual waiting ages for bags I was escorted to my transportation, a top of the range Chauffer driven Mercedes. The driver offered a tissue (I was excited but not so much so that I needed a tissue) this is the way to travel. When I got to the hotel, my car door was opened for me by one gentleman, my bags collected from the boot by another and a young lady greeted me. She said she would take me up to my room, and escorted me up in the lift to the 36th floor. She explained everything the hotel had to offer, gym, pool, spa, sauna, restaurants etc. Everything you could want from a five star hotel. At the 36th floor, straight to my room. She showed me in. Wow! It was tremendous. Very opulent. She asked me to sit down and I thought 'hold on this is taking service far too far, I am a married man with a baby on the way'. It turned out that she only wanted me to complete my checking in details, no waiting at reception for me. To be fair I found it all a little disconcerting, getting treated like a God just because I had paid to stay. It doesn't really sit well with me. Just because I have a bit of money in my pocket doesn't make me any better than anyone else.

I spent a whopping 60 hours in Dubai, which is crazy really because by the time I got used to the three hour time difference I was ready to fly home and get used to UK time again. It's amazing how big a difference three hours really can be. Going to work at 9 am in Dubai is still only 6 am in England, and in the Isle of Man it's 20 years ago still, so three hours really doesn't make that much difference does it? I miss home and especially Nikki as we spend most of our time together. We have great fun, never argue and things are just right. So when I am away we miss each other terribly. It's easier being the one away as you are generally kept busy (especially in less than 60 hours in a foreign land). The person left behind has a normal life that is far from normal, because there is a big gap. Nikki went away for work last year and I didn't like it one bit. I was lonely and really bored! I won't moan about the shortness of the visit to Dubai, as it was my choice to cram all the stuff in and stay away as little time as was required. It makes for a hectic schedule but I want to be there for Nikki as much as possible and see as much as possible, feeling the little one move (kick like a mule according to Nikki). As I've waited 40 years, I am going to make the most of it. The thing is, my job's great and going to places such as Dubai and South Africa where the work I do is enthralling and the relationships I get to build become so much stronger than if I'm at the end of a phone thousands of miles away. Seeing different cultures has been an amazing experience that maybe I wouldn't have had without the need to go for work. Witnessing the differing cultures of Africa and the Middle East has been brilliant. Also work pays the bills for the idyllic lifestyle I'm lucky enough to have. Now it will have to stretch to the substantial amount of nappies that mini me is going to use, especially if they are as full of shit as me!

In 60 hours though, I got my fair share of things done. Two full days in work, one night out and one and a half hours skiing. Yes you heard right. Skiing - in Dubai! They have an indoor ski area that rises hundreds of feet and includes a full blown ski lift. For about 25 quid you can hire skis, trousers and jackets and get a lift pass for two hours of skiing or snowboarding. You can even get lessons if required. The only things you had to purchase extra was gloves and a beanie hat. I made a mistake I thought I wouldn't need a hat, it would be all right, but after a couple of runs I found it was freezing and one was definitely required, (well it was 90 degrees outside). I thought when in Dubai do what the locals do, Ski!! It was good to be fair. It took about four minutes on the ski lift to get up to the top and then about a minute to get down from top to bottom. It was challenging enough for me due to the tightness of the run compared to the usual wide expanses that I'm used to on a mountain, but it was the closest thing you will ever get without going to the mountains. I had been skiing in the February to Lake Tahoe in California USA when it was 50 degrees Fahrenheit (very pleasant) so this was back to the days of freezing cold skiing. On that visit I really got my confidence and thoroughly enjoyed it so this was a great opportunity that I just had to take up. The snow, even though artificial, was great and I didn't fall flat on my arse once (yes I am that good at it now). My knees were a bit buggered the following day though. If you are over to Dubai, take a day off from the beach and have a go.

By the way there goes Istanbul again. I can see it on the downward Sky Camera from the plane. Technology is wonderful. It keeps bringing Istanbul back and I can picture Stevie G lifting old big ears again and again. So it really all does come back to football.

I thought Dubai was to be my last trip away but I had to find a way to escape the endless pre baby decorating. The house is a three-bed semi but feels more like the Forth Bridge, as the painting never seems to stop. That is one of the stupid facts I picked up on my way to here. They never stop painting the Forth Bridge near Edinburgh because due to the weather up there every time they finish painting they need to start again. The other useless tit-bit I trot out on a regular basis is who won the cup in 1927? It's Cardiff City by the way and the only time the cup left England. You'll never guess where I learnt that one from? It was 'It ain't half hot Mum' and don't ask why. That line was trotted out when Cardiff

City unbelievably made the 2008 Cup Final so I know it's true.

—∿—

Well six flights in four days and two time zones and I have only been to Jersey and Guernsey. The time zones refer to the pace of life in Guernsey, which appears to make the Isle of Man seem like it's at the cutting edge.

The island of Guernsey is tiny, it's six miles by three miles (and that's if the tide is out). Still costs you a tenner in a taxi though from the airport to the Capital St Peter Port. The richest people you seem to meet on these islands are (surprise, surprise) taxi drivers (I hope they never find out who they have in the back of the cab though). The funny thing is half of them are Scousers with a similar story - went for a season's work in the seventies and been there ever since. At the start of the conversation you can just detect the touch of scouseness that makes you think they may be from the Royal Borough of Bebbington on the Wirral. By the end of it they are back to being from the tough end of Huyton or Kensington (Kenny). By the way, so am I. The professional in a suit travelling on business is replaced by the lad who goes to the match. They always get a tip and the journey flies. The catalyst to the change is always the question 'which part of Liverpool are you from?. As soon as I say 'do you know Walton Vale', their guard goes down and they know they don't have to pretend to be from a nice suburb to impress me. Travelling to the Islands for me is classed as missionary work and I love to meet other missionaries on the way.

There is the odd exception such as this morning when the taxi driver said to me 'what's a Manchester lad doing in the Isle of Man?' Cheeky get! He was soon put straight and even though he tried to get off the subject he didn't perform well enough to get his tip. I have been mistaken a number of times for being Scottish, Irish (both understandable considering Liverpool's roots) and even Welsh but never a Manc. The Welsh one was highly embarrassing as I was in a lift in Las Vegas with three posh mates (from the leafy suburb of Mossley Hill and they felt far superior for it as well) when this fat Welsh get said "I know you three are from Liverpool but what part of Wales are you from?" and directed it at me. Well they were pissing themselves weren't they, until I pointed out they must have sounded more Scouse than me and they wouldn't be allowed back into their privileged leafy suburb when they got back to the UK.

It's not just the cabs you meet Scousers in, it's the offices and also flying between Islands. It's amazing when Maggie Thatcher's screaming scull Norman Tebbitt told everyone to get on their bike and look for work, loads of Scousers got on a plane instead and headed for Jersey. It wasn't just a Scouse migration - there are thousands of Scots and Irish in the Islands too. Unemployment in the eighties affected every working class area not just Liverpool. You may say it was the best thing that ever happened because they all seem quite content with their lot and are earning money you'd find difficult to get in Liverpool. You may be thinking about the plane I mentioned - well I was travelling to Guernsey for the day from Jersey and that is an adventure in itself. I like to think that fate exists in all sorts of different ways and you really fall upon good things by just opening your mouth. You see loads of people who never say a word on a plane or on a train and to be fair they are the poorer for it. Don't get me wrong I am not like the nutter on the bus you can't get away from, it takes two to tango, and both parties must be fairly open and interested in someone else to start a conversation. As a society the British are not that good at it actually. I find us as a race to be fairly insular and suspicious overall. That is why if you're not insular you stand out, and like-minded people can tune in right away, whilst the rest of the plane is desperately trying to tune into your conversation secretly wishing to get involved.

The flight to Guernsey is fairly special and something everyone should try at least once, unless you don't like flying. Actually you really need to like flying and even then it is a bit of a leap of faith. The leap of faith is required because a small plane is the way you get there if you need to go and can't take all day about it. Anyone reading this who is used to going on holiday to Spain, Greece or the Canaries may think the planes they go on are not that big when you compare them to a jumbo jet. Well the Trilander plane you travel to Guernsey in is smaller than a Ford transit van I'd say. About 5 feet wide and maybe 20 feet long, so you certainly are flying on a wing and a prayer. The scary bit is that there is only one pilot - what happens if he croaks when airborne? The good bit is that you only fly at a thousand feet and it takes a little under fifteen minutes. When they call your flight, you are taken on to the tarmac to stand by the plane. Your boarding card has a number written on it and you have to wait for your number to be called by the airline staff 1 and 2, 3 and 4, 5 and 6 - you get the picture. Usually I don't mind who I get as most people on the plane are travelling on a days business between the two Islands, but sometimes I get the nutter and it is the longest fifteen minutes of my life. Inside the plane it can't be described as luxurious in any way, it looks like they have taken the off cuts of your grandma's old couch and cut it into bits and smashed it into place with a hammer. Oh, I forgot to tell you, that you actually have to climb into the plane through a door on the side of the fuselage, and it is one of seven doors on the side. Access is gained by using a step they kindly place on the floor for you. It is one step away from gaining access like they used to in the Dukes of Hazard (arse first through the window)

My travelling companion today was still to be decided, and as we took to the tarmac, I wasn't particularly fussed as I was armed with a copy of the Times (well the sports section is great in it). A fifteen minute journey during which you can't usually hear yourself think because of the sound of the propellers so no great loss if I got someone who couldn't be bothered talking that early in the morning. As the numbers were called out '5 and 6' and I headed towards the aircraft, a lady was soon by my side and with a nervous smile we greeted each other with a good morning and being a gentlemen I offered her the opportunity to enter the aircraft first. I didn't realise though that there was no elegant way of entering for a lady so I averted my gaze. As we got in she turned and apologised for her inelegant entrance to which I replied 'don't worry love I deliberately looked the other way'. Immediately the question on her lips was 'which part of Liverpool are you from?' All of a sudden a soft accent became Scouse and I chirped 'Walton Vale, why where are you from?' She replied 'Huyton' and the next obvious question for her was 'Are you blue or red?' She must have had her fingers crossed as my response of red was met with a beaming smile. Needless to say this was going to be a great fifteen minutes with one of my own.

The lady was called Brenda and by the time we hit the runway at Guernsey I had found out that she spent most of her spare time following the Mighty Red Men around Europe and the itinerary in the near future would be taking in Bordeaux, and she had recently returned from Istanbul. It comes back to what I said before, from just an incidental or accidental meeting you meet great people who can inspire you even further. When I told her about this book, and what it was about, her interest was so warming, that yet again I feel that I need to write this story for all people like Brenda and myself for whom the passion remains so strong. As she lives in Jersey she can relate totally to my position of watching from afar and being unable to do anything other than curse and keep your fingers crossed when the Mighty Reds were playing. She said that she usually turns the telly over if the other team look like scoring and turns back over when the danger has gone, and it generally works! Well I have my own habit, which is that I leave the TV and go into the kitchen and pretend to do something until the danger passes. The other thing I do is go upstairs to the toilet when the other team are attacking or have a dangerous free kick. It might have something to do with the fact that I am shitting myself, quite literally obviously. These things work though as the opposition very rarely score.

Superstitions are another thing. Lucky shirts, trainers, underpants anything that I have been wearing when the Reds have won. I defy anyone to say they don't do the same. The one superstition I really keep to is when I am flying away from the Island to watch the Reds I always say hello to the fairies (or the little people) at The Fairy

Bridge (a famous landmark in the Isle of Man). Don't laugh, it always works and we won the European Cup, nothing to do with Stevie G or Jerzey Dudek it was all down to the fairies and me. Sounds a bit gay that though so I won't go shouting it and definitely wouldn't want it to be a headline in the Liverpool Echo.

Brenda, by the way was one of the select band of people who managed to get to every game in the European Cup run which resulted in that glorious night in Istanbul. You have to take your hat off to people like her who spend fortunes following the Reds, surely devoting all their spare time in the process. One of the things that people like Brenda have to do is also get off an Island first, no quick day trips. It has to be planned and results in a number of days off work, at least four flights, and a hell of an expense. Fair play to them all, they were fortunate, as was I that it resulted in glory. Others often are not so lucky. I remember lads at Peterborough who would travel to the outposts of English football for nothing in return. Carlisle in the LDV Vans Trophy on a wet Wednesday night doesn't carry the weight of a European Cup Final, but then again neither does Macabi Haifa in pre-qualifying, especially away in Ukraine. There is always someone there though, sad, mad or just plain passionate, you choose your own word. I have done my own share of 4am returns home following a wasted away trip to watch the Reds and do you know what? If I wasn't married with a baby on the way I would probably still be doing it. I loved my time doing it and it was cut short by circumstances, but if I was still doing it now, I would not be who I am and as happy as I am. The way I look at it is I had a wonderful time doing that and now I have a wonderful time doing something else, with a little fix of the old days thrown in to the mix. You can't do everything in life but you can be a little greedy at times can't you? Wait until my little one grows up then I will have a great excuse, trips to football. I will sell the benefit as the child's education, boy or girl, it's a great lesson in history! The baby is not even born yet and I am mapping out the future, at least until Nikki hears about it.

I once read a great book by a guy called Alan Edge called 'Faith of Our Fathers' which claimed that football was the one constant in life and, it could become your mistress. I like to think that it is the best stopgap that you can get in your life while you are either waiting for something or you have lost something. You can always go back and football will be your mistress, your friend or your confidant.

The 2nd of November 2006 will live long in my memory and football is firmly knocked of its shelf, if getting married had not done that already ('it had love honest!'). 2.15am and a wonderful little boy was born, get in there! I wasn't bothered if it was a boy or girl to be fair, as long as the baby was healthy and Nikki was okay. But a boy was a bonus especially with footballer's legs and an eye for goal, he was breastfeeding and scored immediately. Nothing else mattered except this little bundle blinking into the light and staring up at his Mummy and looking into the lens of the video camera at his dad. No crying just interested in everything. After sixteen hours of Mars Bars and Lucozade Sport, I was knackered, and Nikki said she was a little tired too, well done love.

Charlie is his name and very fitting it is too. It means 'free man' so Nikki reliably tells me and he is his own man. This book was originally written for me to share with my child. In the process of writing it, Charlie has come along and he now has full ownership of it. I can only write it when he is not around and as such it has taken me a lot longer to write than I thought. But this is for him and I hope one day when he can read it himself he will be proud of his dad's efforts. The weight of responsibility I felt on his arrival is unbelievable; I am responsible for his moral upbringing, his honesty, his self-belief and most of all his passion for the Mighty Reds. At just two weeks old he was watching the glorious night in Istanbul and the Cup Final glory in Cardiff. He is sung to sleep with Liverpool songs in the style of a lullaby (not that of a club singer I may add) and he loves it when his dad sings him the proper song at Kop sound levels, especially the 'Fields of Anfield Road'.

He is the future, he is my future and he is Liverpool's future, he will certainly know what it means and how it feels to be a follower of the greatest Club in the world.

Now that's what I call new beginnings!

—〜—

12

Nou Camp or bust

How does a married man with a 15-week-old child get to go on his own to watch the Reds in the Champions League in Barcelona? Make a big thing of Valentines Day the week before? Promise to take the family on holiday, including the mother in law? Look after his son on a Saturday night so his wife can go out? Or marry the right woman? All of the above! Well not really, I just married the right woman and it was a pleasure to do the other things, and yes I actually did them.

As with Istanbul, Nikki made sure I went to Barcelona. I have missed out on so many trips with the Reds over the years and she is making sure I get to what I can. The deal was if Liverpool got a decent draw in the last 16, she was fully behind me going. Well Barcelona is what I call a decent draw, don't you? The past two European Champions going head to head, it doesn't get much better does it? The other draw I was looking for was Real Madrid. That was the draw I know thousands of Reds would have liked. Real Madrid were not in the best of form and the city was a new and great place to go with a wonderful football stadium. Well I am getting the best of both worlds, I am going to take in Madrid and Barcelona in two days. How does that happen I hear you ask? I blame the Internet.

The Internet is a wonderful thing. No longer do you get ripped off by having to travel on expensive day trips organised by the club, you can get anywhere you want in any way you want. Following my sojourn to Istanbul, there was no longer any appeal in a day trip to Barcelona. A day trip isn't exactly a day trip for me anyway, everywhere from the Island has to be a three day trip. The day trip would have cost £250, going from Manchester at 7am on the morning of the game, (therefore having to leave Liverpool at 4am), and getting back to Manchester the following morning at 3am at the earliest, you could forget that! I started looking for different ways to get there.

As soon as the Champions League draw is made, the web sites of the no frills airlines get battered before they clock on to the fact an English team are playing abroad. As soon as they realise, the prices go through the roof. First of all, I had to get off the Island, and cheap flights are as rare as a decent England performance under the charismatic Steve Mclaren, it would cost about another hundred quid, so in total £350 for a day out was a bit steep. I was looking at options ranging from 6am flights from Luton to Gerona (an hour from Barcelona), Stanstead to Murcia and a four hour drive, Reus to Luton returning at midnight on the Thursday night meaning four days off work. One of the strangest was Frankfurt to Barcelona for a whopping 6 euros return. The problem was it would cost me two hundred quid to get to Frankfurt after having to take a Planes, trains and automobiles journey to get there.

I then remembered my air miles? I have been flying with British airways for three years to Jersey and London, and having completed over forty flights, I thought I should have had enough air miles to get to Australia, never mind Barcelona. Well it turned out I had just enough to get me to Barcelona, which was a great result. Well it would have been if I could get a flight, BA had done their homework, and the day of the game and either side were blocked out meaning I couldn't use them. They had done me again, after missing out on using them flying to England to get to Istanbul when I missed out by an hour. What's the use in having them if you can never use them? One last thing to try was to fly somewhere else and get a cheap flight to Barcelona. Calling Madrid! It worked, I could get to Madrid from the Island for just the cost of the tax, about £70 (cheers Gordon Brown Chancellor of the Exchequer at the time). The flights from Madrid to Barcelona are plentiful with a flight virtually every hour and for only £60. So instead of day trip for £350 I was looking a three day trip for a hell of a lot less.

Now all I had to do was get a hotel in Madrid and try and get tickets to see the mighty Real Madrid against Bayern Munich, which would be an absolute bonus. The draw had been kind and Real had been drawn at home the night before Liverpool were taking on Barcelona. The Santiago Bernabeu holds eighty thousand, so it should be a piece of cake to get a ticket. Some piece of cake - it's murder trying to get one, they are like gold dust on the Internet and when you find them, they're £150 a throw. There is no way I am paying three times the amount I am spending on watching the Red men the following night against the European Champions.

I am definitely not paying that much towards David Beckham's final pay packets at Madrid. I will just have to blag my way in, or jump in with the Germans from Munich. You never know, the Spanish will probably think that I am German as they have no chance at understanding Scouse.

As is normal with my trips abroad, there is a ticket fiasco to talk about. It should be straightforward shouldn't it? I want to go, I buy a ticket, I go! Ta-Dah, as simple as that, but its not anymore, because of the loyalty card Liverpool introduced, rightly so, to protect the fans who travel regularly. There is very little chance to actually get a ticket if you can't get to the European games. Because I live on a rock in the middle of the Irish Sea and have a job, which now limits my opportunities, it is a real struggle. So I have to covertly get tickets from my sources, which will remain nameless to protect their fan cards from being taken off them.

It started off really straightforward. One of my mates, who goes away in Europe, was able to get a ticket because of his travels this year, but due to financial constraints Barcelona was a step too far. He guaranteed me my name was on it as soon as he got his hands on it. True to his word, he excitedly rang me and duly informed me that he would get the ticket the morning of the Liverpool/Everton Derby game.

Here the story really starts, with the Reds having to settle for a draw with that small club across Stanley Park (as Rafa Benitez chose to refer to Everton after a Derby game). My mate decides to drown his sorrows and, to cut along story short, the ticket ends up as a pile of soggy paper.

Okay that's not enough information. Try this because it's true, maybe not believable but true, honest. He heads home and picks a manhole to go swimming in - ignoring the barriers, he heads feet first down a bloody big hole filled with water. He heads off home on the train still dripping and squelching as he sits uncomfortably in his own mess. Well, it wasn't the first time, manhole yes, sitting in his own mess, no. He gets home, trips on one of his daughters' toys (yeah right) and then falls from the top of the stairs, cracking his skull on the banister and gashing his head open.

What about the ticket? Well I'm getting there. He heads to casualty, and his jacket, covered in blood heads to the washing machine. The ticket is destined to become a mushy mess. Nightmare! He makes a drunken phone call to me where I think he is taking the piss, it's so ridiculous, it just can't be true.

Sunday morning arrived and it was true and the ticket can't be reissued, well bugger it I will go without a ticket. I would get in, I am quite confident about that. It doesn't make him feel any better though poor sod. He worries too much about me, ridiculous accidents happen, and they always happen to him. As it was, one of the other lads came through for me big time, and ticket sorted I could look forward to Sunny Spain.

Monday night was spent checking and double-checking everything. The time of the plane, the tickets, my passport, my credit cards and cash, throw some socks and clean undies in, and I was sorted for my trip to the Nou Camp. I must have checked ticket, passport and cash about twenty times, well I could get by wearing the same undies for three days straight (don't tell Nikki). I went to bed dreaming of victory at the Nou Camp.

In six hours time (5.15am), the alarm would ring to signal the start of my journey. Charlie had other ideas. He was obviously more excited than me about my journey and he couldn't wait. The baby monitor burst into life at 4 am and there was no sending him back to sleep. He started laughing and not even a chorus of 'We won it five times' would settle him. He was awake to see me off. When I left for the airport, he was still giggling away, and the none too impressed Nikki wished me a great time through somewhat gritted teeth. She could see what her three days alone would look like, and it wasn't as good as my three days were going to be.

—⁓—

An evening with Capello

I was on the red eye to Manchester at a little after 7am, so I left the house at six for the fifteen minutes drive to the airport. With the modern wonder of online check in I only had to turn up and walk through security due to the lack of baggage, well how much space do three pair of undies take up? As you know now there is a famous Isle of Man custom, which is where you have to say hi to the fairies on the way to the airport. Now I don't care what you think, it really works (Istanbul was a prime example) I can't remember a time when we got beat when I asked for the fairies help. This trip was to be no different, besides it also makes sure I came home in one piece.

I thought I would be the only one going to the match, but even in the Island there were lads on their way however they could. I never saw the dozen or so lads again anywhere I went, so god knows which way they went to get there. The bonus is that the flight time to Manchester is a mere 35 minutes, but even before I settled into my seat the captain was announcing a 20 minute delay. The worry was that if the delay became any longer, then the connection, which was tight anyway, would become unmanageable. It would put the whole trip into disarray. We were still expected to arrive at 8am though, which would give me plenty of time to make the connection to Madrid.

Bonus, landed on time, that's one worry out of the way. I wouldn't miss my flight to Madrid, so all my plans are still spot on. It only takes a little thing like missing a plane to bugger things up. Forty minutes in Manchester and then on to sunny Spain, just enough time to wish my dad happy birthday, 72 years of age and still moaning like mad about the Red men. He is still amazed that I can get time off work during the week to fly to Spain, and that I can afford it. As always, he wished me safe travel and told me to look after myself. Even though I am a big boy, he still worries. Now I have the little fella, I know what he means. I can see me being the same when Charlie grows up and follows the Mighty Reds.

How big do you think the plane was? A holiday jet to Spain? Well you would be wrong it was absolutely tiny, one seat on one side of the aisle and two on the other, holding about 60 people in total. The pilot didn't really impress me when he said we were going to be delayed by twenty minutes, but he tempered this with the fact that this was one of the fastest aircraft at Manchester Airport. The reason I didn't believe him was that he followed the statement by saying it would take two and three-quarter hours to fly to Madrid. That threw me as I thought the flight would be less than two hours. I sat there gob smacked and thought how stupid I had been thinking that Spain was two hours away from us. I settled down behind a couple of plane spotters.

How did I know they were plane spotters? I had seen them at Manchester, with their binoculars and note-books, noting down planes as they landed or took off. 'That one's got two wings and some wheels'; 'So's that one, and that one and that one'; 'There's a white one'. Oh how the hours must fly by! When we landed in Madrid and took the bus to the terminal they were at it again. I just don't get it! Do you?

The flight wasn't without its scares. As we headed over the Pyrenees and hit the jet stream, the plane lurched and dropped, then again and for 20 or 30 minutes (well seconds but it felt like minutes) the plane bounced all over the place. The woman opposite me went white and nearly broke her husbands hand by squeezing so hard. Even the stewardess put her Hello magazine and nail varnish down and breathed deeply, looking somewhat concerned. Its funny, all sorts of thoughts go through your mind when things like that happen, is it one flight to many? Did I really need to go? That tea is burning my lap.

Drama over and we edged nervously into Spanish airspace and on towards Madrid. Now is it me, or do most places look the same as you fly in? As you drop through the clouds, row after row of industrial units, cheap housing and thousands of cars greet you, you really could be anywhere. As we landed, the plane's taxi to its stand took an eternity, and the pilot still managed to park nowhere near the terminal building. The bus that collected us turned into a spotter's paradise, I swear they were going to wet themselves with joy. They nearly climaxed as we had to wait to cross a runway as a jumbo jet landed, they didn't even check to see if they had already spotted it, once again what pleasure can you get? It was as bad as the train spotters in Crewe in the old days, just shows how advanced we are now with our travels. Air travel is the new rail travel without the shit carriages and smell of piss, well British Airways are trying their best to catch up with British Rail but are not quite there just yet. Barajas Airport (pronounced Barajas Airport, yeh like I'd know anyway, I've only just about got past Hola!) is magnificent, well the new Terminal 4 is. It is a planners dream and must have cost hundreds of millions of euros to build. It's so new, there is still wet paint. From the arrival gate there was no long walk to the baggage claim area, no we got a tube train. Oh yes, and then a long walk to the baggage reclaim. I wouldn't mind I didn't even have any baggage. I needed a rest by the time I got out of the terminal.

—⁂—

Its 1.30pm and now to the city and destination Bernabeu. Real Madrid are at home to Bayern Munich in the Champions League. I thought I would get my disappointment out of the way early on, if I couldn't get a ticket I would find a decent bar in the city centre, bit of Tapas, couple of beers and chill out for the night prior to my exciting day tomorrow. The wondrous Internet had not promised tickets unless I wanted to pay at least three times my Barcelona ticket. I wasn't that interested in seeing the fading giants of World football that I would have to prostitute myself on the streets of Madrid just to afford a ticket. Preparation on the plane made sure that I knew I had to get to Terminal 2 and then the Metro in to the city, change at Nuevo Ministeros and one stop to the Bernabeu. Piece of cake! To be honest, Madrid makes it easy for you to get around quickly and in clean carriages as well. It didn't feel at all claustrophobic like the London Underground. The design of the train ingeniously creates one whole carriage and you can walk from one end of the train to the other, so even when they are really busy, there's never a crush. I thought I would be the only one going to the Bernabeu but I was joined by half of Munich who had just jetted in, back packs and all, direct from Germany. The Germans were in two camps, one wore combat gear or khaki green bomber jackets (their naughty boys) and the other wore Bayern Munich branded gear with a backpack and Lederhosen. The Germans walked round wearing the tightest trousers I have ever seen. I was half expecting them to squat into position and start slapping their thighs as an oompah band serenaded the onlookers. But no, they just looked as if they were freezing their bollocks off, and as the trousers were so tight, they were already looking like walnuts. I was in the train carriage with some of their normal fans from the way they were behaving. Their excited chatter, whilst in German, was the language of any excited fan, the trip of a lifetime for many.

After a swift Metro change, we arrived at the Santiago Bernabeu stop and headed for daylight. Coming up from out of the ground, within 50 yards you are confronted by this monstrous concrete clad stadium. It was just about seven hours to kick off but you would swear it was only two hours to go. The streets outside the ground already thronged with people; the souvenir sellers were doing brisk business in anything with Madrid on it, from a million David Beckham shirts of varying quality to the standard scarves, flags and hats. There must have been about 50 scarves to choose from, the dual Real Madrid and Bayern Munich one being a big seller.

I thought there would be no chance of a ticket, but in a vain attempt to secure an evening's entertainment I headed to Gate 42 where the ticket office is (Got on t'internet to find that out too). There were queues at the windows so I decided to ask the guard if they were they selling tickets for tonight. 'Habla Inglese Signor por favor' (roughly translated as do you speak English please sir). Thank the lord he did because I had no more Spanish left in me after that. He asked me how many did I want because I may not get five or six together, I only wanted one. He told me which window the guy spoke English at and within seconds I was standing in possession of a 70 euros ticket in what they classed as stage 2, not the best but not the worst and not in the gods. As I was sorted there was no time to waste around the ground now, I was going to head into the city, sort my hotel, and then see a bit of what Madrid had to offer.

The Metro was straight forward, no changes, and within fifteen minutes I was once again heading into the Winter Sunlight at Place de Espana in the heart of the old city. I walked up Gran Via, Madrid's main street, a bit more glamorous than Church Street in Liverpool, more like London's Oxford Street. I found my hotel, a Best Western just off the main street in what looked to be a dingy side street, but as I found out later, that was only because it was siesta time. I walked straight into reception confident as you like, as the Internet had made things so easy it was a breeze. 'Hola Habla Inglese' oh yes English speaking again, bonus! I proceeded to pass over my booking confirmation and wait for my room key. I had spent hours deliberating over rooms on numerous Internet sites, comparing rooms, prices and availability and this was the best bet for me. The girl went through all the room cards ready for that night, nothing! Then she tried again. She did but still nothing, so she buggers off and speaks in Spanish, how rude, to her colleague, then loads of shoulder shrugging, huffing and puffing and more Spanish. Oh just get on with it, how difficult can it be I have a reservation for tonight, the 20th of February, for one single room for 60 euros. Well let me tell you how difficult I made it for myself as the girl politely, almost apologetically, pointed out that I (yes me, master of travel) had actually reserved a room for the 20th March (not February). Dickhead! My frustration turned to wanton embarrassment as I could picture myself sleeping with the tramps in the cardboard homes on the Gran Via. By the way, their cardboard homes were something you may see on Grand Designs but they still smelt of piss and contained the obligatory moth eaten Alsatian with three legs and a plastic bowl round its neck. I was ready to beg but unbelievably, even though it was my own fault, they looked after me. 'Gracias, Gracias, Gracias' (I was really stretching my vocabulary now).

I headed up to my room rather sheepishly and I realised I had been sweating like a pig and really needed to get some food inside me. No time to waste in the room (yeah I know minger) just enough to hear that every time someone had a pee or a dump upstairs, I was going to hear about it. The waste pipe ran within the wall between the bedroom and the bathroom and I could hear every log banging against the side of the pipe on its way out of the building.

The streets of Madrid were bathed in a watery sunlight that belied how cold it actually was out there, so layering was the key. As the day went on, the zips on the hoodie and the coat found their way up around my double chins. By about 4pm it was nudging towards freezing. By this time I had taken advantage of the local Tapas offering, well a quarter pounder with cheese at McDonalds was as close as it got, bit of quick sustenance is always on hand. Madrid is vibrant, with a touch of the arrogance that London has, but only a touch. I had my mini guide (£3.50 from Waterstones, complete with Maps), which became my bible for the afternoon in order to see as much as I could before heading back to the Bernabeu. At least kick off was not until nearly nine o'clock local time, so I had enough time to see a fair bit. I headed to Puerto del Sol in the centre of the old city and I was met by hordes of Bayern Munich fans, all in combat jackets and a mix of denim and Third Reich combat trousers. When I say hordes, there were about a hundred of them all crowded round a six pack of San Miguel. They didn't actually seem to be doing anything except posing in their ex-army gear for the locals to gawp at, who didn't really bother. The usual vans of Riot Police were within arms length, but the van inhabitants were spending the afternoon yawning, waiting for Munich to give them a song or some excuse to draw their batons (as if they need one). Twenty four hours later in Barcelona, anywhere there happened to be more than ten Scousers, then noise, generally singing, would be bursting into the air and letting everybody know about their presence.

With nothing happening here, I headed into the back streets and around the sights the Palacia Real, the Puerto del Sol area and the Plaza Mayor (pronounced My-ore, not Mare as I called it in my Scouse accent). Besides the random Bayern Munich fan, the streets were fairly normal for a Tuesday afternoon. A couple of hours wandering was enough for me and it was time to head back to the Bernabeu for the evening. I gave myself a couple of hours as everyone tends to get there early, or so I thought. The Metro was comparatively empty and as I rose from the ground once again (makes me sound like Jesus) the streets were only a bit busier than earlier in the day. Night had fallen and the magical night match atmosphere was very much present. Car horns were blaring with their owners trying to knock over the errant day tripper trying to get a great snap of the stadium. Police Sirens blared around the concrete towers (sounding just like the Italian Job), weird how the sirens in Europe have a noise totally different to the UK police sirens.

As I knew my way around the stadium, I headed towards Gate 36 where I would be going in but the metal shutters were still down and access was denied. I took a stroll towards the side of the stadium where I assumed the players arrived and I found myself next to a barricade where a full scale military operation was in progress to greet the arrival of the teams. To my left was about 200 yards of cordoned off road, behind me was TGI Fridays doing a roaring trade, to my right was a rather large roundabout that's main purpose in life was to cause motor mayhem, and right in front of me was yet another souvenir stall doing a roaring trade. From the way the police were acting, any minute now the Real team would be passing my way, so I thought I might as well hang on.

Forty minutes later they arrived and I had put up with pissed up Spaniards breathing and burping on me, some woman laughing like a horse with the teeth of a young Celine Dion (go on, picture it) and dozens of ignorant Spanish gits bumping in to me. On the road it was no better, as the police were making a simple task of holding back the crowds so the team could get through into an art form in chaos. Too many chiefs controlling too many pricks in my book. They didn't have a clue and they were turning back anything in a vehicle, even those with a big blue light and siren blaring, until the top man told them to let the ambulance through. It was probably for a policeman who had fallen off his horse, because I have never seen such poor horsemanship in my life, or was it such poorly trained horses, probably both.

You might ask why did I stay if it annoyed me so much? Well at 41 I still get quite excited at a teams arrival and probably wanted to see who was on the coach, could I see Beckham, Gutti or Raul? Ruud Van Nistelroy already had some copper on his back (well he looks like a horse doesn't he?). It was worth the wait as, when the coach came from my right hand side, the klaxons blared, the crowd cheered and the scarves recently purchased from the stalls began to twirl. As the coach passed me a thousand cameras burst into life, and strobes of translucent light pounded the coach. I could actually see …. no one I actually knew, all I could see was the side of a big coach with the Madrid crest on it as it sped past at 30 miles an hour. A let down, yes as always, but I still do it, every Cup Final I will do the same.

Excitement over I thought I would get into the ground, find my seat and milk the atmosphere. The turnstiles lead right on to the street, hence the metal shutters which stay firmly shut until they are ready to open. They would be dead easy to bunk five minutes before kick off with a big crowd. The turnstile reads your bar code and you're away into the stadium, so I hurried through into the stadium following the signs to my seat. Bonus! It was right ahead of me and I could see the pitch through the tunnel ahead of me. I came out in the big blue seated arena with the lushest green pitch I have seen in years. 'Hola Habla Inglese' works again as the steward directs me to my seat. There must be some mistake, its right in front of me and only twenty rows from the pitch behind the goal just to one side and in line with the corner flag. But surely I was going to be in the gods spotting dots due to the cheapness of the ticket? The atmosphere was incredible, yes incredibly quiet with the most noise coming from the touchline to my right where a huge number of film crews and presenters were ready to go live for their own version of the Champions League special. There was no one as vibrant as Andy Townsend and Ally McCoist when they did it for ITV. There was 'Der Kaiser' himself, Franz Beckenbaur, looking every inch the Teutonic God he undoubtedly is. This Cathedral of football was deserted except for a couple of thousand Germans already singing their hearts out up in the gods at the other end of the stadium. This is why I had seen hardly any of them in town. They had got off the plane and come straight here to get the best view. There was no point really as the Spanish don't allow you a good view as an away fan, Madrid, Barcelona and Valencia, from my own personal experience, put away fans in the furthest part of the ground where they have as little influence on the proceedings than if sitting at home watching the game on Sky.

I got as far round the pitch as I could, to within touching distance of the tunnel, just in time for the 80 year old Oliver Kahn (well he goes down for the ball as quick as an 80 year old) to come out for his geriatric warm up. It started to rain heavier and it looked like the rest of the players, and Madrid in particular, didn't want to come out and ruin their immaculately coiffured barnets. Eventually, Madrid emerged and within spitting distance was Beckham, Roberto Carlos, Ruud 'the Horse' Van Nistelrooy, Casillas and the tiny (for a centre half) Cannavarro and the Blonde God Gutti. Every one of them world famous, and all warming up within twenty yards of me. When I say spitting distance, I don't mean literally, but the dirty Catalans did the following night, spitting at Steven Gerrard. I wandered back to behind the goal and watched Casillas put through his paces by what I would describe as the worst goalkeeping coach I have ever seen. Even I could kick a ball better than him, and I can't say Casillas was stretched whatsoever. He was lucky he wasn't called on for some time in the game, and then his first action was to take the ball out of the net.

On the way back to the goalmouth I spied a red flag up in the gods 'Maloney's Bar – LFC'. Scousers get everywhere! The flag was draped over the real Madrid sign and was a certainty to get moved sooner rather than later. I wouldn't like to be that steward, as Scousers never give up, the flag got moved and reappeared time and again. From my position I could see the lads blagging the stewards. 'Non comprende' always comes in useful, blissful ignorance when you are in the wrong is a wonderful Scouse trait.

Realising I was starving again, I headed to the food bar, past the man selling cushions, which you can throw on the pitch when you are pissed off, Goodison had them years ago, but it used to take them ages collecting them all in, so they gave up and obviously flogged them to Real Madrid. All the butties looked a bit worse for wear but I thought I'd try the least dodgy one, the ham looked alright, so here goes 'Hola, Habla Inglese' No not this time, only Spanish, what was I going to do, blag my way in Spanish? Well I had learned enough by now. I got the ropiest butty going, it was like bacon but not bacon, it was spiced pork loin, and all I can say was it didn't give me the shits so there can be no higher praise. Kick off was approaching and the atmosphere was as dead as the butty, then literally two minutes before the teams came out, the Madrid crowd burst into life, well just about. They certainly don't believe in wasting their energies in their support of the team.

Being used to the wonderful mosaics the Kop produce, and the ever endearing sight and sound of the Kop in full voice for "You'll never walk alone", Real Madrid's efforts were certainly second rate. Even though they were coordinated by a man on a megaphone and another on a microphone, the best they could do was hold some bin bags above their heads. At least the game lived up to its billing of two great teams and it produced a classic. With Beckham pulling the strings and pulling his team mates up by their boot laces, Madrid took an early lead through the man they just can't drop, Raul (ask Michael Owen who admitted he doesn't even look for Madrid's results – says it all doesn't it) and the fans stopped moaning about Capello and his team and cheered them on, well at least until the Germans dragged themselves back in to the game with a looping header from the Brazilian defender Lucio. The Germans in the top tier could be just seen going ballistic and slapping their thighs, tightly constrained within their lederhosen.

The looping header was good enough for the Germans, so the Spaniards took advantage themselves with a header going to the back post, leaving Kahn stranded and Raul jumping into the defender and putting the ball in. Munich, prompted by the waif like Hargreaves, were giving as good as they got and they forced Casillas into two great saves. Then just before half time, Ruud the Horse put them in front from a great free kick from Beckham. I sat there thinking 'get Barca out of the way and we would take either of these'. Even though it was a great game, they were both crap, really poor shadows of what you would expect from allegedly two of the best teams in Europe. The Madrilenos (Madrid fans) were now getting behind their team at last and the atmosphere was now excellent. Half time changed all that. The atmosphere went dead and the second half failed to live up to the excitement of the first. With the excitement waning, the crowd became restless as the Germans took control and looked to be the more likely to make a break through. It just wasn't going to happen though, and Madrid edged closer to victory and the obligatory time wasting substitutions which are such a part if European football. The Germans were still giving it a good go and brought on three attackers.

With just about five minutes left, I decided to make a move, something I would never do it when watching the Reds. I thought I would get to the Metro before the crowds and take the chance to get in to the city, otherwise I may be there for hours (as it was to be the following night in Barcelona). As I headed to the Metro, I heard a roar from the ground and I gathered Madrid had scored a fourth. But it must have been a groan not a roar as the Germans had scored a second through Van Bommel who, after being abused all night due to his Barcelona links, thoroughly enjoyed his goal and his celebrations did nothing to endear him to the Real Madrid crowd. How do I know? I had made the right decision, and within fifteen minutes I was in the city centre and I saw the goal back in the hotel as I was eating my tapas from KFC. I was fading fast now after Charlie's early morning wake up call, and tomorrow was going to be a long day and night, so wiser to get my head down than sample the night life which was only just starting outside. As I lay my head on the pillow another log banged down the pipe and I dreamed of the Nou Camp.

—⁂—

Cilla wants her teeth back!

So said the banner unfurled on the Ramblas late in the afternoon with irreverent humour linking the well known professional Scouser Cilla Black (lorra lorra laughs) and the wonderful Ronaldhino, then still at the height of his powers. The banner was proudly displayed, showcasing the ability of a Ronaldhino look-alike ball juggler. It must have been an easy way to make money, but a short career once Ronaldhino moved on, unless he followed the Brazilian to Milan.

Match Day and what a match! Would it live up to Real's match the night before? Of course it would, and as it turned out, a million times better.

7am is an early start for a kick off at 8.45pm, but I still had to get to Barcelona. Sleep had been interrupted by some Germans shouting in the hotel corridor, probably four floors up, but it sounded like it was right outside my room. Marble floors are not the best soundproofing for a hotel, and they had scored a late away goal that was to prove crucial and take them through. I would be pissed and very loud as well. God help anyone sleeping next to me tonight as I bounce off the walls coming back.

Deprived of sleep, I managed to shower and get my stuff together to be out the door by quarter to eight. I headed out into the crisp Madrid morning, expecting the city to be buzzing into life in the morning rush hour. Besides the tramps going through the bins outside KFC, the Madrid morning had nothing much to offer the intrepid traveller. It was really quiet as I walked down to the Metro to go to the airport. I had been in Madrid for less than eighteen hours and Catalonia was calling. Within half an hour, I was at Barajas Airport and looking for my 9.30am Spanair flight to Barcelona. In eighteen hours, the Metro had been like a second home having spent nearly as much time on it as in my bed. After facing a rather leery Spanish airport security guard who suspected me as a terrorist for having dared carry a small bottle of water with me, I realised I was now starving and it was time for breakfast.

'This foods shite' a voice bellowed out across the café, pure Scouse and obviously disgruntled with the choice, 'Not eating none of this crap' behind me more dissenting Scouse voices. It can't be that bad can it? Yes it was, stale pastries and over brewed coffee were the staple diet in Terminal 2. I looked around and, as an airport regular, even I was disappointed by the choice. I have spent so many hours in Gatwick and Manchester airports over the past couple of years to never be too disappointed, but even I was lost for words. That was until I saw from the corner of my eye the ropey old bird putting out some fresh (well fresher than anything else on offer) doughnuts. Oh doughnuts and coffee, what a breakfast, Nikki would go mad at me though.

Breakfast sorted, I looked for a seat, and there in front of me was a lad who had a Liverpool shirt on beneath a smart leather jacket. He looked like he was one of The La's ('There she goes' the classic pop song). Any chance of a conversation with a Scouser who wasn't moaning about the food, I'd take. 'Anyone sitting here mate?' was met with a big smile and we got talking. Within minutes, we discovered we had things in common and were swapping stories and getting on like the proverbial house on fire. Neil was working in Madrid at the Stock Exchange, and had been for the past ten months, he lived right by the Bernabeu and was really enjoying life in Madrid. He couldn't quite get used to the nightlife where the locals go out at midnight, and after work on a Friday, he still went out at five and got pissed out of his tree, never quite working out why he was going home when everybody was just coming out to play.

When I met him, he was gutted as he had been let down by some of his mates in Liverpool. Promised a ticket, he booked his flights from Madrid to Barcelona only to find out 48 hours before he was due to fly that there were no tickets and none of his mates were even travelling. So there he was Billy no mates in Madrid airport and talking to me, things could only get better! At least I promised to be his mate for the day and he could meet up with my mates in Barcelona. I had been in the same position in Cologne a few years earlier. If you go on your own, you will meet new mates, at least for the day. We are all there with one common aim: to watch the Reds and have a bloody good day out. Neil took the view that instead of wasting the money on the flight by cancelling, it was worth the day out and if he got a ticket, so much the better. I started making calls and texts to my mates who were already Spain-bound, someone might have had a spare.

By the time we hit the tarmac at Barcelona, all Neil's worries had flown away. We disembarked at opposite ends of the plane and boarded a bus to take us the twenty miles to the terminal building (well it seemed like twenty miles). It put the bus ride at Madrid airport the day before to shame. We ended up on the same bus but separated by about thirty Spanish businessmen, all suited up for the day ahead, checking their mobiles and Blackberry's to see who had really been missing them in that all important 55 minutes where they couldn't speak to anyone. They nearly dropped their electronic devices when this Scouse voice boomed 'Keith, I got a ticket laddddd'. The thirty Spaniard captains of industry turned to see this Scouse rock star look-a-like beaming from ear to ear and texting like a demon, obviously to his mates who had let him down in Liverpool, just to rub it in. By the time the bus stopped and we got off, the relief was tangible. Everyone without a ticket always says it doesn't matter if you don't get in but it's not really true. It matters like hell, who wants to travel half way across Europe to not get in and watch it in a bar where no one speaks English or supports your team. Neil had to make his arrangements to collect his ticket and the bonus was that it was free of charge, from a sponsor of all things. So we arranged to see each other on the Ramblas later on, that's the wonder of mobile phones it is so much easier to meet people.

I had to head to town and get my digs sorted out for the night, because I didn't have any. I headed through arrivals, and chose the nothing to declare channel and came out into the arrivals area, which always disappoints me, as no one is ever there to meet me. There were Liverpool fans everywhere and streams of people travelling from all over Europe to get to see tonight's match and most of them were wearing red.

Compared to Madrid, the transport into the centre was poor, still only ten euros but twenty years behind the times. First of all you have to walk miles to the train station from the terminal, and I already had a sweat on compared to the crisp air of Madrid. We were definitely in a warmer climate, even though rain was heading our way over the mountains that surround Barcelona. The train crawled through the building sites and scrub land that passed for the suburbs of the city, a tortuous twenty minutes later (seemed a lot longer) the train pulled into Sants Station on the edge of the city centre and here it was all change to the Ramblas. Transferring platforms was unbelievably difficult, go out to go back into the same area confused the life out of me, was I heading in the right direction or not? Well just follow the Scousers, which was a good call as they had fluked the right way and within minutes we were ensconced in same carriage for the one stop to Placa de Catalunya at the head of the Ramblas. With everyone in the same boat, it was time to swap experiences between eight of us we had; me with my epic journey, one lad travelling from Berlin and six boys who were doing a week in Ibiza and flew in for the day and night and would be back on the lash in San Antonio by midday tomorrow.

We were still all laughing at the fact that all six of them, with no deodorant, would be sharing a double room for the night, especially as that would be luxury compared to the fourteen of them who shared in Dortmund a few years earlier. We headed into the fresh air and sunlight of Barcelona. Well it was grey and ready for rain and Placa de Catalunya is the busiest junction in the city with all the fumes that come with the traffic. Never mind blinking into the light, we were blinking in disbelief as we passed the Sightseeing Bus Stop. There, in all his glory, was Chris Kamara, the most excitable man in the world. He can make a drab 0-0 draw in the LDV Trophy on a wet night in Grimsby sound like the Champions League Final in Istanbul. Well he could if you didn't know it was a load of crap. There he was, about six foot four of him, complete with trench coat that looked worth a few bob, black polar neck and designer shades to complete the picture of elegance. One of the comedians with me shouts 'eh Kammy laddddd. All your bleeding money and you're getting the bus'. Oh he had been spotted and he was delighted and starting hurling one-liners back and forth as we kept moving. To be fair he was good craic and he got as excited as he did on Sky Sports. I can just picture him now on the open top red double-decker, shouting at people by the Gaudi Cathedral the 'Sagrada Familia'. 'This bus ride is amazing!! Never seen anything like it!!! It's the best ride I have ever been on'. Yes, but I bet it was still only as good as a 0-0 at Grimsby in the pissing down rain.

With the others all star struck over Chris Kamara, I headed down the Ramblas towards my hotel. I was walking against a tide of Reds fans all heading up from the statue of Christopher Columbus at the harbour. This is the usual dropping off point from the airport for the day trippers. The bars in the middle of the Ramblas were already doing a roaring trade and skinny white legs in shorts were seen in abundance. On top of the skinny legs were ale guts of varying sizes, neatly wrapped in some form of LFC merchandise, although not always neatly wrapped, with skin often peeping below the shirt and above the belt line. The bars are situated on the side of the street with two lanes of traffic between them, and the seating areas on the central reservation. The waiters could have been left here following the Barcelona Olympics, greying somewhat, but certainly fleet of foot, and no one was without a pint for long. The Ramblas is a mixture of life; bars next to aviaries full of exotic birds (whistling along to Fields of Anfield Road on this day) and those strange fellas who paint themselves gold, stay dead still and then scare the shit out of you by moving when you least expect it. Funny, everyone loves them. I think they should get a proper job, all they do is attract the pickpockets that the Ramblas is famous for. Full of shady gits, and the shout of 'watch your pockets' went up any time they got within five yards of one of our kind. Surely no one was thick enough to get dipped, after all legend has it that Scousers invented the art of dipping, years before Oliver Twist and his mates.

The hotel I was heading for was recommended by Nikki's boss Paul. He went on a skiing trip and stayed there. Work that out for yourself, skiing in Barcelona? He actually went skiing in Andorra, him and his mate on a lads skiing holiday with flights for a penny each way, (well that's a lie as there is always tax to pay, though thirty quid's not bad). Away from the wife and kids he thought he had it made. His wife must have put a word in as there was no snow, and there hadn't been for ages, so his skiing was very limited. Him and his mate had really had enough after three days and hired a car and went on the piss in Barcelona for three days. The Hotel Metropole, which he recommended was clean, cheap and close to the Ramblas so I thought I would give it a go. I had tried on the internet but with no luck and most of Barcelona was booked solid, so if there wasn't a room here I don't know what I would do as there was no plan B. Well there was, but it consisted of staying up all night until I flew home. I had done it in Istanbul just two years earlier, but the years had taken their toll and I was feeling knackered, it was only one o'clock and I was trying to stay awake for the match never mind the after party.

Turn left off the Ramblas by Christopher Columbus, walk five minutes and there it was, the Hotel Metropole. I won't bore you with my only Spanish phrase again, but it got its hourly airing and thank the lord he spoke decent English, 'What you have one room left and it's a single with a bed and a shower? Senor I will bite your hand off!' Within five minutes I was chilling out, waiting for Mongoose to return my call, not sure whether he had landed or not. I thought I might as well make the most of the room whilst I could. No point getting bladdered too early, I was sure I would be having plenty to drink once I met Mongoose. They had Sky News on the TV in the room, but it only kept bleating on about Iraq and how the British were pulling out, like it wasn't three years too late. An hour passed quickly and the belly started rumbling, so I made some room for lunch by having the obligatory new hotel room dump. Well I was paying for all the facilities so I might as well use them, except the bidet obviously, that's just a weird thing to do in my book. I had a safe as well so all valuables were put away from the greedy little gypsies on the Ramblas. All secured, I headed off to find some food. Last time I was in Barcelona I made the mistake of not eating all day and was bladdered by the time I got the Nou Camp. No such mistake today, I was off for some Tapas. Well I am sorry to say I failed again as I settled for a sandwich at Subway, well it's foreign isn't it (I know, its American, give me a break).

The Nokia sound burst to life and deafened the shop, Mongoose had arrived. With his travelling companions, Tommy, Muller and Tony, he was at his hotel, a big 4 star hotel out of the city centre and they were waiting for a cab to bring them down to the Ramblas. Whilst waiting they were annoying an Italian Football team who had made the biggest mistake of all time. Livorno had arrived in town to play Barcelona's rivals Espanyol the following evening in the UEFA Cup. The guy who booked the hotel (who has probably been sacked by now) had booked them into a hotel where a couple of hundred Scousers were staying. They were even more upset by what everyone was promising that if the Reds won, there would be no sleep that night. The Scouse contingent were taking great delight in taking the piss out of one of the lesser known teams in Serie A. As it turned out, the Italians got beat 4-1 the following night but I didn't hear what their excuses were, serves them right as they got the hotel bar closed before the Reds got back that night. See, God works in mysterious yet wonderful ways.

Remember those robbing Gypsies? Well add a couple of the local bar owners to the description of robbing bastards. 8 euros for a two-litre glass of beer when you could get a six pack for 5 euros, from yes, you've guessed it, the gypsies. I arranged to meet Mongoose in the Placa Real where thousands were gathering, a square just twenty yards off the Ramblas, but a million miles away with the sights and sounds of the travelling red army. This was the central meeting point, adorned with flags, empty ale cans and flabby Scousers drinking anything under the watery sun. The atmosphere was great, there was the mandatory 'kicking a ball as high in the air as you can' competition, closely followed by the 'who can you hit on the head with a ball that's been kicked as high in the air as possible' competition. The square was a great place to meet up. I met Phil from Scunthorpe. Scunthorpe? I hear you ask. Well, once again, these boys sit in front of me at the match and go everywhere. Phil puts his money where his mouth is and has been following the Reds for more than 30 years through thick and thin. It turns out he has a villa in Murcia (remember one of the many possible airports I considered) and four of them had driven up from there that morning with only three tickets between them. They had four now but the fourth had cost them 250 euros. As Phil said, between four of them and with the low cost of staying in Spain, it works out OK, and your mate gets into the match, that's what its all about at the end of the day. After a couple of beers, we start to make our move from the rowdy square and up the Ramblas itself. Liverpool songs are getting carried on the air, Songs about Rafa link intricately with songs about Luis Garcia and then "The fields of Anfield Road" and into "Poor Scouser Tommy". All sang by different groups in different bars within a two hundred yards stretch. The locals and tourists alike are out to gawp and enjoy the sights and sounds of the red army invasion. All good natured and all well received may I add. We were popular guests, well we were spending a fortune and giving free entertainment.

Hunger pangs were getting the better of us, and with ale to soak up, the Spanish version of Subway got a call on the way to the next bar. It's only when you stop drinking you actually realise what you have been drinking, then it hits you, the munchies! Starving, and in my hand a hot chicken baguette serenaded by potato wedges with coatings of mayonnaise and BBQ sauce. Oh that hit the spot, well for all of us but Tommy, who said he isn't interested, would he regret that later on? Tony started talking to some tourists from Israel, and he mesmerised them with tales of Liverpool and the wonderful Israelis who played for us, well Avi Cohen and Ronnie Rosenthal. Avi was famous for scoring at both ends the day Liverpool won the league against Aston Villa, and Ronnie was famous for what is described as the worst sitter miss ever, at Villa Park against Aston Villa (of all people). There was an open goal and he missed, we got beat and he never got over it. Forget the fact that one season he virtually won the league for us with crucial goals and he scored a winner in a local derby, he is unfortunately remembered for that miss and that alone. The kid was transfixed, and though not understanding every word Tony said, was obviously very impressed with our Scouse cultural ambassador. He has a lot to offer the City of Culture in 2008.

Muller, in the meantime, decided it was time to take a photograph with his new camera that he didn't have a clue how to use. Not realising that there were tables and chairs behind him he edged back to get us all in with the style of Lord Snowdon, and in true Princess Margaret style, he fell over the table, pissed. We nearly choked and

the shop cliental wet themselves, all except the manageress. She took great exception to the frivolity and the accident in her shop. She started shouting at us in Spanish.
Tony was trying to find out what she said, from her tone
he had assumed it wasn't complimentary. None of the
staff were too cooperative about giving any evidence
against their manageress for obvious reasons. Our
cultural ambassador had discarded the role and was a
complete pain in the arse. Tony had been popular with
all but the manageress, but now they were all glad to
see us go

Neil, remember him? He rang and said he was up the
Ramblas in the Jules Verne, an Irish bar that always get
their fair share of business when we are in town. By the
time we got there, it had emptied out as everyone was
making their way to the Nou Camp to carry on the party.
One more bottle and we were joining the throng on
the Metro. The train bounced all the way to the Nou
Camp, everybody was in the mood and you could
feel something good was going to happen. To be honest,
I don't always say that, usually I am more pessimistic
than optimistic after years of the Reds ruining good days
out with shit performances. Whilst it may have bounced,
it did so slowly as the driver stopped for ages at every
station and more and more people got on. So much so
there was a crush inside the carriage. Tommy ended up
protecting a little lad whose excitement was turning into
panic as the masses filled the carriage. Things are good
like that generally, you make sure the little ones are
looked after, and he shouldered most of the pressure to
the grateful thanks of the lad's dad.

—⧈—

The train arrived at Les Corts station and people exploded out onto the platform and up past the riot police lines into the night air. We threw a left away from the main crowds to find a bar down a side street where we would have chance of having a quick one before kick off. Only an hour to go now, and I was really looking forward to it, all bar the walk up to the gods in the stadium as I had left the oxygen mask on the plane. Mongoose went to the Bank for about the third time, what was he doing just getting a tenner out? We never quite got to understand why he kept going – did he not know how many euros made a tenner, or did he just not want to go the bar? Mongoose said that Banco Santander was, and I quote, 'It's shit, it won't give me any money', he didn't need it so what was he moaning about? Was he going to ruin the reputation of one of the biggest Banks in Europe when he didn't even need any cash? Funnier still, on his quest for cash that he couldn't get, he lost us and only found us after a frantic phone call. I swear he was nearly in tears (he will kill me for that, who cares he will have already spent a tenner for the read).

We found a little bar frequented only by Spanish so Tony went in, who didn't speak any Spanish, and ordered in sign language. Neil who spoke perfect Spanish, well perfect compared to us, stayed outside and started talking to some fella who claimed to be Xabi Alonso's mate. Well if he was, why was he wearing a Barcelona Scarf? Neil asked him, and that wiped the smug look off his face. With only half an hour to go to kick off, it was time to head up to the ground, twenty yards to the bottom of the road, turn right and there was the ground right in front of us all lit up like a space ship out of Close Encounters. The bonus was that we were at the right end and our entrance gates were right ahead of us.

Neil was in the Barca section, so it was goodbyes all round with the usual drunken manly hugs, from a guy who twelve hours earlier none of knew existed, and three hours earlier only I knew existed. He left with great wishes and fondness, top lad, that's what following your team is all about, a common purpose uniting genuine people for the right reasons. I scanned my ticket to ensure that once inside the perimeter fence, I was heading to the right gate, gate 23 and I found it, but we were all refused entry by the stewards, typical of Europe. It never matters what is on your ticket they just push five thousand of you through three turnstiles and if you complain you get a truncheon round your legs. We got in and headed up to our seats, once again don't bother about your seat just sit anywhere. Why do they bother actually giving you tickets I hear you ask, exactly! After what seemed like 50 flights of stairs but was probably only 40, we got to the top tier where they had allocated a whole strip to Liverpool which went from behind one goal and round to just past the half way line. Last time we came they allocated us four individual strips in each corner, what the reason for that is nobody knows.

As we reached the top of Everest, we came out behind the goal but there was no chance of getting in there as it was heaving being the first section you came upon. Mongoose, to redeem himself from his banking fiasco, suggested we go as far right as we could, as no one would be bothered walking that far. How right he was as we ended up in the last but one seated section. We headed through the tunnel to see the pitch bathed in floodlights and the centre circle covered by the now mandatory Champion's League motif. It's all about image and that's why it takes two days to transform each ground to meet the UEFA marketing men's minimum standards. The clubs are handsomely paid to transform their arenas with the correct branding and Champions league advertisers, no local car dealers or double-glazing companies here. Sponsors pay a fortune and get their money's worth. Within a matter of minutes, the teams were with us, arriving to the Champions League tune, even "You'll never walk alone" is brought forward at Anfield to accommodate it, that's sacrilege. We had just found our vantage point two rows from the back of this huge stadium as the teams kicked off. The players were dots and it takes more than a few minutes to actually see what is going on all the way down there on the green carpet. I finally found my eye sight range after thirteen minutes, just as Barcelona put the ball in the net, oh no, it was going to be a long night. Barca kicked into gear and started ripping at the Liverpool defence like a pride of lions picking at a barely alive beast they had just hunted down. The movement was excellent and, even from where I was, Ronaldhino could be seen looking one way and passing the ball the other way. It may be an old trick, but the Liverpool players were falling for it. Some desperate defending and the passion of Jamie Carragher ensured that the Reds didn't buckle and concede further. The referee, meanwhile, was doing an exceedingly good impression of Jeff Winter and gave Liverpool absolutely nothing, and some of his decisions were to baffle Spaniards and Scousers alike.

Half an hour of being played with like a toy, and Benitez had managed to ensure that his players took on his instructions and nullified the Barca threat. From being the toy, Liverpool started to probe their tormentors and started asking them some pretty testing questions, which they had no real answer for. Going at Barca was Liverpool's best form of defence and a minute before half time we were back level with a strange goal from Craig Bellamy. The Barca keeper, Valdez, seemed to be badly out of position as he took Bellamy's header across the line with is momentum. He looked to push it out, just in case the linesman had not noticed he was a yard across his line. Kuyt was on hand to bury it, making sure that there need be no inquest, though to Bellamy's delight, the linesman had already confirmed his effort counted. The hordes in the top tier clapped politely and shouted hurrah! Must be joking, we all went mad, and the Barcelona Ultras, a hundred yards to our right, didn't take too kindly and started to use that friendly "I will slit your throat" gesture that welcomes you to many European grounds. Sit down you and grow up Senor's.

Sit down was all they had to do after half time as Liverpool produced one of the most commanding European away performances they had ever had. The second goal by Riise was thoroughly deserved, and he was set up by Bellamy, which had a sense of destiny about it. I say that as the week before, Liverpool having no game because of their capitulation to an Arsenal under 10s side in the FA Cup, they spent the week in Portugal training and team building in the sun. The story goes that Bellamy thought the best way to build team spirit was to attack Riise with a golf club. Now whether you ever hear the definitive version of events, it is better to believe that Bellamy took more shots than Tiger Woods takes to go round Augusta.

Mongoose had said less than 60 seconds earlier that Barcelona were there for the taking and how right he was! All he wanted to do was to see Liverpool score at the Nou Camp and have something to cheer about. The last game we saw at the Nou Camp was pretty boring with absolutely nothing to cheer. It was notable only for Milan Baros coming on in an early game in his career for us, picking the ball up on the right touchline. Five yards from the penalty area he proceeded to go on a mazy dribble which took him across the face of the penalty area, to the left hand touchline, running the ball out of play ten yards from the penalty box, and we cheered that! He didn't get much better before we sold him. Mongoose wanted to see where all the Reds fans were dotted round the ground, and there were thousands of them. He got so excited when we scored the first that he forgot to look. The second sparked wilder celebrations than the first but we both looked to see thousands of dots jumping up and down. We were too far away to see the euro coins pinging off their heads, it was just like being at Goodison with the pies flying your way in the Gwladys Street end.

Besides the assistant referee saying there was four minutes of added time left to play, the only real threat to Liverpool was a miss-hit cross that struck the post. That would have been a shame to be denied by a fluke after such a performance, and we could have come away with more goals as well. Watch out Europe, we are panning the big clubs again, remember Juventus and Chelsea (well Juventus are a big club at least). The delight of thousands of Scousers cascaded down from the top tier and the middle and the bottom, they were everywhere. It was only after the Barcelona fans had made their exit, which was underway as soon as Riise scored, that we actually saw how many were in the ground. As Liverpool completed their post match warm down, they were applauded from all over the stadium. It must be great to see the joy you bring to others so many miles from home or at least your adopted home. Things must have been particularly sweet for Benitez, Reina and Alonso who made the move to Liverpool to make us great. Cheers Boys for one of the best nights out ever.

—⋙—

The night hadn't finished yet as we still had a party to go to on the Ramblas. We weren't on the first plane home, and the decision to stay had turned out to be a great one. The police kept us in for about 45 minutes, just enough for us to get our breath back and the streets to clear. After what seemed an age the police allowed us out of the seated area and we headed down the first staircase we saw. At the bottom, there was a metal fence closing off access but that felt the force of someone's training shoe and we just walked out on to one of the ramps that weave down the side of the stadium. We came out a different place than the police wanted us to, and the ramp we were on was above the one that the rest of the Liverpool fans were on. Lines of Riot Police penned them in and the sticks were out already, and one poor unfortunate was already getting a beating to show all the others not to mess. Protestations just met with more raised batons, the riot police really are bastards abroad. At the end of the match, all manner of objects came raining down on us and nothing was done. As soon as anyone moved in their direction, the sticks were out. When I say sticks they are about three foot long and carry some weight, you know if you get hit. As we saw what was going on down below, we moved on quickly so as not to draw attention to ourselves, and we headed to the exits where we thought everyone would end up. They took the escort at the other end of the ground to a different Metro and where the coaches were. Mongoose went looking for Muller and got carried away with the escort. Tony, Tommy and me decided to head to the bar we were in before the game and get a drink before getting the Metro back to the Ramblas. It was already closed, so we headed up to the Metro to go straight back, but there was no chance as we were met by a wave of people coming back out to get air because there were too many people waiting down below ground. So we went to another bar and got a beer to walk with and get a cab, but there was no chance of that either. We were stuck near the ground with no chance of escape for a while at least.

The bar by the Metro looked a good bet for a while. Tommy was now regretting the lack of food and foreign crisps were the best we could do unless he wanted to risk the tapas on the bar. There were only Anchovies left, and there is always a reason why they are left, they taste like piss. We were in there for ages and everybody was in that post euphoric state where you can't quite believe they have won and need to dissect the details. We got talking to some lads who had only arrived half an hour before the game and had to pay 500 euros for two of them to get in. The lads had flown into Perpignan in the South of France that morning and had a five hour train journey to get to Barcelona. The best thing about it was one of them had his twelve year old son with him and only told him the night before that they were going. The youngster was battling to stay awake, as this was obviously the best night of his life so far, his dad was making up for not taking him to Istanbul. There will be fathers in Liverpool for years to come trying to make up for that sin (in the eyes of their sons that is) can they ever be really forgiven?

The young lad wasn't the only one who didn't know he was going until the Tuesday night. Tommy, who was with me, also found out then, and had had to tell his missus he wouldn't be home for his tea on Wednesday.

The bar owner was trying to send out a message to us, see if you can work it out. The TV goes off, one by one the lights go out, half drunk lager mysteriously start disappearing. Yes that's right 'Piss off I want to go home'. Ok, we might as well head to the Ramblas, I already know it should be 8 euros from here. The first cab that stopped asked for 60 euros so he got told where to go right away. The next one said it would be whatever the meter said and true enough it was only 8 euros. Mongoose had been on the phone moaning about being Billy-no-mates in the Irish bars on the Ramblas, so he was very happy to see us again, bar a kiss on the lips, he couldn't have been more pleased. No room at any of the Irish Bars, so a big tapas bar was the best bet. Sorry again, no tapas for me, just beer and more of it. The atmosphere was great in there and Phil from Scunthorpe was in there so we had a great catch up of the day's events. Phil's a top guy who I have known for years in the Kop but never had more than a half time chat, so it was great to see him there. Before long, it was time to go. Obviously not of our own accord, but the riot police asked politely so we offered to leave to make their job easy for them. Well it sounds better than the truth, which was that they came in, took their sticks out, and started to manhandle people through the door. No thank you, I will just leave. As I said, they are the ones who cause problems where there aren't any. It wasn't just that bar, it looked like they were in the act of closing the Ramblas down for the night. As a matter of fact there was no trouble and no likelihood of trouble happening either, just nobody wanted to go to bed on a night like that.

We tottered off down the Ramblas, past the hookers who looked like men, and the hookers who looked like men who were men, and then the ones who were really just ugly women. You need to have your head tested going with something like that, as long as you have a right hand it is always going to be better. Mongoose, Tommy and Tony went to get a cab back to their hotel, whilst mine was within staggering distance. As I am saying goodbye to Mongoose, a prostitute started bothering us and a polite 'No thanks luv' seemed to do the trick. As Mongoose got in the taxi, I turned to walk towards Christopher Columbus and a hand grabbed my elbow. I turned and there was the prostitute again. She said '20 euro for blow job' so I said to her 'I charge more than that luv'. She just said '20 euro blow job' over and over again. After twelve hours drinking and little sleep, I just reasoned simply with her and said 'Listen luv just piss off' and to my amazement she did. A hundred yards on a woman headed towards me and undid her coat under which she had nothing on her top half and started fondling her breasts. At this point I thought, I need my bed, I am seeing things, this can't be happening, what was in that last pint?

—⁓—

Beep Beep Beep Beep Beep .... the alarm was going off already, but that cant be right, I hadn't even got into bed.

I obviously had, and I was waking up with a throat like sandpaper and Johhny Cash's "Ring of fire" playing in my head (very loudly). God, it was only 7am but the plane wasn't going to wait for me, it was leaving at 9.30 and heading back to Madrid so I could catch my UK flights. What seemed like a good idea at the time of booking now seemed such a bad idea. It was going to take me all day to get home and with a hangover worthy of the name. Well I was going to have to grin and bear it. I headed out into the clean air of the streets of Barcelona as the city blinked into life. To the early morning commuters, I must have been a sight to pity with my rucksack hanging off my shoulders and still pissed weaving down the pavement. I had taken the precaution in my sober state of ensuring I had enough water in the room to quench my thirst. At the rate I was drinking it I was going to have to have my own hosepipe ban.

I felt so bad that I wanted to share my pain, so I rang Mongoose to annoy the life out of him. You won't be surprised to hear that he didn't answer. I found out I'd done the trick though and woken him up and pissed him off. They had all day to spare before flying back home. I was on my way and things were not looking good, as the trains were not going to plan. I took the Metro back to Sants station expecting a short wait until the airport train. I had missed one by a minute, that's what I get for not checking the times the day before, I was too busy laughing at Chris Kamara. The next train was twenty five past eight and the last check in was ten to nine, it was going to be tight. I couldn't remember how long the train took but it seemed like an age. As always in Europe, the train arrived on time and departed on time, not like England, but as it did the day before it crawled, it wasn't looking good and I was calculating how much I would have to pay to get on the next flight, would I make the connection in Madrid to London? Was there another flight if I missed it? For once I didn't have the answers. I hadn't planned on being pissed and missing the plane. Then the airport came into sight and the train still couldn't be bothered speeding up. At 8.45 it crawled to a halt and there I was like a gazelle avoiding the wilderbeasts on the platform. Why is it that when you are in a hurry, you get stuck behind dozy gits who just stop dead in the middle of the platform and look for the way out? There is only one way out, it was the end of the line. I climbed the steps two at a time as the clock ticked on, and I was sweating profusely and the sweat stunk of lager, how pleasant! How far was the station from the check-in desks? Phew, they were right in front of me, a stroke of luck just when I needed one. The guy at check-in asked me what the hurry was, I still had ten minutes until check in closed, not according to their ticket I didn't! I headed through Security and picked up the Spanish breakfast of doughnuts and water. I had the munchies now and cheap no-frills airlines don't look after you.

As I headed to the gate, I wondered what had happened to Neil. We didn't meet up after the match, as we couldn't get to the Ramblas in time. I called him to say cheers and goodbye and was greeted with a grunt followed by recognition and an 'Alright ladddd'. He had as good a night as us and had fallen asleep at his gate after going straight to the airport. The adventure was nearly over for us both and my flight was getting called, so I left him to his self-induced coma and headed back to Madrid.

My tortuous route home was to fly from Barcelona to Madrid, Madrid to London Gatwick and then back to the Island. By the time I got to Gatwick, I was feeling much better following a healthy McDonalds in Madrid airport. I say healthy as the Tenerife Basketball team were there, stocking up on Big Macs. All these skinny giants can't be wrong can they? I had forgotten my early morning state until I went to drop the kids off at the pool (that's having a dump by the way) and realised my undies were the wrong way around. Too late now, I was too tired to be arsed to change them now, the Island called me home. It turned out I wasn't the only one, a number of lads from the Isle of Man had been to Barcelona and must have had some weird connections to get home, as I hadn't seen them and they were different to the guys on the Tuesday morning at the start of my journey all those days ago.

I walked into the house at six o'clock after three days, six flights, two great football matches in two of the world's best stadiums, too much beer and too little sleep. There to meet me with Nikki was Charlie, eyes wide open, delight on his little face and a shrill sound in his newly discovered voice. He knew what I had done as a Scouse missionary. That look was far better than anything in the days that proceeded. See football is not the most important thing, it's close but not close enough. The best will be when we share it together.

Oh alright Charlie if I must sing your favourite nursery rhyme once more …. 'We won it five times, we won it five times in Istanbul we won it five times ……'

—⟋⟍—

13

Sick as a parrot

This should have been the chapter where I'd deliver a glorious account of how the Mighty Reds progressed to Athens. How I took a week to get there and back, how I avoided the baton charges and tear gas with a ticket in my hand but still couldn't gain entry and my rightful place to watch the Reds claim a sixth European Cup.

However, I can't do any of the above. Notwithstanding the fact that the Reds fell at the final hurdle, and AC Milan gained revenge for my trip to Istanbul some two years earlier. Why? Because I didn't go to Athens, never had any intention of going and that's why they lost. Well that and a bad slice of luck. I watched the Reds succumb to the Rossienieri in a nameless and soulless bar in Majorca. It might as well have been on the moon as it had so little atmosphere. Besides me and my dad kicking every ball, there was no real passion for the game.

My European sojourn ended on that glorious night at the Nou Camp in March when only fools were dreaming of European glory. If I had been dreaming of European glory, do you think I would have booked a family holiday in Majorca during Cup Final week?

The truth is, the decision was forced on me. The Isle of Man was hosting the Centenary celebration of the magnificent TT races and for three weeks early in June, there was little chance of getting on or off the Island, at least as a family in an affordable manner. Nikki was due back at work in July after Charlie's birth and I had to travel for work so our options were limited, and it was looking likely that we would not have a family holiday. I didn't really expect the Reds to beat Barcelona so it served me right for having so little faith. Too many things get in the way of believing now and that is something you have to deal with. It doesn't make it easier not to be there watching the Reds, but if it's not your choice to go due to other circumstances beyond your control, that makes it alright doesn't it? No! It still got to me. I even looked at flights from Palma to Athens to see if it was possible to get there and back. It was but it would be a five day round trip at a cost of over a thousand pounds. Five days out of a seven day holiday, I would have been strung up. Whilst Nikki is generally supportive and tolerant of my away trips, I think......

After the defeat of Barcelona, Liverpool had a dream draw against a weak PSV Eindhoven side. I quite fancied a trip to Holland, but once again the gods conspired against me. I was in South Africa for the away leg so I couldn't get there. As it turned out I wouldn't have got a ticket anyhow and that was to become a recurring theme. I was planning to go to the home leg with PSV but I came back from South Africa with three weeks worth of the wildies (gastroenteritis to be medically correct). At least I lost a stone and a half (which I didn't even miss, fat get). The bonus was that Liverpool had cruised to a 3 -0 victory in Holland and they were ready to set up another semi final meeting with Valencia or Chelsea. My plan was to get to Valencia if they prevailed, or at least the home leg with Chelsea. After missing out on the semi final two years earlier I didn't want to miss it again. Ticket-wise the latter would be a tougher proposition though. A great plan! Well it would have been had it worked. Chelsea made it more difficult for me by scoring a late winner against Valencia to set up the all English Semi Final. The final still wasn't going to feature Liverpool though, well not according to the English media. I got fed up hearing about how United and Chelsea were going to both the FA Cup Final and the European Cup Final to set up the finals that everyone wanted to see! Who says so? Firstly that all English European Cup Final didn't happen as two English sides needed to actually get there and only one did (the wrong one according to the press). Chelsea didn't make it so the media changed their tune. Now the all English final fell to Liverpool to be runners up to Manchester United. They didn't make it either after getting outclassed by AC Milan in the San Siro. You could hear the pundits crying all night long. The wonderful FA Cup Final of everyone's dreams with the best teams in the country was supposedly a turgid affair. Thankfully I was on my way to Majorca at the time and I didn't have to listen to the sycophantic Sky commentary from Martin Tyler and Andy Gray, or the equally sickly BBC offering from John Motson and Mark Lawrenson for that matter.

The Chelsea semi final was to be my final, and only one thing stood in the way, the small matter of a match ticket. Initially I was quite confident of getting one, even though this was the game that everyone wanted to see. I had only ever been locked out once in all the years of watching the Reds. I thought I would come up smelling of roses as I always did. I had all my contacts looking for tickets and the noises were fairly favourable in the weeks ahead of the game. People I had looked after for years, in one way or another, were all on board to find me a ticket. There were a couple of shouts for tickets but by the time the contact firmed up they had gone. It was starting to look a little precarious, especially as I had booked the time off work and spent over a hundred quid on my flight from the Island. As the game approached the contacts went very quiet, with the exception of Zil, who as usual was trying everything and everybody. Hope started to fade away the day before the game, as I tried to fight the feelings of desperation. There was a final call of contacts, who had gone mysteriously quiet on me, resulting in absolutely nothing. I was flying with no ticket and very little hope. I was still positive, but not as much as I had been. Ronaldsway Airport in the Isle of Man is not massive but there were a fair few Reds waiting for flights to the match and I thought it was worth a try, you never know? 'Hard luck mate, last Saturday I had one', 'Oh yes, me mate had one last night but sold it for two hundred quid'. At least they answered my pleas, which was more than could be said for my contacts in Liverpool. From Liverpool John Lennon airport I headed in to the city centre to try some pubs for any spares.

Now think how you would answer this question to a man who looks far from being a young scally, just a guy desperate for a ticket. 'Alright lads have you got any spares?' Very polite and decent. Responses varied from 'NO' to downright ignorance, some just ignored me. Not one of them was from Liverpool. Now I have never slagged people off who follow us from outside our city, as you will see with Phil from Scunthorpe who I met up with in Barcelona, they pay their money and follow the team and the ones I know are sound. As someone who has followed the Reds, man and boy, being looked down upon by smug outsiders with tickets was a slap in the face. The sting of their attitude towards me shocked me. Anyone who has ever asked me for a ticket at least got the decency of a 'No sorry, I haven't mate'.

From the city centre I headed to my mum and dad's house in the northern suburbs to catch up with them for an hour. I wasn't going to get a ticket in their front living room though, and I hadn't given up just yet. My dad, god bless him, told me all was not lost. He had a plan, and in his mind a great plan! In my mind it was totally unacceptable and I turned down the guaranteed offer of a ticket. Why? After all it was exactly what I wanted wasn't it? Yes, but not at this price. He was offering me his own ticket! Here was someone who had followed Liverpool for over 60 years, been to all the home games this season and he wanted to give his ticket away to me. I couldn't accept that, no matter how much I appreciated the gesture. He tried convincing me that he would just as happy watching it on TV in the club over the road with a few pints. Quite a firm refusal did the trick but the gesture will be remembered forever.

Things got worse as I made my way to the ground. I headed up the hill from Everton Valley, the mighty Kop rising high into the sky ahead of me pulling me up the hill with an almost magnetic attraction. Three hours before kick off, the early May sunshine giving a fair impression of a July day, and the streets were buzzing. There were thousands of people circling, ready in anticipation of another wonderful European night. The atmosphere was electric, I had to get in. Now I had choices to make. Did I head for the ticket office? Take my chances in a pub? Or just plain beg by the roadside? The first pub made up my mind when the barman warned me off the street tickets, as they were already known to be forgeries or stolen. If I was caught with one, I was not getting in to the game.

Also, the prices of tickets varied wildly from £200 to £500 a ticket and I have been around long enough to know who to trust and who not to trust. That night I had no doubt fans buying tickets on the street were going to get ripped off, and all the real tickets had gone. What annoyed me was that genuine tickets had also gone for inflated prices. Whilst longstanding fans, like me, could not get tickets those fortunate enough to get them were happy to sell theirs at inflated prices and rip everybody else off. Liverpool FC really need to review how they distribute tickets for big games like this, far too many end up in the hands of touts. Liverpool still encourage this supply by giving tickets to people with no consequences if they get caught, unlike season ticket holders. While the club impose penalties for season ticket holders if they sell to touts, there are no such consequences to others who purchase tickets. This was before the even bigger debacle of Athens and the ticket distribution for that fixture.

As I neared the Kop, there were pockets of little scallies trying to sell tickets for £400 and they were hunting in packs, surrounding their prey and trying far too hard to convince people that the ticket they were selling was, "dead genuine mate...honest it is not like them fakes that they are selling" (gesturing up the road to the next little pack of rats). Anyone who tries that hard to convince you must be lying. I headed straight to the ticket office, where on a good day, you get the tickets that normal people return to ensure they don't get into the hands of the touts. Was tonight going to be a lucky night? Should I head for the coaches arriving from all over the country carrying our out of town support? After my experiences earlier that day, and the fact that most if not all the tickets on the internet were from out of town-ers I resigned myself to camping outside the ticket office and waiting for that elusive returned ticket.

I made sure the stewards knew I was genuine and that I was first in line for any tickets. They assured me that any one looking for a genuine person would be pointed towards me. I couldn't ask anymore than that, so with my fingers crossed and two and half hours to go I was rooted to the spot watching everyone coming in to see if there was anyone with just one ticket to spare. I was still asking, politely of course, if anyone had any spare tick-ets but once again I was met with stony silence or grunts, except for Scouse boys when at least I got a 'sorry mate' and 'good luck lad hope you get a ticket'. I must admit, with an hour to go, my spirits were starting to falter and deep inside I was resigned to missing what promised to be the match of the season or even the biggest home match ever. As the sun started to drop behind the streets leading up from the Mersey, hordes of excited fans pushed past me on the way into the ground, oblivious to my plight. Killing precious time gave me the chance to reflect as I observed that some of those collecting tickets needed directions as to where to sit. I wondered how this came about. I have been following Liverpool since 1972. I supported them through the dark days of Heysel and Hillsborough. I followed them through the 70s and 80s when football wasn't fashionable and football fans were seen as pariahs and all classed as hooligans. *It made me feel absolutely worthless!* At least they had spent their cash in the Club Shop so from the club perspective they deserve their place at the table more than me. The truth is Liverpool FC, and for that matter Manchester United and Chelsea, would rather fill their ground with people with shopping bags with the club crest upon it than people who hold season tickets. Besides the season ticket, what else do they get out of me? For every match a different bum on the same seat but always with a bag in hand with club merchandise neatly folded away and their LFC credit card. The application just waiting for their details and the transfer of their outstanding balance at 0%, and they could win a signed shirt. The club are no fools. The faithful will keep shelling out £600 plus per season for the ticket, no matter what. We are still people who believe and fight for *our club* regardless of the reality, that it's never been *our club*.

As it turned 7.30pm the only remaining chance was that the ticket office had held some tickets back. My older brother, Ian, called and said he was heading up towards the ground to watch the match in a pub. Even though he had no ticket and knew he had no chance of getting a ticket, he still hoped I would get a ticket but if I didn't manage to get one (or two if I could) we would meet up. At 7.40pm, if it was going to happen it would happen then, and it did. The Head Steward let everybody know there were no tickets and definitely wouldn't be any. People, including me, were literally suspended in disbelief so we didn't move. We thought any minute now there will be some released and the announcement was just to clear the majority away from the ticket office. At

7.45 the truth dawned, there were no tickets. Why was I still there when the match had just kicked off? I didn't know what to do with myself. All the hope had evaporated and I just stood there, all the feelings of the last couple of hours conflicted with one another and drew all the energy from me. Hope and anticipation then despair and disappointment were replaced by total numbness, and all in front of the Shankly statue. It was too much to bear. He would turn in his grave, God rest his soul, to see what the heartless money men have done to our game. It is a disgrace now everything is about money, it is about **"The Experience"** which can only be bought at more exorbitant prices year after year. When will the money men learn that **"The Experience"** is only a replica of the real thing, which cannot be bought at any price. It is driven by the people that they are alienating from the game, it is not the prawn sandwich brigade who make football wonderful, it is the Kopite, the Stretford Ender or the Blue Nose from the Gwladys Street. Look at Chelsea without the Shed, Arsenal without the North Bank and Spurs without the Shelf. The people who made these terraces live and breathe are now in danger of being priced out of the game and the stadiums changed to ensure they will never be welcomed again. No surprise that the northern clubs are fighting it somewhat more than their southern counterparts.

The arrival of our Ian shook me out of the malaise. This was unfamiliar territory to me; being locked outside that hallowed ground listening to the roar of the Anfield faithful, unfamiliar and uncomfortable. We headed to The Albert pub right next door to the ground The Reds still had to make it to Athens. All my feelings of despair faded away as we watched the Reds aim for European glory. Within the pub it was as good as being a hundred yards away on the Kop. The atmosphere was wonderful, shouting, singing and abusing the referee. All part of the match experience, along with the odd bottle of beer or six. Liverpool took a first half lead and comfortably held on to it with few threats from a far superior Chelsea side (well at least according to the 'special one' Mourinho). Liverpool had the better chances to finish the tie, but I think it was always destined to go to extra time and ultimately penalties. Once it went to penalties, I had no doubt we were heading to Athens. Reina in the Liverpool goal is arguably the world's greatest keeper when it comes to penalty kicks. With penalties to spare Dirk Kuyt had the honour to finish the job. As he did, the ground erupted and so did the Albert, pints of beer flew all over the pub drenching everybody giving a rather drunken version of "You'll never walk alone". I grabbed our Ian and said 'let's get in to the ground'. We headed next door as we knew no one would be going home quickly and there was loads of celebrating to be done. There was no chance of any of the stewards stopping us as we sprinted past them and into the bottom of the Kop. What was I doing – I was 41 years of age? The players were still on the pitch as we joined in the celebrations and even though I didn't get in for the actual match I could later be seen on the TV belting out songs in celebration. Now no one actually believes me that I never got in to see the game. To be honest by the time I met up with my dad and Our Kev I forgot that I hadn't been in my usual seat in the Kop.

The morning after, it had begun to sink in a little, add in the well deserved hangover in to the bargain and I was starting to feel pretty fed up by the time I headed to the airport. By the time I arrived at the airport I was getting more annoyed. It served me right I was buying papers, which basically shouted at me 'YOU SHOULD HAVE BEEN THERE'. I know I should have, don't rub it in. By one o'clock I was back at my work desk dealing with a constant stream of people asking me what it was like to have been at such a wonderful game. If only I knew!

As the week wore on I felt my feelings intensify, more annoyed, more upset, more disappointed and more.... well more confused. I was confused because I couldn't shake off these feelings, after a particularly bad defeat it normally takes me a day or two to get over, even a Cup Final loss is yesterday's news very quickly. These feelings were not going away though. It was getting worse and the feelings were eating me up inside, I thought no one would understand this. It was so bad that Nikki kept asking me what was wrong, as usually I am energetic around the house, sometimes hyperactive, but loads of fun (well that's what I think). Nikki knows me well and knew something was wrong. I couldn't keep treating her that way, being off -hand, short and quite morose. It wasn't her fault or Charlie's for that matter, I was wrapped up with myself and missing out on what really counts, having fun with him growing up.

The following Saturday night, as the last mouthful of Chinese stuck in my throat, I thought I have got to stop this now and I did. With the immortal words 'listen love you won't think I am daft if I tell you this will you', I proceeded to spill my guts. Not literally, I had paid for a decent Chinese so there was no way it was coming back up! Before I knew it I had told Nikki how useless and worthless I felt outside the ground on the Tuesday night, and how in the grand old world of Liverpool FC I was nothing more than a tourist now. That hurt like hell, I used to be someone when I watched the Reds. I was admired for my travels, appreciated for the effort I took to help others get to matches with tickets and transport and overall I was one of the few who never missed a game home or away. For five years I never missed a game, home or away, and although that was in the late 80s, it did include the double winning season of 1986. I was living on past glories. For years I had been denying the obvious fact that I didn't deserve to hold myself in such an exalted position as a follower of the Reds. As the years went by, my visits to Anfield and beyond got fewer and far between, starting with fewer away games and then missing home games. As my personal life changed so did my football watching habits.

Football shouldn't be the most important thing in your life. If it is you are missing out. People are the most important things in your life. Nikki and Charlie make me realise that every day of the week. Lost my love for Liverpool? No. Never, I love them but I am not in love with them. I miss them and miss them madly but not enough to do something about it every Saturday. They used to be my one and only all consuming passion, now they come a distant third to my wife and son.

I can now see through football completely. It is not about me, my dad, Our Kev, Zil - the real fans, it is about money. The silver dollar, the pound, the euro - Whatever your currency, you can be bought. When players like Nigel Quashie of West Ham (exactly: who?) are reputedly earning £30,000 per week you really have to question what is going on. I remember when John Barnes was the first £10,000 per week footballer and it wasn't that long ago. I thought I could never spend ten grand a week,

I could give it a good go though. The game is dirty. Everybody knows it and it doesn't take a report costing £1.5 million (by Lord Stevens) to tell us so, we all know it. The only way it will ever change is when people vote with their feet and we are just not prepared to do it, are we?

My season ticket renewal has just landed on the doormat. Six hundred quid and worth every penny, maybe? Well it will be if they win the Premiership. After all I have said, I can't actually walk away and ignore it. This is Charlie's future if he wants it, I will be the proudest man in the world when he makes his own pilgrimage, and joins me on the Kop for the first time. Especially as he will know all the words to our songs, nothing better than a five year old belting out "Poor Scouser Tommy". Wherever we are and wherever they are, Liverpool will always be the Mighty Reds and our team, from father to son. I thank my Dad for my passion and starting me on the wondrous journey. Everybody should at least go a couple of stops on the journey. I wouldn't have missed it for the world, no matter what has happened on the way. My life has been shaped by my journey, I am who I am and I am where I am because of it.

14

Riise ruins the book

Or at least he tries his best!

To be fair there wasn't much he could do, caught in three minds, 'Do I head it? Do I kick it with my right foot which I only use for standing?' or 'Do my strawberry blonde highlights come out well under the flood lights?' As the ball pings in to the top of the Kop net off the aforementioned strawberry blonde bonce, you could hear a pin drop and you just know he chose the wrong option.

Seconds earlier I was there shouting at the referee 'Blow your bloody whistle – it's time', as the clock hit 94 minutes, the four minutes extra time was up. Six seconds was all it took to change a great result into a poor one, and ultimately send Liverpool crashing out of the Champions league enabling Chelsea to exact a painful revenge.

I sat there in the chair and there was nothing I could do. In the living room again! I didn't go across to Liverpool as I was taking my chances the following week in London for the return leg. Our Ian had my ticket and he was helping get me to Moscow if the Reds got there.

We had an injury scare in our house the day before when Nikki thought she had broken her toe falling off her twelve inch high stilettos (she fell down some steps really). Her injury didn't keep her off the bench with me, but I had to be really careful with my constant rising from the couch to berate the referee or celebrate the goal Kuyt scored before half time. Nerves were stretched in our house in case I actually broke her toe (which was in fact only badly bruised). I managed it with consummate ease as Kuyt scored a well deserved opening goal and Liverpool thoroughly deserved their lead and really should have extended it at least twice in the last five minutes. As always, if you don't take your chances, you put pressure on yourself and that is exactly what happened to Liverpool. With the Reds falling asleep from a throw in, Chelsea scored an undeserved equaliser. Our luck had finally run out.

When I went to bed that night I literally had nightmares. I kept picturing the strawberry blonde putting the ball into the roof of the net and it always went in, never wide. Even when Charlie woke up screaming at 2:30am, I couldn't think about his teething, Riise's goal was all consuming. Two hours later, when Charlie finally went to sleep, I still couldn't sleep because of Ginger Nut's own goal.

—✳—

The Champions League campaign hadn't started in a promising fashion with Liverpool only picking up one point in the first nine, it had not been a great start. But the Reds had turned it round in style with three wins on the trot and a hatful of goals, including a Champions League record of 8-0 against Besiktas of Turkey. When we got to the knock out stages it got really interesting, the last sixteen paired us with the famous Inter Milan.

Not since we were cheated out of a European Cup Final by them in 1965 had we been paired with them. We had waited over 40 years for revenge. The game in '65 is the stuff of folklore. Liverpool won the FA Cup on the Saturday for the first time in our history. A stroke of genius by Bill Shankly saw his injured heroes parade the cup before the game. Anfield, packed to the rafters before the game, erupted as the Silverware was paraded in front of them and the Italians were blown away and lost 3 – 1. Inter were a class team and fielded the majority of the Italian national side.

The Italians, stunned by the defeat and the manner of it, resorted to dirty tricks in the return, with the well known Italian behaviours on show - kicking, punching and diving. A referee, many thought to have been bribed, gave some dodgy decisions to give the Italians a 3 – 0 win and knock Liverpool out. The hurt has been passed down by generations and we still feel it. We were looking for retribution!

Regardless of history, this was one of my footballing dreams, I had waited over 30 years to get to the San Siro. Just the mere mention of the stadium name conjures wonder. Following the rebuilding for the World Cup in 1990, it has confirmed its place as one of THE Stadiums in the world to go to. It wasn't just me either; this draw fired everyone's imagination and half of the Kop wanted to go. The low cost airline websites were on fire. Within minutes of the draw you couldn't get out of Liverpool airport and the fight was on for affordable flights from any airport as long as it got us to Milan. Within an hour I was set, and so was Tommy the Butcher, if we could get there tickets would look after themselves hopefully.

We hit on Luton to Bergamo (north of Milan) for just £60, I still had to add the Isle of Man flight going via Gatwick and the train to Luton, which cost me another £120. Throw a night in a hotel for £30 each and we were sorted for less than the cost of a day trip. The Internet's a wonderful thing, it stops you being ripped off by Liverpool's 'travel partners'. If Ryanair and Easy Jet can fly planes at cheap prices two thirds full and still make money, how much do these guys (the travel partners) make out of football fans? It was all booked for us - cheap flights, cheap hotel and an excited bunch of mates, Mongoose, Zil and Effin Tony would all be there, as you may remember from Istanbul it is great meeting your mates in a far foreign land.

That nicely brings me to how the book gets to you. Tony Evans is Football Editor of The Times and the author of a wonderful book about following Liverpool titled aptly "Far foreign land". I contacted Tony by e mail a while before for a little advice, and he said if I was ever in London to give him a shout and have a pint and chat things through. Well replace London with Milan - it couldn't be a better venue, so we arranged to meet by the Duomo (Milan's landmark cathedral). I would be wearing a red carnation (and carrying a can of Heineken). Milan come on!

―∿―

The great day came and so did the worst weather of the winter. Storms battered the Island and the whole of the UK. I woke up to the sounds of the radio telling me that flights out of Heathrow and Gatwick were getting cancelled left right and centre, and the weather was getting worse not better. As I arrived at the airport, I was met by a departure board showing the Gatwick flight as being on time. My luck was in. I bought my luck by wishing the fairies a good morning on the way to the airport and it was working for me. Or was it? At check-in, there was a queue of people who were supposed to be on the first flight out in the morning, whilst I had opted for the second flight at 10.30am, as we were not leaving Luton until 7.30pm. The first one was cancelled and now the second was delayed by an hour at least. We were lucky as at least we had a plane standing at the airport, if we had been waiting on one coming in we would have had no chance. We were only waiting for a gap in the horrendous weather. As we boarded the plane, the airline was true to their word - it was an hour late so I was going to make my connections. They were also true to their word when they told us conditions were awful and the usual request to keep your seat belts fastened through the flight was an order not a request. When we landed, it was like a roller coaster as we could see the sky, then the floor, and then the sky again, and that was only out of my window. As the runway called the plane forward, the pilot battled to control it against the cross winds and did a brilliant job. The rain hammered against the plane as he touched down. One wheel first, then the second a hundred yards or so down the runway, with the nose wheel last to come down. As the brakes were applied, I grasped the seatback in front of me tightly, as if that would save me. As the engines roared due to the reverse thrust, he came slowly to a trundle and towards the gate, the passengers burst into immediate applause. This is rare on planes from the Island as most landings aren't great, but this one was special and everybody knew it. Relieved, 60 happy soles braved the torrential rain to leg it into the terminal, no luxury of an air bridges for our planes.

I took the train from Gatwick right through to Luton and headed to the airport. Within two hours I had my first drink in my hand reliving my near death experience to Tommy as we settled down for a little drinking session and catch up on our lives. By 7pm we had put our worlds to right and caught up on years of missed conversations, which was great and made short work of a pannini that would come back to haunt me the following morning (or maybe it was the ale).

In less than two hours we were facing more death defying landings in Italy this time. As the pilot descended through the clouds, the chattering between the numerous Liverpool fans on board started to hush as he bounced through the clouds. Out of my window I could see little beyond a snow and hailstorm that we seemed to be ploughing through. Mongoose, who was already in Milan, had warned us that the weather was so bad he had to shelter in bars all day to avoid the horrendous rain. As we neared the runway and the lights started to appear I could make out the airport buildings. We were coming in fast and the ground was appearing very fast. About a hundred foot above the ground and the pilot threw the power on and no wonder. We were going to miss the runway. The extra power took us all of 50 foot on to the runway. No applause this time, just quiet and some really odd smells.

No waiting for luggage for us as we were lightly packed so we were straight out into the rain and finding our way to Milan. Mongoose had phoned and there was a party going on right next to our hotel. Bergamo is about an hour north of Milan and a coach would swiftly take us into the centre for less than a tenner. Swiftly wasn't on the drivers agenda though as he took the scenic route though all the industrial estates of northern Italy (or so it seemed). As midnight struck, we entered the city and meandered through the empty wet streets to the Central Train station. Last time I was here was in 1989 and it was baking hot - not this time though. The splendid building hadn't changed at all and neither had the tramps sleeping in the doorways smelling of piss.

The hotel I had booked bragged about being 'just yards from the central station' and I had downloaded a Google map, which should guide us on our way. Unfortunately the map was rubbish and only served to guide us away from the Hotel! After half an hour and with no help from Mongoose who, although drinking next to our hotel, was too drunk to give us proper directions. Eventually we stumbled upon our hotel. As we stood outside our hotel, 200 yards dead ahead was, yes you guessed it, the Central station. By the time we got there the party was starting to die out. Too much ale all day and a willingness of the Italians to close the bar as quickly as possible added up to an early night for most. We got a couple of pints each and started to catch up with Mongoose but it was never going to be possible, especially when the pints were £5 each. As the bar closed around us we were forced on our way onto the streets. The rain had stopped now and besides the small knots of Liverpool fans looking for the next drink, the streets were deserted. There were a few scooter boys checking us out but nothing too sinister. Our main concern was not getting knocked down by a tram. Milan has a classical tram system and it seemed to run all night, eerily with no passengers. As Mongoose was slightly inebriated, for safety's sake we decided to walk him to his hotel, only for him to get there and keep walking as he was looking for the Istanbul Kebab shop (it was an omen). Amazingly he would remember none of it the next day. He couldn't even remember how he received his lovely silk Inter Milan cap. He said it was from the Jurgen Klinsmann era at Inter Milan. It looked more like Klinsmann's silk briefs to me so he may have been right.

Zil had already sent his text at 1am 'Liverpool airport full of dregs like me going to bed down with eight bottles of Grolsch'. What would he be like in the morning? A fresh new day would bring the answer.

—∞—

As we woke in Milan early on the Tuesday morning, the day could not have been more different from our arrival, a beautiful spring day with warm sunshine bathed the northern Italian city. As breakfast settled somewhat uneasily, we checked out and met Mongoose. The day's previous beer or maybe that Pannini were starting to give the warning signs. I knew what was coming and headed to the local pharmacy to make sure, if the inevitable was to happen, I was prepared. Not to be too coarse but you get to know your bowels and their behaviour. Try asking for Imodium in an Italian chemist, just do exactly that, because it works, it's Imodium there too. Thank the lord for worldwide brands. Years earlier I had laughed at the name Snickers when we were in Milan when we had good old Marathon in the UK. Now I was thankful for the brand recognition. These little beauties were going to be worth their weight in gold. They were and I remember the moment well. One of Milan's main sights, the castle, held one attraction for me. The toilet! As it was early in the morning the experience was not too bad. Usually by mid afternoon you don't want to go near a public toilet. No wonder after I had been. Armed with a pocket full of toilet paper (sorry if anyone went without) two Imodium and a delicate walk back to the lads, the last thing I was looking forward to was the match.

Milan has great food booths which sell decent food and beer at prices considerably cheaper than the bars and there was one right by the castle. In the warm sunlight in our shirtsleeves, the round was four beers and one still water, which was drank very slowly. That was mine as if you couldn't guess. Zil had arrived and remarkably chipper considering a lack of sleep and copious amounts of Grolsch. What a lovely experience, this is what European travel is all about, chilling and chatting. The red masses could wait, this was European pavement café culture at its best. Liverpool fans were dotted all over, seeing the sights, sipping (yes sipping) beer and acting like the ambassadors for the European Capital of Culture, which we are. The Milanese didn't even give us a second glance.

As we headed through the main thoroughfares of Milan, past the expensive shops, the scarf sellers started pestering us and Tommy stopped to get one for all of 10 euros. With me being the seasoned traveller, I counselled him that he shouldn't buy the first one he saw, as surely he could do a deal. Point taken, but he didn't believe me. Well he should have done as a hundred yards down the road I got the same scarf, half Inter half Liverpool, for just 5 euros, what a bargain! Do you think I rubbed it in? Of course I did, big time. Our jolly little band headed to the main square where Milan's famous imposing Duomo is positioned. Initially we said we wouldn't stay long as if there is ever going to be an issue it will be somewhere like this. The mix of people was great though, Liverpool fans, Inter fans (looked like out of towners to me) and tourists who were milking in the atmosphere. Songs burst out of Italian and Scouse throats at regular intervals and the carnival occasion was enriched by trays of Heineken, at a marvellous price (for Milan that is).

As Zil and Mongoose lazed in the afternoon sun quaffing beer, me and Tommy headed into the Duomo and then up to the roof for a look at Milan from the roof tops. Looking across those roof tops, we could still hear the singing from all the ants a couple of hundred feet below. With the stomach settled now I chose the best remedy for my future health, as many cans of Heineken as I could manage. It's amazing how resilient the stomach is. I wasn't disrespectful on top of a church though - I waited until I got down. By the time we got down the square was full of people and Robbie and his little fella Craig had arrived. Robbie had a huge flag with him, based on our European cup wins, and was looking for someone to take a picture of him in front of Duomo. It was worse than taking a photo of the bride and groom at a wedding. Gormless gets kept getting in the way, why is it that no one ever notices anyone taking a photograph? After five minutes we had two half decent shots at least, and a hundred of random dozy sods walking in front of the flag.

I then realised that I had lost the five euros scarf, obviously much to the delight of Tommy. If I wanted another I would have paid ten euros in total, the same as him and the exact amount I gave him loads of grief about. The challenge was to get a scarf for less than five euros and I actively took it on, wow it was hard work. None of the sellers would budge below five euros, not even five cents below. The others in my band were offering to throw in the five cents but that was not allowed as it would still cost five euros. After an hour of hard bartering and annoying the life out of everyone who tried to sell me one I got one with a five cents discount, I did a lap of honour. I didn't even realise now that the square was emptying out and people were on the way to the ground. I still had to meet Tony from The Times, who I had arranged to discuss my book with. It was a matter of putting a face to a name and a quick chat. He strolled across the square with a mobile phone to his ear as I directed him in amongst the fans still milling around the monuments. He was as good as his word. He took time out to meet up, no book talk but it was great to put the face to the e-mail and the voice. No sooner had we met and shared our cans with him and we were on the move via the metro and off to the San Siro.

The train bounced its way to the San Siro with Fernando Torres being feted all the way to our destination, rightly so as it turned out to be later on. As we came out of the nearest Metro station to the ground, the late afternoon sun had gone and the night air crackled with anticipation as only it can do for European nights. As we emerged from the Metro the food and drink outlets became the source of focus. Forget a bus to the ground, another cold beer and a pannini was the order of the day. Had I not learnt my pannini lesson? I needed food. All I had all afternoon was two Imodium and ten cans of lager. It hit the mark and allowing for the lies of the police saying it was an hour's walk to the ground and to wait for a tram we headed through the streets with the Milanese towards space ship San Siro. It couldn't be an hour away you could feel it drawing you near. A spaceship is exactly what it looked like as we came out of the dark around the final corner and we feasted our eyes on this huge mother ship lit up in front of us. It stands on its own, unlike Anfield, which has terraced houses clinging on to its base. The sheer size of it was awesome. As we headed towards our part of the stadium the sheer size of the Liverpool following was plain to see, it was Scouse voices in the ascendancy, not Milanese.

The usual chaotic scenes at the turnstiles greeted us. Forget the numbers on your ticket, you're all herded through the same gate and stand or sit anywhere you want. It's always a relief to get inside and away from the more chaotic scenes that occur prior to kick off. Once in, apart from the fact the seats are filthy, full of chewing gum and screwed to the concrete, what a wonderful stadium. One of the best stadium experiences you could ever have, living up to all expectations. The atmosphere was magnificent. Obviously we were enjoying ourselves, but the Inter fans certainly put a show on too. As we were 2 – 0 up they had little hope but they were thankful for one thing. That was the fact that we had beaten their rivals AC Milan in Istanbul. One flag summed it up (and in English too directly above us) 'whatever happens tonight, thank you for 2005'. They hate each other and all through the day we had Inter fans thanking us for beating AC and AC fans gambling upon Liverpool beating Inter and willing us to stuff them. Well we pleased both of them, we beat Inter 1 – 0 and Inter still thanked us for 2005. At the end it was like a great big love-in with mutual respect from both sets of fans, something often seen in Europe but rarely reported.

The only sour note was the length of time they kept us in. It was nearly another 90 minutes before we hit the streets and we were some of the lucky ones to make the last metro back to the city centre. Local police seem to enjoy letting the away fans try and get back in to the city centre once all the public transport has finished. I could swear they all own shares in the taxi firms of big European cities. By the time we got back to the city centre it was as good as closed, one bar near Duomo was opened but we were looking for a host of late bars by the Grand canal, which I was informed would be bouncing. Well it may have been if Inter had won but with the streets deserted, the long walk was fairly fruitless and all we found was a gay bar and a bar that decided that once we sat down and ordered that they were closing for the night. We ended up standing on the chilly street with two pints in hand whiling away the hours. In writing now I must apologise to my fellow travellers for dragging them across the city centre on a wild goose chase, especially Mongoose who cried like a girl all the time that we walked, well he did have his stilettos on! Well in the home of the transvestite he wanted to fit in (now right away before he kills me, that is not true).

We had nowhere to stay and we were trying to find a bar to stay in until we could get the bus back to Bergamo airport, which didn't start until 4am. I never thought it would be that difficult in a big European city but it was. We ended up taking a cab to the central station and having a beer outside from one of the food stands that stayed open through the night. We weren't the only ones, there were hundreds outside and they were all waiting for the first airport buses. There were bodies scattered everywhere trying to either get some kip or provide for their beer induced hunger. The happy band of travellers at the final whistle was now just desperate to go home, and it's a long way home midweek. Even getting to the airport didn't fulfil the need, as sleeping opportunities were limited unless you were totally out the game. Airports aren't great places to be for more than an hour, as they are just not designed for it. By the time our plane landed at Luton it had been twenty-four hours since proper sleep and I still had another six hours ahead of me before I would walk through my door and tell Charlie about Fernando Torres slotting in the San Siro.

—◦◦◦—

The draw on the following Friday was going to be the key to our road to Moscow, a quarter final draw and the draw for the semi final pairings all rolled into one. At least I could partly plan my Red Square experience. It couldn't have been much more difficult with potentially an English affair all the way. Arsenal, Chelsea and maybe Man United to pick up old big ears for the sixth time, this would be the hardest yet. Little chance of away tickets for either of the games but Arsenal at home was going to be great. The first leg really set it up as well with a one all draw, and the tie was fairly even. That was even allowing for a penalty that should have been for the Gunners. Overall I think Liverpool deserved a draw. Finely balanced for the home leg, who was to know what was to come on one of THE great European nights as Anfield.

With the away goal, the confidence that the Liverpudlian's had was palpable, there was only going to be one winner. I took the afternoon off work and with a cheap flight I was in Liverpool by mid afternoon. All you could feel was confidence pulsing through the red half of the city. That confidence went into the game but lasted less than twenty minutes with the wind taken out of the bright red Kop's sails with an Arsenal goal that silenced all but a small corner of Anfield. Liverpool struggled for rhythm as the young Arsenal guns ripped them to pieces with seemingly every attack. Out of the blue, Sami Hyppia equalised with a magnificent header and the pendulum swung again. Half time slowed the momentum a touch but not for long as, early in the second half, the new king of the Kop Fernando Torres gave the Reds the lead with a stunning goal. Often compared to The King of the Kop Kenny Dalglish and so he should be. He is up there with the greatest goal scorers we have had, Rush, Dalglish, Fowler, Owen and Hunt. There was only one team in it then. Although Liverpool were ahead, an equaliser would put Arsenal through on away goals, but didn't seem likely as Liverpool looked like adding a third and putting the game out of sight. Then, out of the blue, Walcott used his Olympian pace to rip the Reds apart and break the hearts of the majority of Anfield. It looked to be step too far as Adebayor put Arsenal in command with the additional away goal, with ten minutes to go. With hardly time to register our disappointment, Liverpool got a penalty, hotly disputed on TV as always, but Gerrard kept his cool to smash the ball into the back of the Kop net and people tumbled all around me. 'Now just hold on to it boys' was the shout as Arsenal tried to summon up the energy to equalise again but with seconds left, Ryan Babel the new super-sub took the ball from a long punt out of defence, and beating Fabregas to the ball calmly slotted the ball past the keeper in front of a sea of delirious Kopites.

As the whistle blew the tremendous noise signalled relief and unbridled joy, this was the way to head to Moscow, we don't do things the easy way. My legs were weak and my head was booming, that's the effect one of those games has on the fans. What must it be like for a manager? One of the greatest European nights, we just need to add it to the list of European great nights which is growing every year

Due to the way they draw the ties now, we knew Chelsea were next and it would be at home first, which was a big change as the previous years ties all ended up at Anfield, this time we would have to finish it at their place. That was no problem though, this was Europe and we were Kings of Europe.

—◊—

Now picture this. Torres slots in the equaliser against Chelsea at the Bridge and the Reds are back in it. The Liverpool supporters erupt and there I am tumbling across seats in my best pin striped Marks and Spencer suit. Well, alter that picture a little. I am still in my best pin striped suit and stumbling not tumbling but I am in a ropey pub in Earls Court with loads of other unfortunates who didn't make it past the police man-to-man marking on the Stamford Bridge turnstiles. Even Roman Abramovich would have struggled to make it past that lot.

The idea of going to Chelsea started off really promising because, as luck would have it, that day I needed to be in London for a meeting. The meeting was in Mayfair hence the pin stripe suit, but after the meeting my focus would be on tickets for the evening's entertainment at Stamford Bridge. Tickets were at a premium and were not going to be easy to come by. With so many irons in the fire, surely one would come up trumps, I couldn't be locked out again, it couldn't happen two years on the trot, could it? Well yes it could and it would, but at least I had a go and I wasn't the only one to miss out, hence the mass of company in the boozer in Earls Court. Throughout the day the irons were pulled out of the fire and thrown in the bin, as contacts failed one by one. I did get the chance to meet Tony from The Times for lunch and he is a big part of the reason as to why you are reading this. As the Football Editor of The Times he was a great person to ask if I was on the right track. After putting the face to the name now it was down to business and thankfully he found my Istanbul chapter an enjoyable read. A couple of pints and a lovely Turkish meal (well after Istanbul it has been really popular for Liverpudlian's) cheers Tony! Before I knew it and having put the world and my book to rights, Tony was off to edit the evening's events at Stamford Bridge.

Still ticketless, it was off to see Zil in Trafalgar Square and the legendary pre-match sing-song prior to Champions League Semi Finals with Chelsea. It wasn't happening though, Trafalgar Square was dead with no Liverpool fans to be seen and surprisingly the surrounding pubs were quiet as well. The driving rain had put paid to any party, as had police action in previous years I believe, which stopped people enjoying themselves. Zil was in a boozer that seemed to sell only home brew, well who really calls them micro breweries. Its home brew and tastes like it too. There were tickets in there though. Blag (fake) ones but they were tickets. Look at them from twenty yards with one eye closed and they would pass as real but close up? To be fair, they were not that bad but I spotted a flaw right away - the hologram was the wrong size. If I could spot it so would the police who were man-to-man marking at the turnstiles. The police were on alert due to mass bunk-ins from previous years and they were not going to get caught out tonight. Tony had warned me about the proposed mass bunk in and besides, getting in with fakes causes overcrowding, and we all know what happened in Athens in 2006, it just causes mayhem and potentially crushes and we know the real cost of that. To me, it wasn't an option. I would rather miss the match. Some of you may be thinking 'mug!'. Well that's up to you but we are all different. Thirty-five quid with every chance of getting a tug and with what I do for a living it is not really something to take a chance on. Records of any type are frowned upon, especially police ones (even though I do own De do do do de da da da da, a classic if ever I heard one, cheers Sting).

Hope was starting to fade now as it turned 5 pm, and I headed up towards the ground and caught up with my mate Mark who is a Chelsea fan. I have never held it against him, but I owed him to at least to turn up for a pint on his patch. Why did I owe him? Well a couple of years back when Liverpool played Chelsea in the FA Cup semi finals at Old Trafford, we arranged to meet and he volunteered to come up the Liverpool end of the ground to meet me and Our Kev. Well he only turned up in his Chelsea Shirt and with every step he took through the red throngs he was roundly abused. Abuse is a strong word, as some of it was light-hearted banter, but some of it was vicious abuse. Shouts of Chelsea rent boy whilst starting off light hearted ended up as vitriolic abuse of two guys who didn't deserve it, they weren't mouthing off, and they took it with dignity. Whilst I defended them and showed they were clearly with us, I am embarrassed to this day about the level of abuse directed at my friends and even though I apologised, I was embarrassed to be associated with some of our fans. No matter how we classify ourselves, there is a small minority who let us down, they are there in every club so there is no mightier than thou feeling from me or anyone. We all know it's true. So here I am on his turf all dressed up, yes but in a suit not a red shirt, I'm not as mad as him. One stop from the ground and after a couple of pints we headed to the ground and see if anything was going.

The only thing going at the ground was a good old soaking in the lashing down rain, and the local police moving us on, away from the turnstiles. The mass bunk-in of previous years was never going to happen and neither was a spare ticket. The nearest I got was eighty quid for a Ford Complimentary ticket, yes complimentary tickets being sold, shock! It happens at every big game, these tickets get in the hands of the touts and it's anything for a quick buck. These are the people who ruin football for the ordinary folk and feed the black market not normal people. I was ready to pay the eighty quid but I was second in line to someone who was thinking about it. For me, no thinking, the guy soon made his mind up to buy and the chance was gone. At that point I was relieved I didn't do the old forgery as people were getting marched away for interrogation. Others, meanwhile, were boxed in by lines of police in a bike shed. An 'over the top' reaction? Maybe, but in previous years Reds fans hadn't covered themselves in glory or won any friends down at Stamford Bridge. For me, my night was over as far as live football went and with 10 minutes to kick off, I headed back against the tide of fans streaming to the ground. I was not the only one trudging away, there were lots of lads who were now going to make the most of the trip to the capital. Earls Court was a good bet due to its proximity to Stamford Bridge and the high volume of pubs, the match would certainly be on and probably only steps away from the Tube station.

It was a good call, 50 yards from the Tube and even though I missed the first ten minutes of the match, I was in sight of a TV screen with a bottle of beer in my hand. It didn't go according to plan though and Didier Drogba got his own back on Rafa for calling him a diver, with a quality finish that made the job harder. By half time the Reds were not really in it and it looked we were going out with a whimper instead of a fight. The second half was a different story and Fernando Torres sent the West London boozer into a state of pandemonium. Ale went everywhere and the pin stripe suit was starting to look more like one from George from Asda instead of Marks and Sparks. With the equaliser there was only one team in it and I was dreaming of Red Square again. The pub was bouncing and Fernando Torres, Liverpool's number 9, was being lauded on high. As extra time neared, my bet of 1 – 1 and penalties looked like coming true. As we burst out of the pub at full time to get some fresh air or a fag, the texts started coming thick and fast. All my red mates were forecasting glory.

Within minutes of the restart it had gone disastrously wrong and we were 3 - 1 down and out. They really should have learnt their lesson when Chelsea had one disallowed, but no the defence stayed asleep and Drogba rubbed more salt into the wounds with the third and killer goal. Whilst Babel pulled one back it was only ever a glimmer of hope and we fell at the last hurdle. The pub that was bouncing only half an hour before now emptied out quickly and quietly on to the main road. Truth be told, I was a little relieved as the prospect of United in Moscow wasn't exactly a cheerful thought, having been to a Cup Final with them, they are never great days. You are always looking over your shoulder and concerned about what happens next, to say the two sets of fans don't get on is somewhat of an understatement. Red Square could have been red for the wrong reasons and the travel experiences would have been fraught with difficulties I think. Well it made me feel better thinking that way and also it saved me a thousand pounds.

From Earls Court by tube, I had to change at Victoria to head back to my cheap hotel at London City airport, well there was no point paying through the nose for a good hotel after drinking all afternoon is there? When I arrived I had an attack of the munchies and obviously Victoria station would be ideal for some rubbish, yet still filling food. Who cares about nutrition when you are in your early forties? Who cares about the mixture of spicy Turkish food, numerous pints and bottles of beer and what might send me over the edge. Normally Nikki would, but tonight I was sleeping alone and would only have myself to worry about. As I staggered up the steps, the concourse was fairly quiet and the Burger King sign directly ahead of me was calling me forward, and at a pace somewhat faster than my legs could carry me. I wasn't the only one, any mainline train station in London at that time of night has its fair share of people in need of sustenance.

Chicken Royale in hand, I headed back to the Jubilee line for the journey back to the east of London. Chelsea fans were now heading up out of the Tube lines for trains back to the Home Counties. They were miserable, but still had their blue and white flags in hand. This was the new football fan. In days of old, these people wouldn't have been Chelsea fans who were something to be wary of. These were new money Chelsea, getting to Moscow meant little, or so it seemed! On the tube there were quite a few Chelsea fans and even though I wished them luck in Moscow against United, they didn't acknowledge me. Six middle-aged women who had been to see Billy Elliot in the West End were showing them how to enjoy themselves. As the train emptied out towards Canning Town, it was approaching midnight and now I was actually gutted we hadn't made it. The Chelsea fans that I saw ruined it, they were not real football fans, they should be bouncing for days, we did, so did United but these Chelsea fans were quiet as doormice. There were still Chelsea fans on board as I hit the Docklands Light Railway and that was strange in itself. Chelsea fans in the East End of London, well the Docklands is not the real East End is it, it's all a bit plastic and new money. Twenty years ago you would never have found Chelsea down there unless they were scrapping with West Ham.

Midnight chimed and I checked in to the Travelodge, which seemed to be a home for refugees looking at the foyer and bar area. It seemed to be full of men in alcohol induced stupors, sleeping kids and a woman surfing the internet with three kids sucking their thumbs, hours past their bed time. I was past my bedtime too and a couple of bottles of water in hand, I headed for my room. In broken English the receptionist offered directions to the room. Down in to the depths of the basement, along the corridor that smells of dog pee, and your room is on the right. We have had the heating on all day so its ninety degrees and given the TV remote control to someone and not been bothered replacing it, so you can't set your alarm for the morning flight. Well she never said any of that really, she grunted and gestured to the right for me to find the room and all of the above for myself.

As always, sleep didn't come, I still couldn't get it out of my mind. I just kept picturing the strawberry blonde blasting the ball into the roof of the net and it always went in. That was a week old now but will live with me forever. Now the delicate combination of Turkish, Burger King and beer guaranteed it wasn't the quietest or most aromatic hotel room I had ever stayed in.

Thursday morning came round far too quick and I flew back home for 48 hours to spend some time with Charlie and Nikki before I jetted back to South Africa to work for a week which was to bring me back down to earth. Instead of looking for a rough guide to Moscow I was looking forward to my summer holidays. I know how Steven Gerrard felt! Normal life knocks the disappointment out of your system a little but as I sat in a bar in Johannesburg on a wet Sunday afternoon watching Liverpool play Manchester City with nothing to play for, the season was over and I looked to forget about football. Well until August at least.

Will I be excited? Oh yes even at 43.

Will I be entertained? Possibly.

Will I be disappointed? Maybe, hopefully not.

Will I be passionate? Oh yes more than ever.

Will it run my life? No way!

Who am I kidding of course it will, see you on the Kop. I will be the one in red shouting my head off. Be sure to say hello and order another copy of the book.

The journey continues

The book started with a journey to Istanbul for one of the greatest nights of my life and my journey continues. Which way will it go? I don't know, and that's what life is all about and what makes it so intriguing. Whichever way it will go I will embark upon my journey with the passion and belief I have carried for over 40 years. My journey has become a family journey now but my extended Liverpool family still calls me home to spend time with them. Whether it is behind the Kop Goal or up in the gods in the Bernabeu, cheering on another famous victory, I will love every minute and keep on supporting my first true love.

Get on board for the next journey. It's going to be a great ride, and remember - every journey starts with that one small step out of the door and usually out of your comfort zone.

I still have my dreams, and yes I still have songs to sing!